Red Lines, Black Spaces

Red Lines, Black Spaces

The Politics of Race and Space in a Black Middle-Class Suburb

Bruce D. Haynes

Yale University Press
New Haven & London

Designed by Mary Valencia
Set in Veljovic Book type by
Tseng Information Systems, Inc.
Printed in the United States of America.

Library of Congress Cataloging-in-Publication Data
Haynes, Bruce D., 1960–
Red lines, black spaces : the politics of race and space in a
Black middle-class suburb / Bruce D. Haynes.
                                      p.   cm.
Includes bibliographical references and index.
ISBN 0-300-08490-0
1. African Americans—New York (State)—Yonkers—
History.   2. African Americans—New York (State)—
Yonkers—Social conditions.   3. African Americans
—New York (State)—Yonkers—Economic conditions.
4. Middle class—New York (State)—Yonkers—
History.   5. Social classes—New York (State)—
History.   6. Ethnic neighborhoods—New York
(State)—Yonkers—History.   7. Yonkers
(N.Y.)—Social conditions.   8. Yonkers
(N.Y.)—Race relations.   I. Title.
F129.Y5 H39   2001
974.7'277—dc21
2001026308

A catalogue record for this book is
available from the British Library.
The paper in this book meets
the guidelines for
permanence and durability
of the Committee on Production
Guidelines for Book Longevity of
the Council on Library Resources.

10   9   8   7   6   5   4   3   2   1

Contents

Tables

Foreword

Books as good as this one do not really need introduction. I accepted an invitation to contribute to these pages, however, because I thought it might be helpful to try to locate Runyon Heights within a tradition of scholarly research to which both Bruce Haynes and I belong.

American sociologists have been engaged in the study of communities for more than a hundred years. Indeed, a strong case can be made that the field drew its first and most important intellectual nourishment from that pursuit. One of the first research reports in this country that can properly be called sociological was *The Philadelphia Negro,* by W. E. B. Du Bois, published in 1899. That extraordinary work appeared well before its time, however, a victim of neglect, and the idea of community studies did not pick up momentum again until the 1910s and 1920s when a remarkable group of sociologists at the University of Chicago undertook to study the new forms of social life that were then appearing in the city around them. Robert E. Park, the dean of that group, looked upon Chicago in particular and modern urban areas in general as "a mosaic of minor communities," a sprawling cluster of "natural areas." His students fanned out over the city, bringing back reports on such neighborhood enclaves as hobo jungles, gold coasts, skid rows, bohemias, slums, boardinghouse areas, ethnic ghettos, and a wide array of other urban spaces. (There may be at least a minor irony here in that those early field-workers took it more or less for granted that they were learning about the anatomy of the city in general from studying this convenient specimen; but the growth of Chicago in the 1920s turned out to be a unique development in the history of urban America, and the information they worked so hard to gather is now of far more interest to historians concerned with that particular moment in time than to sociologists interested in the nature of cities generally.)

In the decades that followed, community studies of a similar kind can be said to have formed the center of the sociological enterprise. The work of Robert and Helen Lynd (on Middletown, 1929, 1937), W. Lloyd Warner and his associates (on Yankee City, 1941, 1945, 1947), William Foote Whyte (on Cornerville, 1943)—these being but prominent examples from a much wider shelf of material—continued to look in on the American urban scene. In more recent times the focus of urban community studies has largely shifted to the inner city, which has proven to be a remarkably rich source of good sociological work. It almost seems unfair to single out particular persons or works in so brief an accounting, but the field reports of social scientists like Elijah Anderson, Mitchell Duneier, Herbert Gans, Elliot Liebow, Jonathan Reider, Carol Stack, and Gerald Suttles have had a major impact on many and can serve as a representative list.

In the meantime, a different set of sociologists had been engaged in studying small rural communities, primarily in the American South. A number of important monographs came out of the University of North Carolina in the 1930s, to be followed by such classics on the rural South as *Caste and Class in a Southern Town,* by John Dollard (1937), *Deep South,* by Allison Davis and his colleagues (1941), and *Blackways of Kent,* by Hylan Lewis (1955); and such classics on the mountain folk of Appalachia as *Children of the Cumberland,* by Claudia Lewis (1946), *Little Smoky Ridge,* by Marion Pearsall (1959), *Stinking Creek,* by John Fetterman (1967), and *Shiloh,* by John Stephenson (1968). This brief sampling, too, has to be understood as a personal one, for the list from which these titles have been drawn is long and rich and varied.

The sociologists who fanned out across the urban surfaces of Chicago in the 1920s and 1930s assumed that they were getting an advance look at the American future. But their colleagues studying the rural South took it more or less for granted that they were getting one last look at a disappearing way of life. The people of the countryside were drifting into urban centers even as the culture of the city was reaching out into the hinter-lands. One of the better known titles on the shelf I mentioned a moment ago caught that feeling perfectly: *Yesterday's People.*

The flow of migrants from the rural South to the urban North through-out this century has been a major preoccupation of sociologists and de-mographers for a long time and will have to be another story for another time; but this preoccupation may be one reason so many of the commu-nity studies that have appeared in recent years focus on either end of the axis along which those vast shifts of population have taken place—rural hills and farmlands at one pole, the central city at the other. The fact of the matter is, though, that no sooner had the tides of modern in-dustry done their work and drawn vast multitudes into the urban cen-ters than a kind of reverse undertow took over and carried many of those from the inner city who could afford it out to the edges of the city—the areas that would soon be called suburbia. That, too, is another story for another time. What is important for our purposes here is that American sociologists took what turned out to be a brief interest in that new form of social life in the 1950s and 1960s, when books like John Seeley's on Crest-wood Heights (1956), William H. White's on Park Forest (1956), Herbert Gans's on Levittown (1967), and Bennett Berger's on "working class sub-urbs" (1968), appeared in print. The demographic center of gravity, so to speak, has continued to shift toward the suburbs (carrying with it most of the industrial plants that once sustained life at the city's core, inciden-tally), but unless I have been looking in all the wrong places, the attention of sociologists has returned to those outer poles—the rural countryside and the inner city. Runyon Heights was taking form at the same time as Crestwood Heights, but none of those earlier studies touched on the sub-ject of black suburbanization.

That makes Runyon Heights doubly distinctive. It deals not only with a modern suburb, but with one consisting almost entirely of African Americans.

One of the first population groups to move out into the suburbs was second- and third-generation European immigrants—people whose par-ents and grandparents had earned a secure niche for themselves in the New World by working in the mills and foundries that once formed the city's core, and in the process had made it possible for their offspring to move to the relative comfort and safety of the suburbs. Another group, very like the first economically, was made up of black Americans who had succeeded in business or in the professions and the skilled crafts while living in the inner city, and whose income allowed them to entertain the same middle-class aspirations. They were part of a cruel circularity, though, as Haynes's account makes clear. The drift out to the suburbs deprived the inner city of many of its steadiest, hardest-working, best-trained, most seasoned families—people from whom the rural newcomers might have learned and from whom they might have drawn community leadership. And the drift to the suburbs isolated those who did make the move, leaving them cut off from the rest of the black community by their relative affluence and their middle-class dreams, and at the same time cut off from other families making the same move because they were black.

The paths along which most white people made their way out to the suburbs were formed by the opening of new roadways and rail lines. The paths along which the people of Runyon Heights made the same journey, however, were formed not only by new transportation routes but by the policies of lending institutions, the effects of restrictive covenants, the behavior of realtors, and all the other workings of racial segregation. This situation created African-American enclaves in a suburban landscape that was otherwise white, and exactly because these enclaves appeared to be so distinct to their neighbors—"racially identified spaces," Haynes calls them—blackness became the prevailing "collective identity" of Runyon Heights and places like it. From the beginning, the residents of Runyon Heights came from a wide range of social and cultural backgrounds—the urban North, the rural South, half a dozen Caribbean countries. They spoke a variety of languages, observed a variety of cultural traditions, adhered to several different religions, and came from a number of different social class backgrounds. Those differences, though, all but disappeared in the stark reality of what others perceived as their shared blackness. As a result, Runyon Heights developed a degree of communal feeling and political cohesiveness that might never otherwise have been its lot. In the end, a remarkable circle closes: Runyon Heights is defined by the blackness of the people who call it home, and yet, at the same time, the racial attitudes of those who draw that boundary participate in creating the concept of blackness itself. As Haynes elegantly puts it: race makes place, and, in doing so, place makes race.

—Kai Erikson

Acknowledgments

This book originated as a Ph.D. dissertation in sociology at the City University of New York Graduate Center. Most of the fieldwork was done and the data were collected between 1991 and 1993. Crucial funding for the research came from the President's Dissertation Year Fellowship offered under the Minority Access Graduate Networking (MAGNET) Program at the City University of New York Graduate Center.

Many individuals provided material, moral, and intellectual support for the research and writing of this manuscript. I am especially indebted to the Runyon Heights community. Without the willingness of residents, past and present, to share their lives with me, this study would not have been possible. I have attempted to preserve their viewpoints and experiences to the best of my ability, while providing a historically accurate and balanced picture. I take full responsibility for any errors or misrepresentations that may have made their way into this study.

I am indebted to Stephen Steinberg, Andrew Beveridge, and Bill Kornblum for their guidance and encouragement throughout my graduate career. They played an especially important role by giving critical feedback and insightful commentary. I wish to thank Andrew Beveridge, in particular, for always having faith in my abilities as a social scientist.

I owe many thanks to my wife, Syma Lee Solovitch. Editing numerous drafts, she was a patient yet demanding critic. Her fresh intellectual perspective and keen literary skills helped to transform the jargon of sociology and my vague ideas into a coherent manuscript. Like many spouses of academicians, she also provided critical emotional support during the long process.

I was fortunate to have the support and expertise of Susan Arellano, senior editor at Yale University Press. I am also indebted to Kai Erikson for his unwavering support during my tenure as a junior faculty member at Yale University. In addition to Kai, a number of colleagues also offered criticisms, suggestions, and intellectual feedback. I'd like to especially thank R. Richard Banks, Juan Battle, Jennifer Eberhardt, Paul Gilroy, Brian Hayashi, Gerald Jaynes, Robert Johnston, Phil Kasinitz, Charles Lemert, Phil Schaap, and Joseph Soares. The many librarians who helped me track down rare documents and obscure materials were an invaluable resource in reconstructing the community's past. Special thanks to Elaine Massena, reference supervisor of the Westchester County Archives; to Jeffrey Williams, Michael Rebic, and Lee Ellman of the Yonkers Planning Bureau; and to Milton Holst of the Runyon Heights Improvement Association. I am also grateful to the following institutions for providing access to their records: the Yonkers City Planning Bureau, the Yonkers Historical Society, the Yonkers Public Library, the Westchester County Archives, the Westchester Historical Society, the Westchester County Department of Land Records, the Westchester County Board of Elections, the Schomburg Center for Research in Black Culture, and the New York Public Library.

Thanks also to the hundreds of individuals who offered time, information, encouragement, and support: to my friends and supporters at the council's Enterprises Community Mental Health Center in Harlem, New York, especially Antoinette Adams, Ida Morris, and Juanita Jones; to the staff, faculty, and students of the African-American Studies and Sociology Departments at Yale University; to my friends at the Graduate Center and Hunter College, and especially to Paul Attewell, Robert Carter, Lindsay Churchill, Debra Davis, Susan Fisher, Charles Green, Charles Kadushin, Hylan Lewis, Neil McLaughlin, Thelma Nesbit, Erol Ricketts, Benjamin Ringer, Catherine Silver, Pamela Stone, and Sharon Zukin. Finally, this

Acknowledgments

book is dedicated to three influential persons in my life: the late Jay Schulman, my graduate mentor, who showed me that the roles of scholar and activist could indeed be reconciled, and my parents, the late Daisy Alexander and George E. Haynes, Jr., for their love, encouragement, and confidence.

Introduction

I think that we're fighting hard to say, "Hey, I'm a person of color."
People in Runyon Heights say that more. They say, "Hey, I'm just
as African-American, I'm just as black as you are. I just happen to
live in this house over here." That's all the difference. . . . Most of us
are one or two paychecks away from there [poverty]. I don't think
the people have forgotten that—those who live in Runyon Heights.
And when you look at some of the things they do, you can see they
haven't forgotten that.
      —Thirty-one-year-old male resident

Red Lines, Black Spaces is a case study of Nepperhan–Runyon Heights,[1]
one of the first middle-class black[2] suburbs in the New York metropolitan region. Runyon Heights is nestled in the northeast section of Yonkers,
New York, on the banks of the Hudson River, in the southwest corner of
Westchester County, just north of New York City. During the early years,
the community was known as Nepperhan. By the 1940s, the Runyon
Heights name had become increasingly common. The original settlement
is sometimes called "old Nepperhan" by residents. The name Nepperhan

comes from a local river, first called Neperah or Nippirau (written Nippiorha in the British Royal Charter) by the original Nappeckamack Native Americans who inhabited the area. "Nepperhan" translates as "rapid flowing water" (Allison 1984). I will call the community Nepperhan when speaking of the early years and Runyon Heights when speaking of the last fifty years or so.

Runyon Heights, located on the east side of Yonkers amid predominantly white communities, is home to some thirteen hundred middle-class African Americans. As such, it is more than a historical anomaly. The community is the product of eight decades of black suburbanization, from the period just before World War I, which greatly expanded housing opportunities and initiated the first period of private home ownership by the American working class, through the middle-class suburban expansion of the post–World War II era. As a result, the community's history sheds light on the ways in which contemporary suburban residential development was shaped by race and class.

The neighborhood of Nepperhan–Runyon Heights is, in many respects, like other suburban home-owning communities. Residents are mostly concerned with maintaining good schools, safe and clean streets, and their middle-class suburban lifestyle. Racial subordination created unique problems for the African-American middle class in Yonkers, however, and the residents of Runyon Heights have had to resist political, economic, and social forces that threatened to transform their neighborhood into a ghetto. They have fought against school gerrymandering, employment and housing discrimination, and attempts by city government to address public housing needs by repeatedly targeting the area for low-income housing projects. Paradoxically, these political battles have tended to promote both class solidarity and racial pride, as residents seek political power and residential stability through the community. Strong community ties have been forged in the heat generated by conflicts involving race and class.

The case of Runyon Heights also details how the creation of racially defined residential space after the turn of the century helped racialize American society in general and provided the foundation for racially segregated educational, social, and religious institutional life.[3] The organization of communities by race, in turn, meant the politicization of racial identity. Residents had little choice but to identify common political interests, and thus the community became the framework for exercising political power. Racial consciousness provided a basis for social solidarity and mobilization, while partially insulating residents from the daily slights of overt racism.

Although racialization encouraged a sense of community that at times transcended residential boundaries, the material interests of this home-owning middle class also made it necessary to maintain a degree of physical and social distance from the black masses who came to dominate the west side of Yonkers. Runyon Heights residents were in the awkward position of negotiating the politics of race and class while relying on both for constructing community solidarity, community identity, and political mobilization. The story of Runyon Heights sheds light on the tensions stemming from the black middle-class embodiment of the political interests of race, on the one hand, and the material interests of class, on the other.

At one level, the community is a model of working-class mobility, reflecting the significance of regular employment on the development and maintenance of a stable middle-class community. At another level, Runyon Heights opens a window onto the racial and class forces that shaped America's suburbs and reveals the community basis for group interests. Residents, who have mobilized to challenge the structures that have led to the subordination of the community, are at the same time engaged in negotiating a course between the racial antagonisms they experience with white mainstream society and the class antagonisms they experience with the black working class.

Nepperhan was first settled in 1912 by black working-class Southern migrants and West Indian immigrants. The early settlement of the community represented a significant historical transition in the residential patterns of Americans of African descent. Nepperhan was one of the original working-class trolley-car settlements in Yonkers, and after World War II it became the only stable community of predominantly middle-class black American homeowners in the city.

The community is sociologically significant beyond the suburbanization patterns it reveals: embodied within its history is the legacy of government-sponsored educational, residential, and occupational segregation. Yonkers was the focus of a landmark ruling handed down in 1986 by United States District Court Judge Leonard B. Sand on the housing and school desegregation suit brought by the United States and the local chapter of the National Association for the Advancement of Colored People (NAACP).[4] Judge Sand ruled that the city of Yonkers and its agencies had intentionally segregated blacks in both housing and public schools. The implementation of racially biased policies by federal and local agencies created a unique set of dilemmas for black middle-class suburbanites that helped to structure the physical boundaries of the community and consequently shaped the development of group interests among residents.

The resulting racial homogeneity of Runyon Heights is striking. According to the 1990 census, the area, as defined by census tract boundaries, is 78 percent black and contains 1,378 persons. But that definition ignores local community boundaries and includes portions of the neighboring and predominantly white Homefield community. If we define the community as the locals do, the area is even more racially homogeneous.

By common standards, today's Runyon Heights is a middle-class community. The median family income in the area was $43,500 in 1990, while the median family income for the entire city of Yonkers was $43,305.[5] At the national level, median family income for all families in 1990 was only $35,353. When racial differences in earnings are taken into account, white median family income rises to $36,915 while black median family income falls to $21,423.[6] Whether by comparison with other black Americans or by comparison with the nation as a whole, Runyon Heights residents are distinctly middle-class.

The Reagan-Bush years were financially advantageous for the average resident. Between 1980 and 1990, Runyon Heights experienced a 38 percent real gain in family income (Table I.1), while the average gain in the city of Yonkers was only 20 percent. Home ownership, as well as income, is often looked upon as a qualification for inclusion in the suburban middle class, and indeed 56 percent of Nepperhan homes are owner occupied. Owning a home is not only a defining characteristic of the American Dream but a significant source of family wealth among the middle class (Oliver and Shapiro 1995, 108). While endowing the owner with status and social respectability, it also aids group solidarity by fostering common interests related to private property.

Runyon Heights is further distinguished by the fact that it is surrounded by many virtually all-white working- and middle-class residential areas. In 1990, the Homefield community, which borders Runyon Heights to the north, was 92 percent white and only 7 percent black. In fact, Runyon Heights is one of only two census tracts on the east side of the city with a black population greater than 10 percent (Map I.1).

Though often ignored by scholars, black suburbanization actually began in the early 1910s and has continued throughout the century. Paul Douglas (1968) identified the presence of black suburbs around north-

Table I.1: Demographics of Runyon Heights, 1980–1990

	1980	1990
Total population	1,270	1,378
Total # families	324	352
Total Hispanic	26	96
Non-Hispanic Black	987	1,085
Non-Hispanic White	238	214
Total # households	469	478
Total units	482	491
Renter-occupied units	191	202
Vacant units	13	13
% Units owner-occupied	58	56
Incomplete plumbing	9	0
Median rent	$203	$475
In 1990 dollars	$322	NA
Median family income	$19,853	$43,500
In 1990 dollars	$31,467	NA

Source: U.S. Census of Population, 1980 and 1990.

ern cities like New York and Chicago in 1925, but his work was largely overlooked by scholars for another four decades. Social scientists Karl E. Taeuber and Alma F. Taeuber were the first to cautiously note moderate black suburbanization in the 1960s (Taeuber and Taeuber 1966, 133). Their analysis, like most studies of post-1960s suburbanization, relied on census data in mapping aggregate demographic trends. These techniques often overlooked isolated enclaves. Although the 1970s ushered in renewed interest in black suburbanization (Farley 1970; Connolly 1973; Pendleton 1973; Taeuber 1975; Kaplan 1976; Schnore, Andre, and Sharp 1976; Downs 1978; Guest 1978; Massey and Denton 1988; Wilson 1987), quantitative analyses of demographic shifts have shed little light on the processes of working- and middle-class black suburban community formation and development. Only recently have sociologists and historians begun documenting the history of black suburbs (Rose 1976; Wilson 1992; Wiese 1993). Since World War II, most research has focused on the urbanization and subsequent ghettoization of the working class and poor. Even the most widely cited studies of American suburbs have failed to note the establishment of black homeowners in suburban areas (Gans

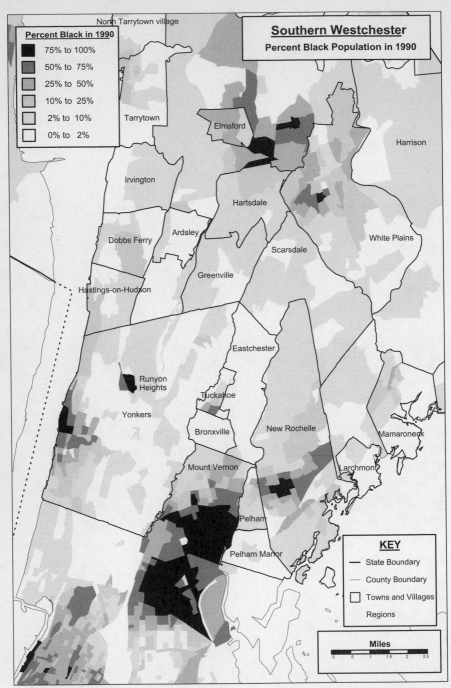

Percent Black in 1990

75% to 100%
50% to 75%
25% to 50%
10% to 25%
2% to 10%
0% to 2%

North Tarrytown village

Elmsford

Harrison

Tarrytown

Irvington

Hartsdale

White Plains

Dobbs Ferry

Ardsley

Scarsdale

Greenville

Hastings-on-Hudson

Eastchester

Runyon Heights

Tuckahoe

Yonkers

Bronxville

New Rochelle

Mamaroneck

Mount Vernon

Larchmont

Pelham

Pelham Manor

KEY

State Boundary
County Boundary
Towns and Villages
Regions

Miles

0   .5   1   1.5   2   2.5

I.1 Southern Westchester: Percentage Black Population in 1990

1967; Berger 1968; Jackson 1985; Rieder 1985; Zunz 1982), and the most significant studies of the black middle class have failed to deal in any detail with suburban community formation and development (Frazier 1962; Kronus 1987; Ball 1983; Landry 1987; Cose 1993; Feagin and Sikes 1994). Recently, two studies of black middle-class urban communities have been published: Mary Patillo McCoy's *Black Picket Fences* (1999), which is a study of Chicago's South Side, and Stephen Gregory's *Black Corona* (1998), which examines New York's working- and middle-class neighborhood of Corona-Elmhurst. Suburban black middle-class communities like Nepperhan, however, remain unexplored.

Contemporary discourse on the black middle class began in 1957, with the American debut of E. Franklin Frazier's scathing critique, *Black Bourgeoisie.* First published in France two years earlier under the title *Bourgeoisie Noire,* the work established Frazier as the preeminent scholar on race and class in America and touched off four decades of debate on the economic status of the black middle class. In *The New Black Middle Class* (1987), Bart Landry updated Frazier's work by considering black employment gains made in the post–civil rights era. According to Landry, despite recent progress, Frazier's central assessment still holds true. Although the black middle class continued to improve its occupational position in relation to whites, its hold on middle-class status remains marginal at best.

Even before Landry entered the fray, sociologist William J. Wilson had renewed scholarly interest in what had become known as the race versus class debate with the publication of his controversial book, *The Declining Significance of Race* (1978). Wilson's central argument was that class background and status have increasingly become the best predictors of black life chances and that racial discrimination has become less of a determining factor. Scholars responding to Wilson argued that race remained significant in the lives of middle-class blacks (Pinkney 1984, 53; Hacker 1992, 44; Cose 1993; Feagin and Sikes 1994). During the 1980s, Wilson, Landry, and others noted the recent movement of the black middle class from central cities to the suburbs (Pinkney 1984, 106; Farley 1987, 142; Landry 1987). For Wilson, urban decline triggered black suburbanization, which, in turn, contributed to growing concentrations of urban poverty (Wilson 1987).

The renewed interest in black middle-class suburbanization over the last decade was sparked both by a concern with the middle class as a barometer of black economic progress (the Frazier debate) and by a concern with middle-class geographic mobility as a partial explanation for increases in urban poverty (the Wilson debate). The suburbanization process in America is generally recognized as having begun in the nineteenth century, when industrialists purchased farmland and transformed rural areas into country estates (Zukin 1991, 138). But suburban areas did not become a focus of community research until after World War II, when planned suburbs became a national phenomenon, although blacks participated from the beginning. Gans's *The Levittowners* (1967), Berger's *Working-Class Suburb* (1968), Williams's *Black Workers in an Industrial Suburb* (1987), and Rieder's *Canarsie* (1985) are among the classic studies of post–World War II suburban residential areas.[7] In the suburbs they study, Berger and Gans ignore the experiences of African Americans, as well as the fundamental role of race. Although both Williams, in his analysis of labor relations in an industrial suburb, and Rieder, in his study of growing conservatism among suburban Jews and Italians, discuss the role of racial inequality and discrimination, neither examines an African-American middle-class community.

In the mind of the average American, the term "suburban" does not evoke images of persons of color, particularly African Americans. Sociological scholarship has done little to change this picture.[8] Gans's *Levittowners*, perhaps the most widely cited study of an American suburb, epitomizes the racially naive descriptions of most suburban community studies. It is a fact that Levittown developers excluded black residents, yet the work barely mentions the centrality of race in the organizing and structuring of community boundaries. The conspicuous absence of discussions of blacks and of the significance of race in the sociological literature on suburbs has had two fundamental consequences. First, the public is left with a distorted image that, on the one hand, defines the suburbs as white and middle-class and, on the other hand, ignores the central role of state and civic institutions in fostering the racial homogeneity of mainly white suburban communities. Second, the exclusion of blacks from portrayals of American suburbanization leaves the false impression that blacks have been too poor, politically weak, or lacking in industriousness to make the transition to the good life with the rest of America. While Kenneth Jackson's *Crabgrass Frontier* (1985) focused on discriminatory state policies in structuring suburban development, *Red Lines, Black Spaces* is the first study to detail local processes of suburban racialization.[9]

American urbanization and suburbanization trends have remained strong since the nineteenth century, transforming the nation's political and economic landscape. By 1920, Americans who lived in cities outnumbered those in rural areas for the first time in our nation's history (Roberts 1995, 128). As central cities became congested, so many urban dwellers headed for the suburban periphery that by 1970, the suburban population actually exceeded the central-city population. The rural landscape that once surrounded the central cities was replaced by a succession of suburban developments and strip malls. Today more than half the nation's population lives in one of 39 urban areas and their suburban extensions, called megalopolises by urban statisticians (Roberts 1995, 21, 122).

Over the past century, residential discrimination and the lack of stable employment opportunities have restricted black suburban settlement. Yet the trend toward black suburbanization has steadily increased since the civil rights movement and subsequent federal antidiscrimination efforts. The 1964 Civil Rights Act expanded middle-class employment opportunities, and the 1968 Fair Housing Act removed many overt racial barriers to suburban housing. The new black middle class has led the urban exodus (Jaynes and Williams 1989, 7, 89; Wilson 1987, 7, 136). According to Landry, the African-American share of the suburban population grew steadily, from 4.8 percent in 1970 to 6.1 percent in 1980 (Landry 1987; Farley and Allen 1987). In the New York metropolitan region, blacks represented 8.2 percent of the suburban population in 1980 (Massey and Denton 1993, 68). Other scholars report a 40 percent increase in black suburbanization between 1980 and 1990, following a period (1969–1983) of growing economic polarization between the black middle class and the black poor (Farley 1984; Beveridge and D'Amico 1994; Dawson 1994, 39).

Most of these new middle-class black suburbanites have settled in previously established racial enclaves like Nepperhan–Runyon Heights (Farley 1987, 144). Even with expanded employment opportunities and increased financial resources, residential segregation remains a significant barrier to full equality for the black middle class (Jaynes and Williams 1989, 9, 26). Unlike Asian and Hispanic Americans, black Americans continue to suffer from extremely high segregation rates, regardless of their socioeconomic status (Massey and Denton 1993, 87–88).

Scholars have noted that though blacks continue to lag behind whites on measures of unemployment, labor-force participation, income, occupation, and wealth, the black middle class has nevertheless experienced unprecedented growth since the 1950s (Farley 1984; Pinkney 1984; Dawson 1994, 29–36; Oliver and Shapiro 1995). By the 1980s, as earlier progress toward parity with whites slowed and the black middle class continued to lag behind in relative and absolute measures, its members were nonetheless outdistancing the black poor. In fact, growing intraracial inequality may have encouraged the black suburban trend of the 1990s. Suburbanization by this "new black middle class" is likely to continue in the twenty-first century, as urban decline and growing inequality persist unabated.

Although late nineteenth-century Yonkerites who lived downtown can be considered suburban when compared with residents of New York City, the environment in which they lived was actually a small version of any northeastern manufacturing city, complete with cold-water flats, poverty, crime, congestion, and a sizable working class employed in local industry. Yonkers also contained its own region of undeveloped farmland outside the downtown area. The Nepperhan–Runyon Heights community emerged within this suburban ring, then called "the country."

Black Americans were largely excluded from the great twentieth-century suburban expansion. Nepperhan–Runyon Heights is obviously a notable exception to this pattern. As families settled in Nepperhan, word of home-ownership opportunities spread to other family members and friends. A few persons who grew up in the neighborhood ended up marrying the guy or gal next door, and in some cases their children did the same. The result was a tight-knit community of extended, multigenerational families. In one sense, the community gives some idea of what might have happened if more black Americans had had opportunities to secure stable employment, suburban housing, and a decent area in which to raise their children.

But Nepperhan is more than an American success story. It highlights the central role of race in the shaping of contemporary social and political organization. There is a pressing need to understand the racial organization of twentieth-century American life as our society becomes increasingly polarized by class, race, and place, and the suburbs have been one of the least studied of the social arenas in which these forces have been played out.

The dominant paradigm used by scholars to explain race and race relations in the twentieth century has drawn on the ethnicity-based theories formulated by the Chicago School during the 1920s and 1930s under the leadership of sociologist Robert E. Park. Preoccupied with cultural contact between groups and with processes of assimilation in the urban milieu, the ethnicity model emphasized the presumed natural progression of group contact and treated both racial and ethnic groups as natural or organic cultural groups. Park and his colleagues predicted that the new black migrants would, like the waves of European immigrants that had preceded them, be absorbed into the city. This "race-relations cycle" model ignored the impact that state-sponsored residential racialization would have on developing communities, and on the politicization of racial consciousness.

Race became a central organizing principle of both the central city and its suburban fringes. Segregated communities became political and social units that linked individuals to both civil society and the state. Runyon Heights residents were concerned about race because race was used as a determining factor in the distribution of societal rewards and goods. Individuals decoded and represented the racial dynamics experienced in community life and made efforts to organize and redistribute resources along racial lines (Omi and Winant 1994, 56).

In his study of African-American politics *Behind the Mule,* Michael C. Dawson maintains that African Americans' perceptions of racial group interests, which he characterizes as "linked fate," act as a constraint on class divisions and determine black political behavior (Dawson 1994, 195–196). Though Dawson notes the historic link between economic subordination and racial subordination, his analysis of national voting trends does not capture the way in which group interests are shaped by pressures from the local community. Whether race or class interests prevail at any one time depends on how residents assess the impact of a particular local or national issue on their community. In Yonkers, racial interests were informed by both the national political climate surrounding racial policy and local civic and political confrontations in which race was used as the basis for the unequal treatment of community residents. At times, the group's collective racial interests seemingly came into conflict with their material self-interests, as when residents resisted the placement of low-income housing in their neighborhood. Residents' evaluations of the collective interests they had as middle-class suburban homeowners intersected with their evaluations of the impact of race on community life. Local community interests often became the basis for determining individual interests.

Urban and suburban residential segregation over the past century have held significance for racial consciousness in other ways, too, for segregated communities like Nepperhan were the first communities to draw the diverse members of the African diaspora together. Modern capitalist society underwent a phase of industrialization that spurred the movement of people between and within urban and suburban communities, and both racial and class lines were used in segregating the industrial landscape.

Increased concentrations of Negroes in metropolitan areas inspired the formation of a new consciousness for Americans of African descent. Although urban communities like Harlem have been widely recognized for their contribution to black social, cultural, and political life, the significance of the New Negro consciousness in suburban communities has gone largely unexplored (Lewis 1981; Watkins-Owens 1996).[10]

Nepperhan was one of many contemporary community contexts whose structuring along racial lines led to the politicization of racial consciousness. In the suburbs, however, where access to residential space was determined by class, as well, we can witness an ongoing negotiation between the racial and class interests of residents. As suburban Nepperhaners pursued the American Dream, their racial community provided a specific framework for transforming the daily slights of racial subordination into politicized group interests.

The term "community," as it is used in this study, implies "place," but it also implies the constellation of personal connections and the sense of historical continuity that individuals internalize. These contacts with others are structured, filtered, and interpreted through local institutions (families, churches, schools, political organizations, voluntary civic associations), forming a multidimensional basis for group consciousness and the articulation of group political interests.

The story of Runyon Heights is one of a successful struggle for community by a group of stable, working-class African Americans who fled the congestion of New York City long before the postwar suburban boom, the urban crises of the 1960s, or the middle-class urban exodus of the 1980s. In addition to its historic role in the process of American suburbanization, Runyon Heights affords a unique opportunity to look at the relationship between class and race, and the articulation of group interests in twentieth-century America.

1

Race and Place in
Industrial Yonkers

Beginning in the middle of the nineteenth century, Yonkers experienced
a period of unprecedented industrial expansion that affected both population growth and future residential development. It became a city of immigrants and migrants in search of work. During the second half of the
nineteenth century, a racialization of Yonkers' housing and employment
markets took place; the development of black residential concentrations
among both the working class and the middle class paved the way not
only for the formation of the so-called Negro ghetto in southwest Yonkers
(Getty Square) but also for the east-side black home-owning community
that would come to be known as Nepperhan.[1]

In Nepperhan, residents were brought together by both racial status
and class position: in the housing market, race determined which housing
was available, while class position determined residents' ability to purchase property. The development of segregated suburban housing markets linked race and class in contemporary geographic space, creating and
reinforcing racially based group boundaries.

Transportation and Industrial Growth in Yonkers

The industrial development of Westchester County was made possible by advances in urban transportation in the 1840s. Jackson (1985) describes how the steam ferry, the omnibus, the horse car, the commuter railroad, and later the cable car transformed the landscape of American cities in the nineteenth century, allowing both people and freight to travel greater distances in a working day.

East-Coast cities developed primarily along waterways. Situated on the banks of the Hudson River and bordering the northwestern end of New York City, Yonkers was uniquely placed to take advantage of the advances of the nineteenth and early twentieth centuries in industry and transportation. To the north, Yonkers adjoins the village of Hastings-on-Hudson and the town of Greenburg; to the east, the Bronx River.

By the 1840s, regular ferry service carrying passengers and freight between New York and Yonkers promoted the expansion of industry and population. River travel by steamboat was slow and costly, however, and was thus restricted to well-to-do commuters. Cheaper, more efficient transportation would be a prerequisite to working- and middle-class residential expansion away from the waterways and downtown industries.

Before industrialization, farming was the main occupation for local workers. Oats, wheat, hay, peaches, apples, potatoes, walnuts, pickles, chestnuts, and corn were produced locally and shipped to New York City along the Hudson (Johnson and others 1962, 19). During the early nineteenth century, once extensive water power became available, Yonkers inaugurated light manufacturing, to make use of the extensive water power available.

Beginning in the 1840s, the growth of railroads and of local industry coincided with the arrival of two distinct groups of people in the burgeoning area: wealthy industrialists, who began purchasing vast tracts of farmland outside the central village, on which they built country estates, and skilled and unskilled laborers, most of them immigrants from southern and eastern Europe, who found work in local industry.

Until the end of the nineteenth century, Yonkers was a walking city. Most industrial workers lived in the downtown areas, close to their workplaces. Commuting was a time-consuming as well as an expensive affair, and many local estates were built to serve as summer "country" homes. Those who maintained their place of business in downtown Yonkers but lived outside town had to be able to afford either horse-drawn railway or private coach service.

A period of industrial development was ushered in along the railways. By the 1860s, the railroad suburb had been born, and by the turn of the century the industrial suburb had come into its own (Goldston 1970, 30; Zukin 1991, 138). As the industrial cities expanded and transportation became more rapid, suburbia was pushed ever further from the urban core.

In the American mind, nineteenth-century suburbia was becoming a place not only for the wealthy but for the aspiring middle classes. Yonkers was one of the first American cities to take on the suburban label, a result of its proximity to New York City. W. E. Baxter noted Yonkers' growth as early as 1855 (Jackson 1985, 36). Suburban areas like Westchester County expanded rapidly. With the coming of the great locomotives and the proliferation of the railroads, the village of Yonkers evolved into more than a mere extension of New York City, as industry took advantage of the available resources. The manufactured goods now produced in Yonkers were easily transported north and south by rail. Much of the manufacturing took place along the Nepperhan River.

When the village of Yonkers was incorporated in 1855, the population was 7,554 (Allison 1984, 149–150). A mere seventeen years later, the village was incorporated as a third-class city with a population of 18,189 (Johnson and others 1962, 26, 43). And by 1910, the U.S. Census tallied 79,803 persons, a 66 percent increase over the previous decade.

The proliferation of the railways facilitated residential expansion to the north and east, while making commuters less dependent on the Hudson River ferry for transportation. Grand Central Station opened in New York City in 1871, Penn Station in 1910 (Jackson 1985, 94). Three separate railroads traversed Yonkers and connected it to northern Westchester and New York City. The New York & Harlem Railroad (New York Central Harlem Division) was running by 1844, touching Yonkers' eastern boundary (Jackson 1985, 20). The Hudson River Railroad (Metro North Hudson Division) began its route along the western edge in 1849, and the New York & Boston Railroad was founded in 1869 (Allison 1984, 156–160).

After a series of mergers and acquisitions in the 1870s and 1880s, the New York & Boston Railroad was eventually incorporated into the Division of the New York Central and Hudson River Railroad Company (Barlow 1980, 2). The single-track line began operation in 1881 (Allison 1984, 392). Known as the Putnam Line, or the Put, the railway cut through the center of the Nepperhan area, running parallel to Runyon Avenue to the west and Moultrie (Merril) and Touissant (Wilson) Avenues to the east. The line originally carried passengers as well as freight from Brewster, New York, proceeding south past businesses along Saw Mill River Road and Nepperhan Avenue in Yonkers, moving through what would become the Nepperhan community, through Van Cortlandt Park in the Bronx, and on to upper Manhattan. The small wood-frame Nepperhan Passenger Station, which gave the area its name, remained active until May 1958. Other communities would also develop along the railroad's fourteen-and-a-half-mile route.

Until the 1890s, only the wealthy could afford the luxury of country living outside the downtown Yonkers area, and only the professional and business classes could afford the railway commute to New York City. The average worker had to live in the city where he was employed and within walking distance to work. By the late nineteenth century, the monthly cost of the commute from Yonkers to New York was five dollars, nearly half the weekly wages of the average male worker (Johnson et al. 1962, 20). The burden of commuting was especially heavy for the small minority of Negroes who lived in Yonkers and worked in the least skilled, lowest-paying jobs as foundry workers, coachmen, domestics, servants, and cooks (Bogart 1898, 290).

From Walking City to Trolley-Car Suburb

Although railway expansion prompted industrial development, it was advances in local transportation that spurred suburban residential development. In 1866, the first horse-drawn-railway tracks in Yonkers were removed in order to widen its main street, Broadway. In 1886, the Yonkers Railroad Company was granted a franchise to lay horse-drawn-railway tracks in the downtown area of the city. They were quickly replaced by electric cars in 1893; in 1896 the company was consolidated with two other lines, and tracks were extended to Tuckahoe Road, one of two major arteries connecting east and west Yonkers, close to the Nepperhan area. Tracks were also laid down along Broadway from Yonkers to the Kingsbridge section of the Bronx (Allison 1984, 228–392). With the new electric trolley, travel speed increased to fourteen miles per hour, four times the rate of the horse-drawn systems (Jackson 1985, 115). This allowed workers to live farther from the center of town without increasing commuting time to work. With the advent of the elevated subway train on Broadway and 242nd Street in Kingsbridge, which connected with the Yonkers trolley from Getty Square, a relatively inexpensive commute to New York City had been established. The trolley paved the way for the suburban residential development outside downtown Yonkers that would occur after 1910. The Yonkers trolley system later became a part of the Third Avenue Railway Company, the last survivor of consolidations, bankruptcies, and competition in Westchester County's transportation industry.

Population Growth and the Racialization of Labor

Industrial expansion and population growth after the 1850s transformed the ethnic composition of the city. Many Irish immigrants came to work on the Croton Aqueduct. Scottish, Slavic, and English immigrants found work in the carpet factory of Scottish immigrant Alexander Smith (Weigold 1984, 77). By 1880, Yonkers, with approximately 19,000 residents, had expanded from a village of 900 acres to a city of 17.5 square miles (Allison 1984, 169–227). After 1890, as Yonkers, like the rest of the northeast, was becoming increasingly urban, thousands came from Eastern Europe in search of work. Between 1880 and 1920, Yonkers' population expanded by more than 500 percent, although the black population remained small. Out of 32,033 persons counted in the 1890 U.S. Census, only 533 were designated "colored" (Table 1.1). This broad and ambiguous category included "persons of Negro descent, Chinese, Japanese, and civilized Indians" (Allison 1984, 266–267). Although the "colored" population was growing, it still accounted for only 1.9 percent of the 100,176 city residents in 1920. Growing steadily, but more slowly than the city at large, the black population still represented fewer than 5 percent of Yonkers residents as late as 1960.

By the 1890s, Yonkers boasted a diverse industrial infrastructure and a multiethnic and multiracial workforce. Major employers included Otis Elevator (1854), the Waring Hat Manufacturing Company (1879), the Alexander Smith Carpet Factory (1865), and the Habirshaw Cable & Wire Company (1886).[2] Yonkers industry also included sugar refineries, rubber companies, breweries, and silk, plow, chemical, and wool factories (Johnson et al. 1962, 26–37).

After the Civil War, industrial employment in Yonkers resembled what scholars have labeled a split labor market, where better jobs were reserved for a labor aristocracy that was defined in racial terms. Workers who were socially and politically classified as white developed a consciousness that emphasized their place as free laborers in the market, and organized themselves along racial lines to exclude nonwhite workers.

5

Table 1.1. Population of Yonkers by Race, 1890–1990

Year	Total population	Total black population	Black percentage of total population
1890	32,033	533	1.7%
1920	100,176	1,940	1.9%
1930	134,646	*(NA)	—
1940	142,598	4,108	2.9%
1950	152,798	4,955	3.2%
1960	190,634	7,663	4.1%
1970	204,298	12,627	6.2%
1980	195,351	20,583	11.0%
1990	188,082	26,465	14.0%

Source: Data from U.S. Census.

White workers' anxiety toward nonwhite laborers culminated in the passage by Congress of a series of exclusion acts beginning in 1882 that placed stringent restrictions on Chinese immigration for twenty years (Ringer 1983, 644; Omi and Winant 1986, 65; Takaki 1989, 111).

Racial restrictions existed in Yonkers in a wide range of industries. David Roediger, in his study of the American working class, The Wages of Whiteness: Race and the Making of the American Working Class,[3] describes how European workers became white workers by defining themselves as a collective in opposition to black workers. White workers claimed the designation "hired hand" and rejected the term "servant," which had previously been used to refer to African slaves (Roediger 1991, 49). They also avoided menial jobs in domestic service, the performance of which was considered suitable only for so-called Negroes, who found few alternatives. As early as 1830, white workers had largely abandoned jobs in domestic service (Roediger 1991, 55).

All European immigrants were regarded as "white" by the dominant society, even though many of them had individual physical characteristics associated with being of African descent. Their ignorance of American language and culture did not bar them from exercising the civic and social privileges that accompanied the "white" political classification. As they adopted Anglo-American culture, they and their children increasingly assimilated into "white" America. As a result, once they had settled in the industrial cities of twentieth-century America, the non-English-speaking European immigrants were granted honorary membership in the white group. That acceptance was crucial in the areas of housing and employment. Their children benefited from the process of public education and were assimilated into the cultural, social, and political mainstream, unlike their darker brothers, who were consistently excluded, regardless of their degree of cultural adaptation.

Zunz (1982, 398) argues that as "occupational bonds began to replace ethnic bonds in the white community. . . . Blacks were drawn into an ever growing ghetto, irrespective of their social status." Zunz fails to acknowledge the significant fact that ethnic Europeans were able to forgo ethnic bonds for occupational ones only by excluding black workers from the industrial labor market. White inclusion was dependent on black exclusion. More than occupational bonds united workers; whiteness mattered.

Within the American social order, structural inequality, property, and racial representation are intricately linked (Dominguez 1986). The development and maintenance of a consciously white identity among European immigrants in industrial cities were contingent on the perception that black workers posed a threat to the industrial labor and housing markets. The maintenance of a strong Negro identity, by contrast, was predicated on the discrimination the group continually experienced, which helped foster group sentiments and racial consciousness. While black racial consciousness is made manifest by a rigid system of racial subordination and exclusion, white racial consciousness is dependent on the presumed threat of the black "other." The benefits of inclusion within the white group are taken for granted, and white racial identity is invoked whenever blacks threaten to challenge the political, economic, and residential norms of white privilege (Waters 1990, 18). Whites become preoccupied with maintaining racial privilege; blacks with eradicating racial inequities. Both groups tend to ignore the historical role racial ideology has played in the exploitation of all American workers by industrial capitalism, as well as the role of the state in fostering social inequality along racial lines and fostering racial animosity in civil society (Fields 1982).

The American labor union movement itself was initially based on the exclusion of Negro and other nonwhite workers. As early as 1899, W. E. B. Du Bois cited the hiring practices of business owners and the policies of unions as major factors contributing to the exclusion of blacks from industrial and skilled occupations in Philadelphia (Du Bois 1973, 323–333). Before the merger of the American Federation of Labor (AFL) and the Congress of Industrial Organizations (CIO) in 1955, AFL unions in construction, skilled metal trades, and railroad work routinely segregated and marginalized black workers across America in Jim Crow locals (Raskin 1986, 16). In 1920, AFL membership topped four million workers. At the same time, some national unions totally excluded black workers by writing color bars into their constitutions (Galenson 1986, 44–50). In that sense, the workers' movement in America was, at its foundation, racially delineated; class identity was itself racially stratified while racial identity was linked to occupational and residential differentiation.

Unlike other unions across the nation, the left-leaning CIO was founded to aid mass-production workers and, in including Negro workers from its very inception in the 1930s, reflected the significant numbers of black workers already in mass-production industries (Raskin 1986, 16; Galenson 1986, 57). The AFL, which began to organize skilled workers in 1886, continued to exclude black workers until 1936, when it chartered the all-black Brotherhood of Sleeping Car Porters, headed by A. Philip Randolph.[4]

Labor's marginalization of the black worker occurred with the active participation of U.S. government policymakers (Johnson 1943, 104). Discrimination was the norm in the segregated armed forces, and the government regularly avoided drawing up contracts with black-owned businesses. Woodrow Wilson appointed black social scientist George E. Haynes, founder of the National Urban League, to head the Bureau of Negro Economics in the Department of Labor in 1918, but he also segregated federal employment and greatly reduced the number of black civil servants (Dawson 1994, 31). It was not until June 1941 that President Franklin Delano Roosevelt issued Executive Order 8802, barring discrimination against workers in the defense industries and government regardless of "race, creed, color or national origin." This act was a response to the threat by A. Philip Randolph and other black leaders to organize a march on Washington. Later that year, Roosevelt signed Executive Order 9001, which barred discrimination in the awarding of defense contracts. Consequently, to the dismay of more radical leaders, Randolph called off what would have been the first mass demonstration for civil rights at the Capitol.

The labor movement remained a largely conservative influence on race relations in America, in its effort to allay anxiety among white workers rather than to provide a vehicle for democratic antiracist agitation. In fact, the labor movement failed to endorse the seemingly universalist agenda of Martin Luther King, Jr.'s, March on Washington in 1963. Although United Automobile Workers Union representative Walter Reuther attended the march, the AFL-CIO refused to support the interracial demonstration (Ringer 1983, 458).

Black Labor and the Black Ghetto

Though slavery had officially ended in New York State in July 1827, Yonkers employers continued to restrict the small number of black workers to menial and domestic jobs or service roles. Some of the city's largest employers openly practiced discrimination against black workers. By 1920, Yonkers boasted more than one hundred mills and factories, among them the Alexander Smith Carpet Company, the largest industry in early twentieth-century Yonkers (Halliburton 1987, 25). Smith employed more than 6,500 people in 1909, nearly one-third of the city's working population (Weigold 1984, 77), but a woman who has lived in the community for seventy years said flatly: "Alexander Smith didn't hire blacks, period." Later she said, "Yonkers just wasn't hiring black people, so you had to work in New York." Her comments were echoed by other residents interviewed. Informants reported that Otis Elevator and Habirshaw were the only large companies to employ Negroes in any significant numbers before World War II, and at Otis most of them worked only in the foundry.

Ernest Bogart's study of working-class Yonkers at the turn of the last century, *The Housing of the Working Class in Yonkers* (1898), provides empirical verification of the experiences reported by informants from Runyon Heights. Bogart identifies six streets where most black workers resided: James, John, Elm, and School Streets, and Palisade and Vinyard Avenues.[5] Yet none of the residents of James or John Streets, where black workers made up approximately 90 percent of the households, was employed in carpet manufacturing or in hat manufacturing, Yonkers' second largest industry. These two industries alone accounted for 28 percent of the local workforce. According to Bogart's survey, only 8 percent of the "coloreds" on James and John Streets were employed in manufacturing of any type, by comparison with 32 percent of workers employed in manufacturing citywide.[6] Only foundry work was available to black male workers in Yonkers industries. Black workers were excluded from the most stable and lucrative jobs in the local industrial economy.

Relegated to traditional "Negro" occupations, which were characterized by low pay and heavy labor, even the best-educated black workers were banned from employment in better-paying skilled jobs. Many worked in service-oriented jobs as domestics, porters, expressmen, or coachmen. Of 102 employed adult residents of James and John Streets in 1898, 61 percent worked as housekeepers or domestics. These two streets alone were home to 10 percent of the city's Negroes. Bogart's analysis does not provide gender breakdowns, but the high percentage of domestic workers suggests that women made up a significant portion of the Negro workforce. His statistics clearly indicate that in the nineteenth century, black employment was limited to traditional Negro jobs in the service sector of the industrial economy. In industrial work, access was limited to the dirtiest and most menial jobs, "which no one else wanted" (Weigold 1984, 67).

Nineteenth-century residential patterns set the stage for black ghettoization in Yonkers after World War II. Like blacks in other American cities at the end of the nineteenth century, the small Negro population in Yonkers, only 1.6 percent of the city's inhabitants, was concentrated in the older, immigrant working-class neighborhoods of the walking city (Zunz 1982, 57). Nearly half the Negro population lived on the six streets identified by Bogart. These streets came to form the heart of the postwar black ghetto in Yonkers. On James and John Streets, 89 percent and 91 percent, respectively, of the households were "colored." Elm was 29 percent colored, while School Street and Palisade and Vineyard Avenues all had concentrations of less than 8 percent. Of the fifty-seven "colored" households identified by Bogart, 60 percent lived on either James or John Street.

Researchers have suggested that black isolation in the wards of major cities, including New York, was relatively low in 1890 (Lieberson 1980, 258). In Yonkers, black residential segregation was more extreme than the segregation experienced by European immigrants. In the working-class districts studied by Bogart, 84 percent of the inhabitants were foreign-born, compared with 69 percent for the city as a whole. Fifty-one percent of his sample were recent Irish immigrants. Although three isolated concentrations of recent Irish immigrants existed on Vinyard, Orchard, and Parker Streets at the time of Bogart's study, residential segregation of Negroes would continue to increase over the next few decades, despite the small percentage of Negro residents in the city. Bogart's study also illuminates the relation between economic marginality and the segregated residential patterns developing in the city at the turn of the century (Bogart 1898, 287).

Table 1.2 shows the marginal incomes of working-class African Americans who lived on four streets in the downtown area.[7] Those streets where

Table 1.2. Average Weekly Income of Working Class Households by Street

Street	James	John	Elm	Palisade	All
Income	$8.73	missing	$11.12	$12.51	$13.27
% Negro Head of Household	89	91	29	8	12

Source: Data from Bogart (1898).

black heads of households were most highly concentrated also housed workers who received the lowest average weekly wages among the city's working class. That is, incomes declined as the concentration of Negro workers increased. Workers who lived on the predominantly Negro James Street received an average weekly household income of $8.73. Workers on Elm, however, where only 29 percent of the population was Negro, earned $11.12 per week, and those from Palisade, where 8 percent were Negro, earned $12.51.

This situation had its own circularity: the segregation of housing and neighborhoods was reinforced by the exclusion of blacks from better-paying industrial work because low wages helped rule out the possibility of a move to more expensive accommodations. In that sense, the housing and labor markets in Yonkers were not reflective of the natural forces of competition; they were deliberately structured along racial lines. The processes by which European immigrants were assimilated and blacks were clustered into segregated neighborhoods were a direct result of that deliberate design.

Bogart's study captures an estimated 251 "colored" persons out of a total population of 533, or close to half of the black population of Yonkers. The makings of a segregated city were already evident by the late 1890s, inasmuch as African-American residents were being drawn into a few streets in the old downtown area while simultaneously being excluded from higher-paying industrial work. The link between residential segregation and occupational segregation has also been noted in connection with other northeastern industrial cities (Hershberg and others, 1979).

Scholars sometimes underestimate the link between residential and occupational discrimination. Olivier Zunz writes (1982, 6):

Blacks were the last group to arrive in large numbers in the industrial city. They experienced a settlement process radically different from that of white ethnic groups, a process which led to the formation of the ghetto. Compared with white ethnic groups, Blacks lived history in reverse: while foreign immigrants ultimately became assimilated into a unified structure dominated by the native white American world based on rank and social status within it, Blacks were increasingly segregated from whites on the basis of race and irrespective of their social status.

Zunz is clearly right so far as he goes, but what he does not articulate fully is that the racial classification system in the United States, one that assigns social and human value on the basis of skin color and other physiological characteristics, is itself a status classification system that is linked to a process of economic subordination in the labor and housing markets. Individuals of African descent have been classified according to a set of observable biological characteristics—thick lips, broad nose, dark tightly curled hair—associated with central and sub-Saharan peoples (those of so-called black Africa), and are placed in the racial category "Negro" ("black"). Those physical attributes have served as a justification for their occupational and residential exclusion. So certain racial characteristics condemn their owners to low-status occupations, and low-status occupations, in turn, reinforce the stereotypes on which the system depends; rather than being viewed as dirty because they were compelled to do dirty work, Negro workers were seen as performing dirty work *because* they were dirty.

We can observe the intersection of racial, economic, and gender subordination in the nineteenth-century labor market in the employment opportunities for Negro women. Negro women were largely confined to domestic activities in the homes of high-status white families. Not only was the work they performed "dirty," but it also removed them from the homemaker role conferred on white women, even those in the working class. Their status, not only as dirty workers but also as custodians of white domesticity, would prevent many Negro women from being able to claim bourgeois status as "ladies." In essence, prejudices about race, class, and gender were fused in the perception of black women's work roles (Higginbotham 1996, 190).

The conditions of working-class employment and housing in late nineteenth-century Yonkers provided the context for twentieth-century suburbanization; suburbanization provided a new context for Negro residential isolation and community development. Studies of segregation patterns demonstrate that racial discrimination is the primary factor determining patterns of residential segregation in cities as well as suburbs (Taeuber 1975; Stearns and Logan 1986; Massey 1990; Alba and Logan 1993; Massey and Denton 1993). Whereas twentieth-century white ethnic economic mobility and suburbanization led to a decline in ethnic concentration in neighborhoods, black mobility and suburbanization resulted in continued, or at times even increased, segregation.

Contrary to popular notions concerning patterns of segregation in the North, employment and housing segregation in Yonkers preceded the massive black migrations from the rural South around World War I. Nevertheless, by comparison with today's neighborhoods, those of the nineteenth century were less segregated. I found no all-black streets in the late nineteenth-century Yonkers ghetto. Lower segregation rates and a smaller population also meant that residential contact was likely to occur more frequently between blacks and whites in the old walking city than in the residential suburb of today. But Negro segregation levels grew dramatically as suburban residential development expanded. Scholars have noted that racial segregation was increasing across the urban North between 1890 and 1930, irrespective of black population gains (Lieberson 1980, 258). In the case of both Yonkers in general and Nepperhan in particular, suburban residential development intensified both class and racial segregation. Industrial changes in the region's postwar political economy only partly explain the "hyperghettoization" that would come to characterize southwest Yonkers in the 1990s; it also arose from the bowels of the contemporary racialized suburb and the devastating processes of residential and occupational segregation that were set in motion during the late nineteenth century.

Demographer Douglas Massey (1990) links economic inequality to racial subordination by calling contemporary residential patterns "American Apartheid." He maintains that today's ghettos are a result of an increase in minority poverty within racially segregated cities (329). Stearns and Logan (1986) find that the racial structuring of the housing market underlies changes in segregation and suburbanization. Research suggests that residential segregation, caused by discrimination in the housing market, and increased poverty, caused in part by discrimination in the labor market, interact to form residential communities that are homogeneous by class and race. Both the black suburb and the racial ghetto are a result of the housing and employment discrimination that have characterized the past century. As a further consequence, black workers have suffered concrete economic disadvantages that have influenced the quality of their community lives. These disadvantages still hold strong implications for the accumulation of family wealth and for the mobility of black workers into the middle class.[8]

Home Ownership and the Black Middle Class

By the 1890s, a small group of middle-class blacks had emerged within the larger black community of Yonkers. They tended to purchase homes and live in or adjacent to the older commercial and industrial area in the downtown section of the city, where the larger Negro population lived. Since the colonial period, Yonkers had always maintained a small Negro population. Still, even with the success of an occasional entrepreneur like Francis J. Moultrie, a well-known caterer and the most prominent Negro businessman of the period, working- and middle-class Negroes' experiences in the city remained qualitatively different from those of European immigrants.[9] Judging from interviews with residents and from historical records, there were no black nurses, policemen, firemen, bankers, industrial foremen, or managers until after 1920 (Esannason and Bagwell 1993, 30).[10] The limitations placed on occupations open to Negroes restricted the growth of a traditional managerial and professional middle class. Middle-class Negroes included a handful of preachers, ministers, musicians, morticians, and doctors who served the emerging black ghetto. Due to the skewed occupational structure, blue-collar occupations like carpenter, coachman, and railroad porter could carry middle-class status, particularly if the individual was a homeowner in a respectable community. Nonetheless, like discrimination in employment, residential discrimination was an assumed part of the local landscape, even for the most prosperous and stable middle-class Negroes.

Thus, home ownership took on heightened importance as a symbol of middle-class status and respectability. The quest for home ownership, a tradition in post-Emancipation African-American culture, is part of a broader historical search for political autonomy and economic independence. The all-black towns that sprang up in Mississippi, Oklahoma, and other border states during the era of the railroads testify to this yearning.

As I just noted, most early black residents were neither successful petty-bourgeois entrepreneurs, like Moultrie, nor professionals; they were working-class, with jobs in the service economy or in semi- or low-skilled blue-collar occupations. In fact, home ownership helped compensate for the marginal satisfaction that low-wage employment afforded blacks, and thus homeowners took on the bourgeois interests of the propertied class. One resident of thirty-four years, a sixty-one-year-old postal worker originally raised in southwest Yonkers, explained the meaning of home ownership to Nepperhaners: "It just gives you a sense of pride in knowing that if I don't do anything else in life, at least you own something. Home ownership, or owning anything, to me just puts a different aspect into your life. And I think that breeds into your children too. Then they want to own something, they want to accomplish more. And there weren't that many communities where blacks were welcomed. You know, over in the other part of town, you couldn't buy a home that easily. Unless you bought it from some Jewish person or somebody who just sold it to you, sort of in the background."

Among the blacks able to purchase private land and homes, most found housing opportunities available only in areas already inhabited by other blacks, usually located only a stone's throw away from the larger and poorer black ghetto. Many homeowners in southwest Yonkers would later find their investments engulfed, first by an expanding population of low-wage and poor black migrant workers, and later by public housing.

Regardless of income or social class, most blacks in Yonkers lived in this "colored" section in the southwest part of town. Homeowners often lived on the outer boundaries of what was in fact a thriving working-class ghetto. After the 1960s, the quality of life in this ghetto would decline dramatically. At the outset of the twentieth century, unemployment was relatively low, and Negroes of every class, status, and color lived within the confines of the ghetto. After 1910, large estates to the east and north of the central city were sold to speculators who subdivided them for working- and middle-class residential developments.

Few developers envisioned the arrival of Negro tenants. In 1920, although the black population was under two thousand, less than 2 percent of Yonkers' hundred thousand citizens, racial discrimination when it came to real estate markets was widespread. In describing the early twentieth-century working-class residential suburb, Jackson (1985) and Zunz (1982) concur that the majority of African-Americans, regardless of income or status, did not escape the confines of the ghetto.

Thus the ghetto was the only option available to the Negro middle classes. According to Zunz (1982, 398), "evading the ghetto may have awarded a different status to a few Blacks—not on the basis of occupation but of residence—for only a short time, because many of these isolated spots of independent black settlements were rapidly joined by an ever growing ghetto." Even W. E. B. Du Bois had prophesied resistance to a

Negro suburban presence in his landmark turn-of-the-century study *The Philadelphia Negro* (1899/1973, 296–297):

> To a race socially ostracized, it means far more to move to remote parts of a city, than to those who will in any part of the city easily form congenial acquaintances and new ties. The Negro who ventures away from the masses of his people and their organized life, finds himself alone, shunned and taunted, stared at and made uncomfortable; he can make few new friends, for his neighbors however well-disposed would shrink to add a Negro to their list of acquaintances. Thus he remains far from friends and the concentred social life of the church, and feels in all its bitterness what it means to be a social outcast. Consequently emigration from the ward has gone in groups and centered itself about some church, and individual initiative is thus checked. At the same time color prejudice makes it difficult for groups to find suitable places to move to—one Negro family would be tolerated where six would be objected to; thus we have here a very decisive hindrance to emigration to the suburbs.

Indeed, Yonkers witnessed the development of three distinct areas of black-owned homes that would later be enveloped by the expanding southwest ghetto. For a brief time, these areas were reputed to have housed some of the city's outstanding citizens. Culver Street, Cottage Place, and Jefferson Street were all short stretches of stable working-class and lower-middle-class housing on the west side of the city. Many in these areas became homeowners after first renting from a white owner. The most unique of the three developments, the Culver Street site, was the property of the Colored Co-Operators of America, an organization of Negro businessmen and clergy founded in 1904 by its grand master, the Reverend John J. Smyer, Pd.D., pastor of Memorial AME Zion Church; F. J. Moultrie was grand treasurer (Allison 1984, 430).[11] The cooperative, which doubled as an insurance company (the Ethiopian Life Insurance Company), owned nine three- family flats on Culver Street, a small factory that manufactured house trim, windows, and doors, as well as a grocery store on New Main Street. The Colored Co-Operators faded from the historical record following the Great Depression, although a couple of the Culver Street homes remain standing today in the shadows of public housing projects and auto-repair shops.

Although most residents of these home-owning areas had stable nonindustrial working-class jobs, respondents reported that they were perceived by the broader Negro community, as well as by themselves, as having middle-class status. The growth of these three areas was stymied, however, by their proximity to the expanding working-class and poor populations on the west side of town. Only Nepperhan, the fourth black settlement, located in the eastern suburban area, survived both the Depression and urban renewal. Interviews suggest that a number of private homeowners in the Culver Street and Cottage Place areas were relocated to make way for urban renewal housing projects; homeowners were replaced by the working poor and unemployed. Because Nepperhan was the only residential space available for sale to blacks that was not adjacent to the ghetto, today it remains the only stable working- and middle-class community of black homeowners in Yonkers.

The new twentieth-century residential suburb that was to develop outside the downtown area embraced and even augmented the segregationist policies of its industrial forerunner. Suburban real estate increasingly embodied both racial and class-based distinctions; stable working- and middle-class white families took advantage of suburban opportunities, while largely barring blacks of equal status. The black ghetto would continue to expand, as the black middle class seeking access to suburban housing encountered restrictive covenants and discriminatory social practices. The real story behind the success of Nepperhan was that good land outside the ghetto became available for purchase by blacks.

2

The Peopling
of Nepperhan

Residential development in Nepperhan followed on the heels of the breakup of large estates in lower Westchester County during the early twentieth century. This period has been described as one of degentrification, when New York City financiers purchased property from the descendants of colonial elites (Zukin 1991, 142). Real estate speculation mushroomed, foreshadowing the rise of the residential suburb.

By and large, the Westchester real estate market was limited to European immigrants and their white descendants. During this early period of suburban expansion, African Americans encountered widespread resistance throughout Yonkers and Westchester County. "Coloreds" did not fit in with the county's self-image of private suburban country clubs and golf courses. Negroes did establish home-owning enclaves in Mount Vernon and New Rochelle, nearby suburban cities in eastern Westchester that attracted a large African-American population. These communities dwarfed the Culver Street, Cottage Place, and Jefferson Street developments in Yonkers. But in the newly created suburban areas of east Yonkers, racial restrictions nearly completely blocked black home ownership. A unique set of circumstances made Nepperhan property available to Negro home seekers.

From Country Retreat to Residential Suburb

The story of Runyon Heights begins on December 13, 1871, when Charles Runyon, a New York industrialist, purchased sixty-three acres of land from Benjamin Curser for sixty-five thousand dollars.[1] Runyon was president of the Communipaw Coal Company. Like other industrialists of his era, he used his estate as a country retreat—that is, he constructed a summer home on it but left the vast expanse undeveloped.

The following April, Runyon sold small parcels to Reuben Van Pelt and to School District No. 1, Yonkers.[2] The Van Pelt property, on the western side of Saw Mill River Road, was outside the area later known as Nepperhan, and was eventually zoned and developed for industrial use. The school district purchased a parcel of land on the east side of the Saw Mill River Road for construction of a new elementary school to replace the one-room schoolhouse that had stood on the northeast corner of Tuckahoe Road and Saw Mill River Road in the first quarter of the nineteenth century. The old schoolhouse had recently been torn down, and its replacement, School 1, was to be located on Second Street (Allison 1984, 176; it was later renamed Dunbar Street). The school drew its students from a broad geographic area, including Homefield and neighboring Nepperhan Heights, and served residents within as well as outside the Nepperhan area until World War II.

While Charles Runyon was still alive, approximately ten to twelve acres were sold off. By the time the first official map of the estate was drawn, in 1872, the Runyon land constituted approximately fifty-two acres, bounded by Saw Mill River Road to the west, the Odell estate to the north, Tuckahoe Road to the south, and the large Fowler estate to the east.[3]

When Charles Runyon died in 1903, the Runyon estate fell under the directorship of the Runyon family. Deed records for 1910 list the estate owners as Carmen R. Runyon, Arthur S. Runyon, and Charles Runyon, Jr. (executors), Margaret C. Runyon (wife of Arthur Runyon), Isabelle M. Runyon (Charles's widow), and Helen R. Belknap.[4] The relationship of Helen Belknap to the Runyons remains unclear, although she did come to own a small parcel of land adjacent to the estate. The year 1910 marked the beginning of a great transformation in land usage in Nepperhan and throughout the region. The Runyon estate soon became a suburban neighborhood, populated by striving Negroes, among others.

New York Telephone was the first corporation to both anticipate and aid residential development in the area. In February 1910, the company purchased from the Runyon estate the land necessary to place telephone poles in Nepperhan. By the time the first parcels were sold as subdivisions, the Putnam line of the New York Central and Hudson River Railroad had already leased the right of way from the Runyon estate, and the Nepperhan Station near Tuckahoe Road was in active use.

A second estate would comprise the eastern section of the Nepperhan community. It was originally a 40-to-40.25-acre estate belonging to Sarah A. and Isaac V. Fowler.[5] This area begins east of Hunt Avenue and the southern portion of Belknap Avenue.[6] As reported by residents and confirmed by deeds, this eastern section remained largely undeveloped (excluding the southern end of Bushey Avenue) until after World War II.

Before 1900, the area surrounding the Runyon land was not completely undeveloped. By then, Yonkers had become home to numerous boarding schools, a few of which made their home in the Nepperhan area.[7] Residents I have talked to have no recollection of the schools, although their presence overlapped with the settlement of the neighborhood.

Memorial Methodist Episcopal Church was also situated on Tuckahoe Road, across the street from the Baxter School on the west corner of Altonwood Place. The church basement became the home of the first Negro prayer group in Nepperhan. In the 1930s, the church was converted into a rooming house; today a garden supply store occupies the original wood-frame structure.

Archival maps show that, as late as 1931, only the property belonging to St. Mary's Cemetery cut into an otherwise solid forty-acre rectangle of the estate. St. Mary's Cemetery abuts Sprain Road and the eastern boundary of Nepperhan. It was in active use at the time.[8]

The Selling of a Black Suburb

The Hudson P. Rose Company, a small realty agency based at 32 West 45th Street, New York, was the first to regard the Runyon land as an investment opportunity. The company purchased its first parcel from the estate in December 1911.[9] At first, Rose sold land almost as fast as it could purchase it. In December 1912, the company bought the land bordering the railroad tracks. In April 1913, Rose sold this tract to the New York Central Railroad Company, presumably at a profit.[10]

The Hudson P. Rose Company also opened the Runyon lands to Negro buyers, an unprecedented act on the part of a white suburban realtor in Yonkers. Nepperhan residents frequently reported difficulty purchasing homes in other parts of Yonkers and Westchester County. The neighborhood's genesis can be traced directly to the actions of Rose and a few other real estate developers and financiers.

In the end, six developers were involved in the initial period of real estate speculation in Nepperhan: the Hudson P. Rose Company, Henry Southgate, the Beechwood Realty Company, the Queen Mab Company, the Marcy Realty Company, and Wekando, Inc. What is most striking is that these realtors set out to target a specifically Negro market. Many older residents told of reading newspaper advertisements inviting Negroes to survey prospective lots and of hearing stories of land auctions where Harlem residents were invited to survey properties. Since none of the Runyon Heights residents interviewed purchased their homes through these auctions or personally knew anyone who had, it remains uncertain whether any actually took place.[11] Such "outings" did occur during the 1920s for the large Odell estate, located to the north, which would become known as Homefield.

Reports of newspaper advertisements, however, can be substantiated. Both Henry Southgate and the Hudson P. Rose Company ran advertisements in the *New York Amsterdam News,* a Negro weekly, between 1922 and 1925 (Figure 2.1). Rose's advertisement appears on page 8 of the first available issue,[12] dated November 29, 1922, and in every subsequent issue of the paper through April 25, 1923. Deed records indicate that migrants from Harlem purchased land with increasing frequency after 1920. Meanwhile, Henry Southgate was also purchasing lots from Rose. The May 2, 1923 issue, ran an ad for Southgate in place of Rose's. Southgate continued to purchase lots from Rose until the Depression.

It is significant that Rose and Southgate identified the thriving new Harlem community as their target market and also that they used modern print media to attract buyers specifically from the Negro community. From its very inception, twentieth-century suburbanization was a process that employed modern consumer-marketing practices.

Harlem itself contained a diversified population from the African diaspora, as Manhattan's real estate market relegated native-born Negro New Yorkers, Caribbean-born black immigrants, Negro migrants from the South, and immigrant Africans to either the already overcrowded Tenderloin and San Juan Hill areas of Manhattan or the new "Negro metropolis," Harlem. Many had come to Harlem in hopes of participating in the creation of a modern urbanized Negro world. Some soon tired of urban life, however, and sought alternative housing north of "the City."

It has been estimated that, in the country as a whole, up to 85 percent of

December 27, 1922

May 2, 1923

July 11, 1923

BUY NEPPERHAN LOTS!

FORGET Croton Point—No mortgages on the land—Free and Clear of heirs—All your battles have been fought by me. Your troubles are over when you start with me. This property is the best ever offered to you. Backed by one of the strongest companies doing business. There are now 80 houses built and occupied by owners. Ten new 1, 2 and 4 family houses now being built. The improvements on the property are: Sidewalks, Electric Lights, Graded Streets, Public School, Church, Railroad Station, Trolley to Subway Trains to Sixth and Ninth Ave. "L." Time, 23 minutes to city. Prices start at $300 and run up to $1,000 per lot. Terms $25 down. Warranty Deed at $300. I personally assist you in securing your loan to build. Call and see me. My references are 600 satisfied people and my bank.

EXTRAORDINARY OPPORTUNITY—$2,000 down buys flat house located between 7th and 8th Avenues on 128th Street.

TO LET—One five-room and four six-room apartments; electric lights; possession sixty days. No agents. Rents $50 and $70 a month. Location 130th Street bet. Seventh and Lexington avenues.

HENRY SOUTHGATE
112 WEST 130th ST.   Tel. Morningside 8152

October 10, 1923

Real Estate Bargains

$500 Cash Down and Up to $1,500 Cash Down—Brick houses that are located in the best part of Harlem.

Modern and Up-to-Date. See Owner.

Nepperhan, Yonkers—Fine building lots. Loans arranged to build. 250 houses occupied by owners. Well restricted property. New parkway buildng; public school and church; 23 minutes to elevated; 13 minutes to subway. New electric line connecting with Grand Central trains. Small down payments.

HENRY SOUTHGATE
201½ WEST 123rd STREET, NEW YORK CITY
PHONE MORNINGSIDE 8152

May 5, 1925

2.1 Advertisements from the *Amsterdam News*

black suburbanites were once city dwellers (Lake 1981). A few of the first Harlem migrants to Nepperhan settled in the eastern area, which came to be known as the Hill. This section developed more slowly and somewhat more haphazardly than the original Nepperhan area west of "the Put."

The years between 1906 and 1930 illustrate the important role realtors played in shaping neighborhood development and local boundaries.

Although the Fowler estate was sold and subdivided before the Runyon estate in 1906, no record of private land development before 1927 was uncovered. Before the Depression, only a handful of homes were built on the southern portion of Bushey Avenue, although a number of investor-agents attempted to take possession of the Fowler land.

Beechwood Realty purchased the entire estate from Sarah A. Fowler on July 3, 1906.[13] Three days later, Beechwood entered into a mortgage agreement with Woodson R. Oglesby for $25,000. The mortgage balance was to be paid to Oglesby by July 3, 1909.[14] Beechwood apparently defaulted on the agreement and lost the land. In October 1914, the Queen Mab Company brought suit against Beechwood and others in a special term of the New York State Supreme Court. To resolve the dispute, the court-appointed referee, William L. Snyder, decided to offer the mortgaged lands at public auction at the front door of city hall. At the auction, duly held on October 6, the premises conveyed to Beechwood Realty Company were purchased by the plaintiff, Queen Mab Company, for $5,000. On May 18, 1917, Queen Mab sold the property to another New York–based firm, Marcy Realty Company.[15]

After this early period of land sales, the historical record for the Fowler estate becomes clouded. Deed records fail to list Marcy Realty as either grantor or grantee. It is not even clear from the record whether either Marcy or Queen Mab was a part of the Nepperhan Home Building Corporation, which first filed subdivision maps in 1927. Consequently, informants provided the only reliable information on the early settlement of the east side of Nepperhan.

Informants reported that Thomas Keno and his family, who purchased their property in August 1946, were among the first residents on the Hill. Using the Keno name and knowledge of the location of their property, I traced the purchase of their home and worked backward, checking both grantor and grantee listings. What I discovered was surprising. The Kenos had purchased their plot from Wekando.[16] I could not locate Wekando as grantee in the deed records, and no entries for Marcy Realty exist in deed records after the initial purchase in 1917. How did Wekando come to own what turns out to be a large portion of the Fowler estate? Deed records have numerous entries showing that Wekando continued to sell property in the area as late as 1969. In addition, a few lots were sold to the city of Yonkers during the 1940s and 1950s, possibly to cover taxes on the remaining properties. The answer to the riddle was that Woodson R. Oglesby was the president of Wekando.

It seems likely that Oglesby was able to capitalize on the misfortunes of others during the Depression by either purchasing lands from another realtor at a cheap rate or buying them at public auction as a result of the previous owners' having defaulted on taxes. Tax and mortgage defaults were a common occurrence in real estate during the Depression years, and record keeping in Yonkers was lax. After nearly forty years, Oglesby reentered the real estate market in Runyon Heights, although the city retained a small parcel of land. Oglesby's son, Woodson R., Jr., a retired oil geologist living in Florida, indicated in a telephone interview that he knew little about his father's real estate dealings, even though he was listed as vice president of Wekando in deeds filed during the 1960s. The younger Oglesby merely signed the necessary papers and collected the proceeds when land was sold.

Clearly, ownership of the vast strip called the Hill was not an investment that yielded rapid returns for Oglesby, although, thanks to real estate appreciation, it did benefit his descendants. Longtime residents reported that the Keno family had an opportunity to purchase the majority of the Hill area from Oglesby when they first arrived in 1946. Residents, however, exaggerated the extent of Oglesby's holdings in Nepperhan. Indeed, the Kenos did buy a few lots from Oglesby as speculative investments, as did a good many other Negro families who moved to the area during this period. Many other families purchased from the city during the postwar years.

Even though Rose and Southgate had clearly marketed Nepperhan to blacks before 1922, blacks were not the first to venture into Nepperhan. Grantor records indicate that Rose made seventy-two land sales between 1912 and 1917. Most purchasers listed their former address as either New York City or Yonkers. Of those first seventy-two buyers, only six had non-Italian surnames. Obviously, Rose's initial primary market was made up of recent Italian immigrants; why he began to advertise to blacks is a mystery. Perhaps he recognized the potential of this untapped market and envisioned quick turnover and handsome profits. The presence of the railroad station made the area less likely to attract white buyers, who had many other options in the real estate market. Or perhaps he simply wished to afford Negroes the same opportunities as whites. Indeed, given that sales to nonblacks between 1912 and 1917 appear to have been brisk, Rose's focus on the Negro market appears even more curious.

One possible explanation is that the largely working-class Italian Americans who purchased land were either less interested in building a home in Nepperhan or less able to do so than they had been. A number, in fact, bought land for the sole purpose of creating a country garden within traveling distance of their homes in the Bronx. Although the first sale for construction of a private home was in March 1912, when the Hudson P. Rose Company sold a lot to Vito Barattino,[17] by 1920, Barattino had still not established residence in Nepperhan, according to federal census manuscripts and residents. This pattern was observed for many other Italian-American buyers; many bought land but never built homes in the area. In fact, deed records show that some Italian Americans who had purchased lots actually sold them back to Rose, who resold the lots to Southgate or to Negroes. A minority held on to their lots and built homes. Barattino eventually moved his family to Nepperhan in 1928. The home he built on Altonwood Place has housed three generations of Italian-American Nepperhaners. Others families, after living in the neighborhood for a single generation, sold to incoming Negroes.

For whatever motivation, the Rose Company continued to buy land from the Runyon estate, which it successfully resold to black families and individuals. Though it appears that the entrepreneur Hudson P. Rose was the instigator, the Runyon family, by subdividing its property and selling off lots to Rose in small parcels, participated indirectly in selling land to blacks. Whether the Runyons had knowledge of Rose's initial business dealings with Negroes or approved of the undertaking is unknown. Nevertheless, once sales were under way, the Runyons may have found themselves with little alternative but to sell to Rose. Rose, by contrast, was a shrewd businessman. Buying only a few lots at any one time, he protected his own investment, while placing the risk of any larger loss on the Runyons themselves. In breaking with the local norms and selling to Negroes, Rose took a gamble, but he apparently turned a profit.[18]

As far as I have been able to ascertain, the first identifiable Negro to own property in Nepperhan was Joseph Morgan, who bought land there in 1918.[19] It is possible to speculate, on the basis of his previous home address, however, that Arthur Ryce was in fact the first Negro to purchase land, in 1914.[20] Ryce had formerly lived at 168 West 136th Street, in the heart of black Harlem. The American West Indian Association was situated just down the street at 149 West 136th Street, and the entire area was more than 75 percent black as early as 1920 (Watkins-Owens 1996, 54). That Ryce was Negro is nevertheless a conjecture, for race is not recorded in deed records and his name does not appear in either the 1920 federal census or the 1925 New York State census.

In any case, Joseph Morgan and his family were without doubt among the earliest African-American families to settle the area. The Morgans became a significant family in the community's development; four generations of them were active in community organization and in local affairs. Arthur Morgan, Joseph's son, had sons of his own who are noted for creating a social club after World War II called the Sportsmen's Lounge, a popular Nepperhan attraction, particularly for the younger generation. As with many other black families, multiple generations of Morgans populated Nepperhan. Arthur Morgan's children married and eventually purchased homes themselves. Some still reside in the community. Joseph Morgan's great-grandchildren now live in the home he built. This pattern of successive generations buying homes in Nepperhan emerged only among black Nepperhan residents. Most of the children of European-American families in Nepperhan came to settle outside the area as adults.

The Perencheif family also reportedly moved to Nepperhan in 1918, but their presence was not recorded in the 1920 federal census. Family members describe having rented a home on Monroe Street. Other Negro families were reportedly there by 1920 as well. The census takers apparently took little interest in conducting an accurate count of Negroes in Yonkers. The Perencheifs rented housing for a few years, until they purchased their own home during the early 1920s. The 1925 state census was more accurate; the family did appear in its manuscript records, although the records fail to account for all the members of the household who were living there at the time.[21]

As mentioned earlier, realtor Henry Southgate began to buy lots from Hudson P. Rose in 1918 and had purchased more than a dozen by 1925. As Italian-American landowners sold their property back to Rose, new sales to European Americans dropped significantly. During the same period, sales to African Americans skyrocketed.

Several Nepperhan locals told me that, along with real estate brokers, the city itself helped determine the development of the early community. The city of Yonkers first became involved in land sales in Nepperhan during the Depression, when homeowners lost their property and real estate speculators sold to the city. Later, Rose himself sold a few parcels of land to the city in the 1950s and 1960s. The city resold the land at auction. City government's involvement in land sales, however, occurred well after the racial composition of the area had been established through real estate transactions.

What conditions encouraged Nepperhan's evolution into a black suburb? Why did Nepperhan become the choice of African-American home-owners in Yonkers? There is no other area in Yonkers where blacks bought land in such great volume or so far from the ghetto. For unknown reasons, Rose and Southgate broke with accepted business practices and began selling land to Negroes. By exploring a new market, these realtors capitalized on the widespread racial constraints that economically mobile Negroes faced in the local housing market. The realtors' recruitment and land-development initiatives worked to reinforce racial and class homogeneity in Nepperhan and in Yonkers, a central characteristic of the postwar suburb (Jackson 1985, 241).

Many developers, like those in Homefield, made use of deed exclusions or restrictive covenants to bar Negroes from settling in the new suburban landscape (Schwartz 1976, 27). New areas open to residential development in places like New Rochelle, Mount Vernon, Bronxville, and Yonkers regularly placed restrictions on the number of "coloreds." Numerous newspaper articles, dating from the 1920s to the present, have detailed white resistance to attempts by blacks to settle in Westchester County.[22] As recently as May 1997, a white Yonkers man who sold his home to a black family was harassed by neighbors. After calling the man "traitor" and "blockbuster," neighbors proceeded to explode a device that shattered the windshield of the man's car, which was parked outside his former residence on Troy Lane.[23]

One incident in 1926 drew the attention of the local news media. A Negro residential development in Yonkers, proposed by the Paterno-Morales Building Corporation, was redlined and refused mortgages by the Metropolitan Life Insurance Company, the Westchester Lawyers Title and Trust Company, the New York Title Company, the Prudential Life Insurance Company, and many local banking institutions.[24] By the time it was clear that Negro buyers would be unable to secure home mortgages from local lending institutions, fourteen homes had already been constructed, two Negro families had moved in, and a number of other Negroes had purchased lots. Paterno-Morales bought the lots and homes back from the Negro owners. The Negro development in Sprain Ridge Park, located in northeast Yonkers, was aborted; plans were made to "designate" the area for white homeowners.

Lending institutions and developers, regulated by state and federal law, were the first line of offense in constructing the contemporary racially defined suburban community. Government policy ensured the racial structuring of contemporary civil society. Until after World War II, the state not only permitted the widespread use of restrictive covenants by white property owners and racial steering practices by realtors; it was also instrumental in the redlining of black residential areas by private lending institutions, a practice widespread in suburban areas across the nation. Federal Housing Authority policy directly contributed to the practice and consequently encouraged defining residential space by race.

After worldwide economic markets collapsed in 1929, thousands of Americans were threatened with foreclosures on their home mortgages. Under Roosevelt's plan, the Home Owners Loan Corporation (HOLC) and the Federal Housing Administration (FHA) assisted nearly 40 percent of eligible homeowners, refinancing more than a million mortgages between 1933 and 1935 alone (Jackson 1985, 196–203). Both the HOLC and the FDA used residential security maps to define desirable and undesirable areas for investment by the banking industry. Negro residential areas (marked in red) and racially mixed areas were deemed undesirable investments; public policy throughout the 1950s thus supported racial homogenization of residential areas and the devaluation of black-owned property (Jackson 1985, 199–218; Oliver and Shapiro 1995, 40; Palen 1995, 121).

Nepperhaners reported racial steering practices during the early years, along with reluctance on the part of many lending institutions to grant home mortgages to blacks. Studies conducted by the Department of Housing and Urban Development indicate that these techniques were widely employed throughout the twentieth century to bar blacks from suburban housing, even after the passage of the 1968 Fair Housing Act (Stearns and Logan 1986, 31; Massey and Denton 1993, 105; Yinger 1995, 56). Indeed, racial restrictions persist in the suburban housing market: studies conducted yearly since 1990 by the Federal Financial Institutions Examination Council show a consistent pattern of bias against black mortgage applicants. Nationally, black applicants, regardless of income, are rejected at nearly twice the rate of white applicants (Yinger 1995, 81).[25] Overall, black home seekers are given less assistance in locating housing, denied mortgages disproportionately, and steered to neighborhoods with minority concentrations and low housing values.

While Rose and Southgate recruited black buyers, William B. Rice, owner of the Odell estate, had different plans for his development, Homefield. A deed dated 1935 from Curtis Lane, near the Homefield-Nepperhan border,[26] contained a typical restrictive covenant: "The granted premises shall be sold only to and occupied by members of the Caucasian race."

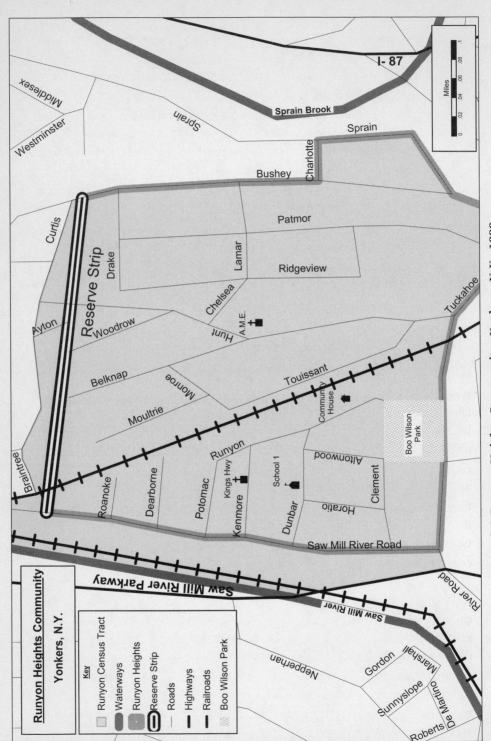

2.1 Runyon Heights Community: Yonkers, N.Y., 1990

Consequently, Homefield, like much of suburban east Yonkers, remained virtually all white into the 1940s.

In addition to racial constraints, class restrictions were implicit for ownership of residential property in Nepperhan because minimum home-building values were specified on individual lots. Newly constructed homes could not cost less than a specified amount, around $1,500 during the early period. This ensured that residential development in the area would favor private homes, which would maintain what was considered the appropriate and respectable character of the neighborhood. By the 1930s, zoning ended the need for covenants regulating minimum housing cost on properties, to exclude the poor. As individual developers carved out their territories with the aid of state-regulated institutions, zoning secured the class character of these suburban areas. The city passed its first zoning ordinances in 1920, following the example set by New York City and other large municipalities. Prompted by realtors' wishes to ensure land values, zoning limited the types of structures that could be constructed in residential areas like Nepperhan (Schwartz 1976, 27–29; Jackson 1985, 242).

Even with respect to zoning, however, Nepperhan differed from neighboring developments. Unlike Homefield, Nepperhan was zoned for both residential and industrial use. The Putnam Railroad had an industrial spur that connected to the passenger line; this established a precedent for industrial zoning in the area bordering the railroad tracks. The remainder of the community was zoned to favor residential development. The railroad and its spur together disrupted aspects of the suburban landscape and helped rob the area of natural appeal; trains were noisy, and people from other areas cut through Nepperhan to reach the station. These factors made the area less attractive. Zoning would later become a major issue in the eyes of community residents, who would rally to upgrade community zoning designations and restrict multifamily housing.

Neighborhood characteristics such as the layout of streets were determined by the developers who subdivided the property. Developers often carved out pockets of streets within their estates. In early Nepperhan, a grid model of street design was favored by developers trying to reproduce the ordered pattern of big cities like New York. Numbered street names (First Street, Second Street) also reflected a distinctly urban orientation in the new development. As the community was settled, numbered streets were renamed to reflect residents' new suburban outlook and racial consciousness. In 1927 alone, five streets were named after notable figures:

Runyon Avenue, Belknap Avenue, Moultrie Avenue, Touissant Avenue,[27] and Monroe Street.

Preexisting estate boundaries further influenced the character and shape of residential development in Nepperhan. A central feature of the community is its geographic isolation. Any visitor to the area will immediately note the numerous dead-end streets. Though major thoroughfares on the west and south, and the Sprain Road and a Catholic cemetery on the east, provide natural boundaries to the area, the northern section of Nepperhan is bordered by a four-foot-wide strip of land adjacent to Homefield. This reserve strip, as it is officially called, separates the two territories physically and symbolically into black and white residential areas (Map 2.1).

The creation and maintenance of this racial barrier were deliberate. The reserve strip was created in 1924 by the Homeland Company, the developer that first subdivided the estate that was to become Homefield.[28] Soon thereafter, the strip was purchased by a local Homefield resident who lived on Storey Lane, just one block from Runyon Heights. Just prior to the postwar building boom that would come to the area, the land was again purchased (in 1947), this time by the local civic association, the Homefield Association. These "four feet of separation," which, according to City Planning Bureau officials, effectively prevented the construction of roads that would have linked the two communities, had the effect of reinforcing the racial homogeneity of the communities.

Thus the geographic boundaries of Runyon Heights were established by preexisting estate borders, state housing market regulations, and the actions of both real estate speculators and the individuals who maintained the reserve strip. The settlement of the area was encouraged by the widespread resistance Negroes faced in other parts of lower Westchester County and the deliberate marketing efforts of real estate speculators. Led by Rose and Southgate, and aided by the constraints that federal housing policy imposed, speculators tapped into desires of working-class Negroes for home ownership and community life and established the pattern for black suburbanization in the city of Yonkers.

3

Working-Class Roots

The 1920s ushered in a period of unprecedented suburban residential development across America. In Yonkers, as elsewhere, inexpensive construction techniques and the availability of land outside central cities made home ownership possible for the working class for the first time (Jackson 1985, 125–126). Before 1920, the Nepperhan population had remained small. The 1915 New York State census recorded a total of thirty-three "white" persons in the Third Election District of the Tenth Ward, a broad geographic area that encompassed Nepperhan. In total, there were seven households, three of which had foreign-born heads: two came from Italy, and one from Germany. Only one person was designated "Negro" in the entire ward, a cook at the Sprain Ridge Hospital.[1]

In the vicinity of Nepperhan in 1920, more blacks lived and worked in the homes of whites than lived in their own households. Federal census takers noted only four independent Negro families,[2] comprising 21 of the 7,905 individual residents of the Tenth Ward.[3] This is probably an underestimate. Nepperhan itself accounted for less than 1 percent of the ward's population. The first Negroes who lived in the area rented on Saw Mill River Road, not far from Nepperhan. Only the most economically stable families would remain; a few later moved into their own homes. Two households were headed by women, each with six children, and two consisted of a married couple and their young children. The female heads of household relied on the income from their jobs as laundress and washerwoman. One of the nuclear families was headed by Thomas Peterson, a laborer in a local hospital. The other consisted of George and Lorrene Wilson and their three children. After living at 564 Saw Mill River Road and later at 646 Saw Mill River Road, they eventually moved to Belknap Avenue and became an integral part of the developing Nepperhan community. In 1920, American-born George Wilson was employed as a clerk; by 1925, according to the New York State census, he had become an electrician. This occupational change reflects the essential role of stable employment in the community's development. In fact Mr. Wilson practiced his trade locally, working on many Negro homes throughout the community.

In addition to these four families, thirty-three black individuals lived in the households of European Americans, where they were employed as nurses, maids, and servants.[4] Officially, fifty-four Negroes in total lived in the Tenth Ward in 1920.

A review of the demographic characteristics of Nepperhan in 1920 reveals a stable, predominantly foreign-born working-class settlement. Ten families, accounting for fifty-six "white" persons, included twenty-three children under sixteen years of age, seventeen men, and sixteen women. According to the census, five of the ten heads of households worked in skilled trades or sales; only three worked as manual laborers.[5] Six of the ten were immigrants, five from Italy and one from France. The remaining four heads of household were native white Americans who had come to Nepperhan from either elsewhere in New York or New Jersey. Only one extended family was listed; the others were nuclear families. None of the women in these families was recorded as being employed, although a number of the sons began working by age sixteen.

These first homesteaders purchased property in the southwestern portion of the Runyon estate, mostly on Runyon Avenue, Altonwood Place, First Street (Clement), Second Street (Dunbar), First Place (Horatio Street), or Saw Mill River Road. These families were actually a minority of those who originally purchased lots in Nepperhan. They did not, however, resell their lots to Southgate and Rose, although most of their homes were constructed after 1920, when the Negro presence in the area was most certainly known. These families warrant further study. They were unique, if only because they were apparently willing to coexist with the growing Negro presence in the area.

In addition to settling on the west side, a few Italian-American families would soon settle at the southern end of Bushey Avenue, on the eastern border of the neighborhood. Many had moved from Arthur Avenue in the Bronx and other traditionally Italian-American areas in New York. Residents of both African and European descent lived similar yet largely separate lives. The two groups rarely participated in common civic and religious organizations, yet both groups sought a primarily rural lifestyle in their new communities. Many plots included large vegetable gardens, as was typical of rural communities of the day. Chickens and goats were as common then as lawnmowers and gas grills are today. For both groups, moving to Nepperhan meant moving to the country. In fact, one nearby area was affectionately called Nanny Goat Hill. One early resident remembers: "Yeah, yes, Sir—living in the country, living in the country. I mean, you had nothing but wide-open spaces. You have got to realize that all these empty . . . there was nothing but empty lots, and all you could see was nothing but goldenrod, daisies, and black-eyed Susans all over the place."

An African-American woman recalled her excitement at the prospect of country living. Before moving, the family would visit their property in Nepperhan, but Harlem was never far from their minds:

Moving to the country was a great thing. I mean, my father was taking us out of Harlem. And we were coming into a brand-new house that my father caused to be built. . . . I remember coming up here as a child, picking the wildflowers. And when I would get back to New York, I'd have these flowers, and the kids would say, "Oh, give me a flower, give me a flower." There were wildflowers growing all over. I picked black-eyed Susans, daisies, and those white flowers, I think they call them Queen Anne's lace. I used to go back to Harlem with these flowers, and the kids thought, "Oh my goodness." And from time to time my little friends would come up here to visit, and from time to time I went to New York to visit them. You know, like stay overnight with my friends.

Working-Class Jobs for Middle-Class Homeowners

By 1925, the foreign-born still accounted for 33 percent of the total European-American population of Nepperhan. Of the fifty-seven foreign-

Table 3.1. Occupations of Employed Men Sixteen Years and Older, by Race, 1925

Occupation	White Men	Black Men
Contractor	3	1
Salesman	1	None
Tailor	1	None
Bookkeeper/Clerical	2	1
Builder	None	2
Clergyman	None	1
Musician	None	1
P.O. Clerk	None	1
Granite Merchant	1	None
Skilled Labor	13	11
Cook/Chef	1	2
Decorator	None	3
Chauffeur	4	4
Coachman	None	2
Porter	None	8
Truckman	None	4
Other labor	17	18
Laborer on Railroad	4	None
Expressman/Messenger	None	5
Farmer	2	None
School worker	3	None
Missing data	2	2
Total employed	49	64
Total males	54	66
% Males employed	91%	97%

Source: Data from 1925 New York State census manuscripts.

born white persons, forty-seven were from Italy. Employment patterns among the early Italian-American residents of Nepperhan closely paralleled those of other Italian immigrant communities. Between 1895 and 1910, 15 percent of new Italian immigrants in America were employed as skilled workers; the majority (77 percent) were unskilled (Weigold 1984, 63). In Nepperhan, thirteen of forty-nine employed white men (27 percent) had jobs in the skilled labor category; another seventeen (35 percent) were classified as "other labor," meaning nonskilled (Table 3.1).

Like the nineteenth-century workers identified by Bogart (1898), black workers in Nepperhan faced a dual labor market. No white men were employed as truckmen, coachmen, messengers, or porters, but nineteen of sixty-four employed black men were engaged in these occupations (30 percent). The category of porter alone accounted for a sizable 12.5 percent. Another eighteen men (28 percent) were nonskilled laborers. Skilled laborers represented 17 percent of the working male population, while traditional middle-class occupations accounted for another 16 percent. Among the middle-class workers were three decorators, one musician, one contractor, one clerical worker/bookkeeper, one clergyman, one post office clerk, and two builders. If we use occupation as a gauge of class, this original Nepperhan group was a mix of skilled and unskilled workers who were clearly blue-collar with a moderate-sized middle-class (white-collar) constituency; yet they were among the most economically stable of black Americans.

The son of a cook and a New York Central Railroad Pullman porter, whose family had settled in Nepperhan in 1929, purchased his own home in 1970. He worked as a wireman for Otis Elevator from 1955 until the company closed in 1983. He recalled: "Well, there was a lot of blacks working there, but at that time most of the blacks worked in the foundry. And there were porters. During the war, blacks started working there. There weren't no blacks working there [at Otis] before the war."

While most European newcomers worked as skilled or semiskilled craftsmen in local industry, many black workers commuted to jobs at hotels and movie houses in Harlem; they were among the first working-class commuters. One woman, who has lived in Nepperhan since the late 1910s, recalled: "Yonkers just wasn't hiring black people, so you had to work in New York. . . . We had a lot of porters. That was considered at that time a good job, you understand. We had a lot that worked in the movie houses. I don't mean the big movie houses. I mean the two-cent movie houses. And still that was considered a big job for a Negro at that time too."

A number of older residents suggested that the first settlers were predominantly Pullman porters and postal workers. In fact, the settlers were most likely to hold semiskilled jobs in the service economy or to be manual laborers. Census records reveal only one postal clerk among the ninety-two employed adult black residents of Nepperhan in 1925. It's important to note, however, that many of the families who remained in Nepperhan possessed better-than-average jobs. Changes in federal labor policy during World War II would later open civil service positions to black workers. These jobs became increasingly available to Nepperhaners in the 1940s and 1950s.[6] The collective memory of residents has constructed a local history that spotlights those workers who held the most prestigious jobs. This romanticized notion of Nepperhan is presented as historical fact in a recent book, *A Study of African-American Life in Yonkers from the Turn of the Century* (Esannason and Bagwell 1993). Interviews revealed that a few postal workers had settled there by the 1930s, many of whom commuted to Harlem's Manhattanville Station on 125th Street. This pattern of attracting an increasingly skilled and educated population would become a defining characteristic of the Runyon Heights community.

The majority of both white and Negro men over sixteen years of age were employed in 1925, and Negro Nepperhaners were a particularly industrious lot; an astounding 97 percent were employed compared with 91 percent of the European-American men. Forty percent of Negro women were employed outside the home, compared with only 14 percent of the European-American Nepperhan women (Table 3.2). Three of the six employed women in the white group were of Italian descent, and most (66 percent) were employed locally in the carpet mills as weavers.

By contrast, Negro women were employed in a wide range of occupations, including social work and teaching; however, 45 percent held more marginal service-oriented "Negro women's" jobs as maids, housemaids, or other servants. None of the Negro women was employed in local industry as a weaver. Like the men in Nepperhan, they encountered a highly segregated labor market. Many worked in hotels or in the homes of wealthy whites in the more exclusive areas of New York City or lower Westchester County.[7] Their experiences were not unlike those of many West Indian immigrants today (Marshall 1987; Foner 1987).

Unlike the small Italian-American population, among whom the men went to work in local industry at the age of sixteen and the women stayed at home, black Nepperhaners, male and female, usually traveled great distances to work. Largely barred from local industry, they were relegated to work as caretakers of white bourgeois society, while they themselves struggled for their piece of the American middle-class dream.

Working-Class Commuters

Dependent on employment outside local industry, Negro Nepperhaners were among the original suburban commuters from Yonkers to Har-

Table 3.2. Occupations of Employed Women Sixteen Years and Older, by Race, 1925

Occupation	White Women	Negro Women
Social Worker	None	1
Teacher	None	1
Nurse	None	1
Merchant	1	None
Dressmaker	None	4
Chef/Cook	None	1
Weaver (carpet mill)	4	None
Drum room (carpet mill)	1	None
Presser	None	1
Maid/Housemaid and Cleaners	None	17
Messengers	None	2
Housework (not employed)	32	38
Retired	None	1
School	3	3
Missing Data	1	0
Total Employed	6	28
Total Persons	42	70
% Employed	14%	40%

Source: Data from 1925 New York State census manuscripts.

lem and even Brooklyn. Although "the Put" whistled through Nepperhan regularly, making a stop near Tuckahoe Road, its high cost made it of limited use to most commuting residents during the early years. At first, residents commuted by trolley, connecting with the New York subway system in the Bronx. The route would continue even after buses replaced the trolley system. After salaries increased and the relative cost of commuting declined, some folks took the Putnam line, which stopped in Harlem. Most, however, remember their parents and themselves making the commute to New York City by trolley. The entire trip cost fifteen cents. One took the #6 trolley from Tuckahoe Road on the southern border of Nepperhan to downtown Yonkers; at Getty Square, one transferred to the Broadway trolley and headed south a few blocks into the Bronx, where one took the #1 Broadway subway to Manhattan. (In use since the turn of the century, the #1 subway is one of the few surviving elevated lines in the city of New York.) The basic commuting pattern of Nepperhan workers has continued, although many began to rely upon the automobile after World War II.

Race Makes Place

As noted in Chapter 2, the earliest blacks in Nepperhan—American- and Caribbean-born—were recruited to the area by enterprising realtors. Both groups tended to have resided in Harlem before making the jump further north to Yonkers. Some had formerly lived in the all-Negro San Juan Hill community in mid-Manhattan, between 63rd and 66th Streets. In coming to the New York area, both the Southern and the foreign-born blacks followed the classic chain migration pattern, in which one or two family members establish households before recruiting friends and relatives to join them (MacDonald and MacDonald 1964). Coming to Nepperhan was a continuation of that migration process.

For many of the earliest tenants, word-of-mouth recruitment seemed to equal if not surpass recruitment through newspaper advertisements. Many residents reported that their families had learned of Nepperhan through friends, acquaintances, or relatives in New York or from other Negro suburbanites already in Westchester County. Nepperhan provided a safe and attractive haven for black home builders, with its country dirt roads, apple trees, and wildflowers. As word spread and the community expanded, Nepperhan became the place to go.

As word-of-mouth reports from residents in other racial communities directed prospective buyers to the area, its racial homogeneity was further reinforced. One resident, the oldest living community member at the time my research was conducted, was a skilled mason who had purchased his land in 1920. He recalled how he came to Nepperhan. In 1914, he had emigrated to Panama from his birthplace in Barbados. Like thousands of others, he was employed by the U.S. government to help construct fortifications for the Panama Canal. Four years later, at the age of twenty-three, he moved to Detroit, finding nonunion carpenter's work constructing the River Rouge Ford plant. Then, he and his wife, who had immigrated from Guyana, moved to West 143rd Street in Harlem. Soon they were looking for property outside the city. After having been ignored by realtors in New Rochelle, they discovered Nepperhan through a local Harlem contact. The mason explained:

I went to New Rochelle because I saw an advertisement for selling land in Webster Avenue, I think it is, and I went over there to see, and they didn't notice me, so I came back. So my wife was down in the store, downstairs from where we lived across the street, telling them that she had went to New Rochelle to look at this land, and they wouldn't even notice her. And the woman said to her, why don't you come go with us to Yonkers, a place called Nepperhan? You may like it there. Sure enough, she built that house across the street there. And that Sunday we came up to take a look around, and to see what's going on. This was the only lot on this street that was vacant, you know, that wasn't sold.

A woman who came to the area in 1929 recalled how her parents came to choose Nepperhan over other areas:

At that particular time, it seems as though most were moving out of Harlem or they were moving on the Hill [the Sugar Hill area of Harlem]. . . . Well, they looked on Long Island for property, but they heard it was damp down there—remember, a lot of black people moved to Jamaica [Queens, New York] in that particular time. Well, my father had two friends who told him how great it was up here, and he bought the lots, and finally he built the house. Across the street was my father's best friend, and he had another friend who lived on Saw Mill River Road. They encouraged my father to come up here. . . . They were friends from Harlem.

As the community expanded, and with it its reputation as a respectable middle-class haven, residents continued to be recruited through family and friends. A Massachusetts-born woman who had been living in the Bronx while training as a nurse recalled her journey to Nepperhan. Her story illustrates the subtle distinctions between working- and middle-class life:

I guess we moved in, in 1939 or '40, I forget which. And it really was quite a community then. And how we happened to settle there: you know, it was right after the Depression, and you could buy any-thing over there for a song. . . . My husband worked in service over in Bronxville at that time. He was a butler for a private home . . . and I was in nursing school at the time. . . . I think he was here the year before I came, and he met a man who was, I think, at that time one of the important members of the Nepperhan community. His name was Paul Bray.[8] And Paul Bray played bridge. . . . I don't know how they met. . . . I was living in the Bronx at the Lincoln School

Table 3.3. Population of Nepperhan by Race and Nativity, 1920–1925

Year	1920	1925
Total Negro	None	195
		(53%)
Total foreign-born Negro	None	14
		(4%)
Total white	56	174
	(100%)	(47%)
Total foreign-born White	12	57
	(21%)	(15%)
Total population	56	369
	(100%)	(100%)

Source: Data from U.S. Census of Population, manuscripts, 1920;
and New York State census manuscripts, 1925.

for Nurses, 'cause I was a student nurse. And my husband was living over in Bronxville because that's where he worked. But he played bridge with somebody, and through playing bridge he met and really became friends with Mr. Bray.

A Yonkers native who worked for Otis Elevator recalled how he came to Nepperhan after World War II: "My brother-in-law, he lived out here, and he told me about a house that was for sale. I came out and saw a real estate agent and I bought it. . . . But my brother-in-law had grew up out here."

Negroes from Brooklyn, Harlem, and west Yonkers flocked to Nepperhan after 1920. Even if allowance is made for the possibility of an undercount, data from the federal and state censuses reveal that the area experienced a metamorphosis between 1920 and 1925, which laid the foundation for its future race and class character (Table 3.3). These census data correspond to real estate records, as well as to the memories and legends of local residents. By 1925, not only had the total population of the neighborhood grown by more than 600 percent (from 56 to 369), but the Negro group had grown at a rate surpassing that of both the native white and the foreign-born white categories. Between 1920 and 1925, 195 Negroes and only 118 whites settled in the area. The 56 European Americans who had constituted virtually all of the district's population just five years earlier now accounted for only 47 percent. The Negro population, by contrast, rose from a handful of families that went unnoticed by census takers, to fifty-one households.

Researchers have argued that the increase in Northern segregation was the result of a perceived increase in competition on the part of the white majority, so that as blacks moved north after 1900, whites increased their attempts to maintain racial boundaries (Blalock 1967; Massey and Denton 1993). Yet Negroes continued to make up less than 10 percent of the population of Yonkers well into the 1970s (see Table 1.1). Competition explains little in the Nepperhan environment, where blacks and whites did not compete directly for housing or work. By 1940, the social life and the community life of the 736 Negro Nepperhaners were completely segregated, and the Yonkers Negro population of 4,108 represented just 2.9 percent of the population of the entire city.

Until the late 1920s, Nepperhan seemed racially balanced and moderately integrated. Residents speak fondly of those early days of sandlot baseball and football games between neighborhood children on lazy afternoons. While the children attended school, played together, and visited one another's homes, parents participated in segregated institutions that structured and limited contact between the races. One resident remembers:

> **Resident:** We had a lot of Italians living here at that time.
> **Interviewer:** When you first moved to the neighborhood, how many blacks were living there? Half and half or . . . ?
> **Resident:** No, personally, a lot of people will dispute me, but at that time it was half and half. Maybe a tip of the scale more blacks. You had a lot of Italians and you have got to realize that with all these houses, there was nothing but vacant land up there. A lot of Italians from the Bronx owned all this vacant land, and what they used to do was plant their gardens, and they use to live in the Bronx.

While black residents perceived a racial balance in Nepperhan, many whites apparently concluded that the area was becoming "too black." Nepperhan was a neighborhood in transition. Tables 3.3 and 3.4 demonstrate the rapid expansion and racial transformation of Nepperhan between 1920 and 1925. Significantly, Central Harlem became a black community between 1905 and 1915 (Watkins-Owens 1996, 41), Nepperhan between 1915 and 1925.

After the Depression, almost all newcomers to the area were so-called

Table 3.4. Demographics of Nepperhan, 1925

	Black	White	Total
Total Persons	195	174	369
Total females sixteen years and older	70	42	112
Total males sixteen years and older	62	54	116
Total children under sixteen years	63	78	141
Total households	51	29	80
Total households with female heads	3	0	3
Total households with foreign-born heads	7	24	28
		(21 Italian)	
Total foreign-born persons sixteen years and older	13	55	68

Source: Data from New York State census manuscripts, 1925.

coloreds. Once the area was identified as a black settlement, many second-generation whites who had been reared in Nepperhan during its early years moved their families elsewhere, some relocating in Home-field. Only a handful of those original settlers remain. The children of many of the early black residents did remain in the community. Thus, over the decades, the pattern of multigenerational residence in the area remained common only among African-Americans.

Racial homogeneity increased in part because of the wide availability of housing choices for European Americans, which contrasted starkly with the experiences of people of African descent, who encountered rampant racial discrimination. While respondents told of being refused mortgages in numerous residential areas in Yonkers and Westchester County, many eventually secured mortgages from regional banks on Nepperhan properties. Runyon Heights proved to be one of the few areas in Yonkers and lower Westchester County where black home seekers could get financing. Sometimes realtors even helped them to negotiate with local banks. Some residents had to look outside Yonkers and the traditional lending institutions. During the early years, a few received help from fraternal associations or cooperative ventures. An early West Indian–born settler recalled: "I had belonged to an association called the Antiguan Holding Company, and I had some money in there. And I pulled it out, so I took mine out and started this work. And then, remember, everything was cheap." Others persistently negotiated with the banks. A retired service worker, originally from North Carolina, recounts his experiences in

1942: "Bronxville bank was the only one that would give me a loan, so when . . . when we wanted to have that repaired, those shingles put on the roof, the banks in Yonkers wouldn't give us a loan. I went to a Bronxville bank, and they gave us a loan."

After FHA policy changes in 1950, some residents who had purchased land from the city did report receiving FHA-backed loans. One resident remembers: "And then, a lot of lots and houses too, the houses that were built, and lots that people bought during the Depression, they lost them. And many of the people who came later bought these from the city. . . . You got the FHA loan, but you didn't buy it from the FHA."

Others used a real estate agent to broker a deal with a bank: "The real estate [agent] had found us a mortgage by time the closing came. We had to pay her a fee, of course, but she had already found the mortgage: Larchmont Savings Bank in Larchmont."

Consequently, while mortgages for Nepperhan homes were sometimes difficult to obtain, securing a mortgage for property outside predominantly Negro areas was next to impossible. In essence, Nepperhan became all-black through considerable effort on the part of white agents, not through an ecological process or even the conscious choice of most blacks.

"Build Your House at Nepperhan, Yonkers"

During the formative years in Nepperhan, land was purchased rapidly, and many new homes were constructed. Many of the early settlers possessed carpentry and masonry skills and played an active role in the construction of their homes and community institutions.

During the 1920s and 1930s, Charles Poe, George Wilson, Shaw Dickerson, Clairbrathe Cook, Mr. Williamson, and Norman Downs were all active participants in the construction of Nepperhan homes. Charles Poe did carpentry and George Wilson did electrical work for local residents. Shaw Dickerson built his own ranch-style home at 25 Moultrie Avenue. Clairbrathe Cook, a brick mason, built two brick homes on Chelsea Place during the early 1930s. Mr. Williamson, a realtor based on 145th Street in Harlem, built a red brick home at 148 Belknap Avenue. Norman Downs, who had joined the United Brotherhood of Carpenters and Joiners of America in 1919 and later became Grand Master of the James H. Farrell Royal Lodge of the Prince Hall Masons in Yonkers, helped in the construction of several homes in addition to his own at 54 Moultrie Avenue. He built two small bungalow-style homes and helped lay the foundation for the Metropolitan African Methodist Episcopal [AME] Zion Church on Belknap Avenue, dedicated in 1928. His specialty was pitched-roof buildings, but he also helped to build a small brick building at 13 Monroe Street, which housed a locally owned market.

It was common for both white and black artisans to build their own homes in working-class suburbs during the 1920s. In *Crabgrass Frontier* (1985), a study of American suburbanization, historian Kenneth Jackson recognizes that inexpensive construction techniques, such as the balloon-frame structure, helped make home ownership possible for the masses for the first time (125–126). Like other scholars, however, Jackson did not recognize that blacks had participated in the home-ownership boom.

> As in so many other aspects of national life, black Americans didn't share in the home ownership boom. Their migration from the plantation south to the urban north led to gains in civil rights, but the pattern of the ghetto—residential segregation, underemployment, substandard housing, disrupted family life, inferior education, and disease—separated the black experience from that of white ethnics. Because of racial discrimination, blacks were unable to enter the housing market on the same terms as other groups before them. Thus the most striking feature of black life was not the slum conditions, but the barriers that middle-class blacks encountered in trying to escape the ghetto.

Both foreign- and native-born Negro residents engaged in a cooperative effort to build their homes in Nepperhan. Barbados-born Norman Downs received help in building homes from friends from "the old country." Downs had made important contacts in Panama as well as through his membership in a New York–based West Indian society called the Mechanics, which drew its members from Antigua, Barbados, Saint Kitts, Trinidad, and other islands. The building of the Metropolitan AME Church was a typical cooperative effort.

Striving black residents in Nepperhan were not initially motivated by a desire to form a black residential community; rather, they sought access to affordable housing and a decent place to raise their families. Racial and class concentrations in Nepperhan, however, reinforced community boundaries and provided a basis for the development of both a strong community and group consciousness.

The West Indian Presence in Early Nepperhan

The enactment of restrictive immigration laws effectively ended Caribbean immigration during the 1920s, but between 1900 and 1920 more than a hundred thousand primarily non-Hispanic Caribbean people had migrated to the United States. A majority settled in New York City and neighboring areas. By 1930, Caribbean-born immigrants, often lumped together under the label West Indian, represented approximately 1 percent of the black population in America (Sowell 1981, 219).

The West Indian presence in America has evoked numerous comparisons between the immigrants and native-born black Americans since the 1930s (Moynihan 1965; Reid 1970; Glazer and Moynihan 1970; Sowell 1981). Some authors have alluded to what I will call West Indian exceptionalism or to what Stephen Steinberg critiques as "the myth of West Indian success"; other scholars have spoken of "the myth of black ethnicity" (Steinberg 1989, 275; Davis 1998). In addition to obscuring differences in mobility among native-born blacks, the exceptionalism model asserts that West Indian culture provided black West Indian–born workers with a decisive advantage over American-born blacks, whose culture was poorly adapted to industrial urban society. In *Beyond the Melting Pot* (1970), Daniel Patrick Moynihan and Nathan Glazer present this myth as an objective social-scientific fact and maintained that "the ethos of the West Indians, in contrast to that of the Southern Negro, emphasized saving, hard work, investment, education" (35). They contend, as did Ira De Augustine Reid more than thirty years earlier, that the comparatively large number of blacks from the West Indies who became leaders in Negro communities is attributable largely to West Indian cultural and family values. Like E. Franklin Frazier (1962), they assert with little supporting evidence that slavery weakened American black families, rendering them unable to adjust to the demands of urbanization (Moynihan and Glazer 1970, 50–52, 114).

Glazer and Moynihan lump together immigrants from the French, British, and Dutch West Indies, even though English-speakers predominated among early settlers in the United States. Consequently, they ignore critical differences in the material backgrounds of distinct immigrant groups as well as material differences between the immigrant and the native-born populations. One major distinction between the groups was that the English- speaking West Indian immigrants were more literate and skilled than the Southern-born migrants who flocked to the cities, a factor that influenced future patterns of mobility (Watkins-Owens 1996).

Ten years after Moynihan and Glazer's characterization of Southern black culture, black economist Thomas Sowell drew a similar conclusion. In *Ethnic America* (1981), using a circular argument rooted in Reid's initial assertion of West Indian cultural superiority, Sowell cited Glazer and Moynihan (1970) as evidence to support the superiority of West Indian values. Pointing out that West Indians had lower unemployment rates, higher incomes, lower fertility rates, lower crime rates, and higher representation in professional occupations by comparison with native-born black Americans, Sowell argued that these disparities stemmed from "their behavior patterns," "culture," and different values (219). Sowell went so far as to suggest that the relative success of West Indians proves that racial discrimination is not a major obstacle to the success of native-born black Americans. According to Sowell, "the West Indian experience itself seriously undermines the proposition that color is a fatal handicap in the American economy" (220). Without directly considering the values of black Americans or the opportunities that were historically open to this racially stigmatized and economically marginalized group, Sowell dismisses the significance of racial discrimination and reaffirms that American society is a meritocracy.

Urban sociologist Stephen Steinberg, building on the work of Reynolds Farley (1987), Nancy Foner (1987), and Roy Simon Bryce-Laporte (1979), provides a comprehensive critique of the West Indian exceptionalism model.[9] In *The Ethnic Myth* (1989), Steinberg asserts that cultural traits fail to explain West Indian economic mobility in American society. Arguing that immigration to the United States was selective, in that it drew some of the most skilled workers, Steinberg details the considerable advantages in social class that West Indian immigrants held over native-born blacks. That many (40 percent) of the West Indian immigrants were skilled and most (89 percent) were literate gave them a distinct advantage over native-born blacks in the job market (p. 276). Sowell (1981, 219) himself points out that West Indian immigrants were overwhelmingly from urban areas, a background that gave them another comparative advantage in the New York regional economy relative to the largely rural native-born black migrant population.

Contrary to the overwhelming evidence presented by Steinberg and others that the West Indian migrants were not directly comparable to those from the rural South, the myth of West Indian exceptionalism lives on in social discourse as well as in the public consciousness. Like many myths, it is partly rooted in reality. Many West Indian immigrants have indeed been economically successful in America. Their presence was also significant in Nepperhan. Although West Indians had advantages over most native-born Southern migrants, they often experienced downward economic mobility once they came to the United States. Nevertheless, precisely because of their relative advantages, they were able to acquire some of the most stable jobs open to blacks. One resident, who had been a classical music teacher in his native St. Croix, settled in Nepperhan in 1926 with his family. He was unable to find work teaching music. Owing to his literacy, however, he scored well on the Civil Service exam and secured what was considered a "good job for a Negro" with the U.S. Postal Service. Other immigrant residents also found it difficult to find work in the fields in which they had been trained. This phenomenon continued throughout Nepperhan's history. One man who arrived in the United States in the late 1950s had been head engineer for an airline in the Dominican Republic but was unable to find engineering work at local airports. He reluctantly drove trucks for a while; frustrated, he returned to trade school to study welding. Eventually, he found work as a maintenance man for a hotel in New York City while working part-time as superintendent of a building in southwest Yonkers. Although these men, like many others, worked long, hard days, the skills they possessed gave them access to the few stable jobs with decent pay available to blacks in the region.

This pattern was typical among Caribbean-born Nepperhaners. Southern-born blacks were at a decisive disadvantage in the job market, unless they came from the most advantaged families. Skills, literacy, and access to stable employment were requirements for home ownership in Nepperhan. For West Indian and native-born Nepperhaners alike, skills and education, rather than "culture," were the prerequisites for future economic mobility.

Many Nepperhan residents believe that a large percentage of the early residents were of West Indian descent; others pointed to the presence of large numbers of Southern migrants. In reality, both groups formed critical components of the Nepperhan community. One resident, the son of a father who was a West Indian–born Pullman porter and of a North Carolina–born mother, remembers those early years: "I think we, as a group, race didn't bother us too much, because we were kind of clannish, and we wanted to keep the original families together. We all kind of held onto our lands—to our families, so it was kind of hard for anybody buying into the area, unless they were a family member or knew somebody."

One Southern-born resident, raised during the 1930s by West Indian foster parents, recounts his version of the West Indian myth as it appeared in Nepperhan.

> There were a few from the South, Virginia—I think there were quite a few Virginians—but the majority of them were West Indians, and another thing the majority of them were postal workers. They worked for the postal service. . . . It seems that they [West Indians] were more industrious. They were more efficient in language, they were more hard-working, and they were, what you would say, they antagonized the black American from the South. . . . They was competitive to the point of no contest, because the West Indians prevailed. They opened up businesses, they bought homes, they bought houses in New York City. . . . And they did quite well because, again, these Southern Negroes were Americans, and Americans carry the connotation of "I am American and I can lay back and I can prosper with a minimum of effort." This has been proven over, over, over and over again by immigrants: Koreans, Vietnams, the Irish, the Italians, whomever. They always outdo the native, or they have been outdoing the native population within the United States.

His Westchester-born wife interjected: "The whole problem was that we black Americans would not sacrifice. Now they [the West Indians] would eat beans and rice for three years, fifty people live in one room, and get their act together, but we have to play the numbers, you know, open a store and buy a Cadillac."

In fact, the majority of Nepperhaners over the years have come from the upper Southern states of Virginia, West Virginia, and North Carolina. In 1925, the foreign-born represented a small minority (7 percent) of black newcomers to Nepperhan (Table 3.3). The West Indian presence in Nepperhan, though small, probably did increase during the 1930s, as a result of continued migration from New York. Still, as intermarriage was common between the native- and foreign-born blacks, many residents have family ties to both the West Indies and the South. The myth of greater West Indian success, widely espoused by scholars and the media and embraced by some residents, is not supported by the historical evidence in Nepperhan (O'Donnell 1994, 4A). Although residents of West Indian origin numbered among the community's most prominent mem-

Table 3.5. Occupations of Foreign-Born Black Heads of Household, Nepperhan, 1925

Occupation	Frequency	Country of Origin	Class
Builder	1	West Indies	ao
Steamfitter	1	Virgin Islands	w
Chauffeur	2	Bermuda	w
		Virgin Islands	w
Cook/Chef	2	Trinidad	w
		French West Indies	w
Porter	1	Danish West Indies	w

Source: Data from 1925 New York State census manuscripts.

ao = self employed
w = salaried worker

bers, there is nothing exceptional about their rate of success. Only one of the original seven foreign-born heads of household held a middle-class occupation in 1925 (see Table 3.5). Like the native-born, most were skilled and semiskilled workers in the service economy.

Descendants mentioned foreign- and native-born settlers' family, culture, and individual perseverance as important characteristics of individuals and the community. Although residents saw race as a factor transcending national and ethnic cultural identities and relied on it for their sense of unity, ethnic identity did not completely disappear. Nepperhaners are proud of their family heritage. Nevertheless, in retelling the collective history of Nepperhan, people emphasize race as the central basis for collective identity. The high rate of intermarriage between the two groups is testament to the transcendence of race over culture, region, and national origin.

It is interesting that hostility between native- and foreign-born residents never developed, either among the first generation of residents or among those who have settled more recently. In the eyes of most residents, community survival has always necessitated racial solidarity. Sociologist Philip Kasinitz maintains that despite underlying tensions between Caribbean-born and native-born blacks in Harlem, race dominated both the life chances of Harlemites and the political discourse of local politicians (Kasinitz 1992, 51–53). "A feeling of commonality, based partially on an awareness of a common history and heritage, but also on an awareness of common problems faced in racist America, helped forge a shared black identity" (50).

Even the tensions between the two groups, when they did occur, can be easily explained as class rivalry between the better-educated and skilled immigrants and the more rural and unskilled Southern migrants. The following chapters will demonstrate how the life chances and political environment of Nepperhaners were marked by concerns over race and class. In a residential environment where community boundaries were defined by race, and class position was threatened by racial subordination, race became the focal point for defending community interests through collective mobilization.

Caribbean immigrants in the community acknowledge their unique cultural background when discussing their family histories. Their descriptions of the community and its members, however, emphasize racial identification over distinctive ethnic or national identities. Interviews suggest that first-generation immigrants maintained the strongest ethnic identity, but their children became increasingly socialized into a context that recognized skin color and "blackness" rather than a specific ethnic culture as the operative social markers of status. Though friendships were forged through church, social groups, and work, race ultimately provided the unifying characteristic and the mechanism for recruitment into the neighborhood. A new community of associations grew up within this locale, structured by the racialized environment and its interaction with the outside world. Segregation, and the relatively small numbers of West Indians, forced them to meld with American Negroes in their communities, and this accounted for the limited disharmony between the groups (Green and Wilson 1992, 121). Nonetheless, ethnic or national identification persists and is evident in the overglorification of Caribbean successes by a few individual community members and their families.

The racial organization of communities linked race and place in contemporary urban America. The line between white and black had become more rigid as Northern urban society adjusted to the influx of free Negro workers. Racial communities provided a framework for a set of common political interests that would come to define black American consciousness for nearly a century.

4

E Pluribus Unum

Social-scientific studies of the general Negro population and of the black middle class in particular have been marred by a major theoretical weakness: insufficient attention is paid to the way racial classifications are constructed (Williams 1990). Consequently, race is rarely explored as a social process. The racial homogeneity of communities is often treated as a natural or ecological outgrowth of membership in a racial group and therefore as self-explanatory. Rather than exploring the critical connection between residential segregation and the construction of racial-group interests and antagonisms, social scientists have treated race in the abstract as an explanatory concept in their analyses, an approach that serves to legitimate racial categorization by demonstrating its apparently natural character.

During the nineteenth century, biologically deterministic explanations of race were widespread in social-scientific work. During the twentieth century, criticisms of biological models of racial difference were expressed by scientists as diverse as anthropologist Franz Boas, during the early part of the century, and Harvard zoologist Stephen J. Gould in his *Mismeasure of Man* (1981). The notion that race is a socially constructed phenomenon has been widely accepted in mainstream social science circles, although such proponents of biological determinism as Richard Hernstein and Charles Murray (1994) have recently drawn public attention and influenced social policy.

Researchers on segregation generally presuppose that racial homogeneity in communities is not "natural," yet their quantitative investigations tend to focus solely on the structural dynamics of inequality and discrimination, even while the debate continues about the appropriate techniques for measuring shifts in census categories. The questions of how federal racial classification affected twentieth-century suburban residential segregation, structured group boundaries, informed group consciousness, and politicized racial identity are overlooked. Because no objective scientific basis for racial designations can be found, social science researchers are left with individual self-designation as a way to establish membership in racial groups, even though the boundaries of racial categories have changed over time. After years of relying on the misguided belief that census takers could accurately determine the race of a respondent through visual inspection, since 1960 the U.S. Census has recognized the social basis of race and required that respondents designate their own racial classification. If race is not a natural category, consistent over time, and if the notion is not supported by genetic evidence, what is the basis for the continuity of black American social life and the deep interracial divisions that persist in American political life (Fields 1982; Dominguez 1986, xv, 54; Omi and Winant 1986, 60)?

While acknowledging the lack of a biological basis for racial classification, investigators of black communities have proceeded on the assumption that it is more or less self-evident who is black and who is white. Without really meaning to do so, they transform race from a temporal sociopolitical category to a universal analytical category. We are left with studies of the "black" middle class that treat racial categories not as sociopolitical divisions but as universal and organic groups, while attempting to describe in largely psychological terms the attitudes and behaviors of a presumably homogeneous group. As Richard Williams (1990) points out, although the structural approach asserts that race and ethnicity are social constructs, it fails to take the point to its logical conclusion—that ethnic and racial distinctions and their signifiers are themselves subjective and arbitrary. What most warrants a sociological explanation, the very existence of racial groupings, is taken as a given. If membership in a racial group is not assigned by nature, then the articulation of racial designations needs to be placed in a historical context that sheds light on the creation and maintenance of racial boundaries. How did race become a central political, social, and cultural axis in America?

To understand how racial differentiation structures the development of group interests, we must investigate communities like Runyon Heights and examine the relation between the racialization of residential space and the politicization of race consciousness. What we know about Runyon Heights supports the contention that group interests directly reflect the saliency of race in local and national political spheres. In essence, racial consciousness comes to the fore politically when people see community interests through a racial prism. At the same time, state policies and market processes have encouraged common material interests among community residents. To cast light on the formation of group interest within a suburban black middle class, it is essential not merely to place the group in its historical context but to decipher the processes that give the appearance of historical continuity and homogeneity to people who display neither (Williams 1990, 8).

Indeed, the very definitions of racial categories and of the people included in them have changed throughout American history; for example, the offspring of Africans and Europeans were once classified as "mulatto," but by the end of the nineteenth century they were increasingly regarded as "Negro." In fact, the growth of Northern residential segregation coincided with racial reclassification and the solidification of the "color line." Urbanization, suburbanization, and racialization encouraged the formation of a new people, both literally and figuratively, from the different strains of the African diaspora whose members flocked to the cities.

As the structural landscape shifted, a new consciousness emerged among the bulk of Negroes who lived in segregated environments and participated in a new popular culture. Instrumental in the shaping of that consciousness were Negro intellectuals who created literature and art and established institutions like the NAACP in 1909 and the National Urban League on Urban Conditions Among Negroes (National Urban League) in 1911. Segregated communities provided a critical site for the reorganization of membership in a racial group and the formation of racial consciousness, by linking racialized individuals politically, socially, and economically, setting the stage for the creation of a common history and identity. Although racial consciousness obviously existed before the modern era, twentieth-century segregation played a major part in the establishment of social and political boundaries that politicized race within the new urban milieu. Race took on an added political significance. As Howard Winant argues in *Racial Conditions* (1994), the institutionalization of racial difference—the refusal to grant blacks basic democratic rights and the exclusion of blacks from civil society—"demanded the organization and consolidation of excluded communities of color" (p. 44). Thus racial solidarity, which sprang from residential segregation, provided the impetus for political mobilization against the very discriminatory practices that had contributed to solidifying the group.

Race and State Policy

The creation, formalization, and maintenance of racial categories by the U.S. Census significantly contributed to the formation of contemporary racial groupings, the social and political mythology of race and racial purity, and the preservation of the racial state (Collas 1994, 5). Yet the state has defined different racial groupings in different historical periods. Even though historical shifts in definition occur, the racial categories used by the census are treated as self-evident facts of everyday life.

Between 1865 and 1920, American society increasingly adopted what anthropologists call the hypo-descent rule and what the courts have called the traceable amount rule—the idea that a single drop of "African blood" was sufficient to warrant classifying someone as "Negro" (Nelson 1986, 319–320; Davis 1991, 5, 113–117; Dominguez 1986, 26–36). During this period, the "one-drop rule" was increasingly enforced by an array of government agencies, market practices, and social norms, and it was eventually internalized by individuals of mixed European and African lineage, even though many were resistant at first.

That the aim of the American racial classification system was the political exclusion of people of African descent is clearly demonstrated by the history of legislation designating any person of mixed parentage as Negro and, ipso facto, inferior. As recently as 1970, a Louisiana law quantified racial designations, maintaining that the possession of 1/32 of "Negro blood" made a person Negro (Omi and Winant 1994, 53). The illogic of this racist law is revealed by the question why 1/32 percent of white blood did not accordingly make a person white. Although the Louisiana law was eventually repealed, "Negro blood" was and still is treated by the U.S. political system as a contaminant of "white blood." At the same time, the one-drop rule makes clear the purported biological permanence and master status of the "Negro race." Once one is "tainted" with Negro blood, one must always be Negro; moreover, all one's future offspring, regardless of their physical features, will also be considered Negro. On the basis of these suppositions, racial segregation seems not only natural but desirable for maintaining the natural social order.[1] Unlike the European immigrants, who were seen as possessing cultural differences that could change in time, Africans were viewed as a mass of savages, among whom any social or cultural differences were outweighed by their overwhelming blackness. Race, and the superficial physiological characteristics that signified it, became a gauge of social worth and civil status.

The racial category of "Negro" developed during the period of Colonial slavery. West Africans, whose varied cultural identities included Ibo, Ewe, Biafada, Bokongo, Wolof, Bambara, Ibibio, and Oyo Yoruba, were folded into a single category, Negro, by a system of labor exploitation that propagated an ideology of white supremacy (Blassingame 1972, 2). The Civil War brought an end to racial slavery and the clear status distinctions between white and black that the relationship between slave and master had specified. In the years following Reconstruction, the reestablishment of white supremacy outside the institution of slavery became a major objective of social and state institutions. The color line became solidified, with the help of the one-drop rule, in both custom and law.

Omi and Winant (1994, 66) characterize our nation's history up until the 1960s as a racial dictatorship during which the state actively enforced racial inequality. Even during the era of slavery, a social and political system predicated on the association between free labor and whiteness, and between slavery and blackness, "free persons of color" challenged the norms of the prevailing social order. At the dawn of the Civil War, the presence of mulattoes, already concentrated in cities in 1850, continued to challenge the notion that clear-cut boundaries between races existed at all: 37 percent of the free Negroes and 8 percent of the slaves were classified as mixed-blood, or mulatto (Frazier 1962, 18–19).

After the solidification of the color line following the Civil War, intermediary racial categories between white and black were no longer recognized by federal institutions. Persons of mixed African, European, and Native American ancestry, save for a few isolated populations, were reclassified according to the new bifurcated system.

The creation and maintenance of the color line by the state gained in importance in the post-emancipation era. The U.S. Census had initially recognized a "mulatto" category but had yet to define the term by 1860. "Mulatto" originally referred to color and had a social definition that implied half black or African and half European or white. The terms "octoroon" and "quadroon" referred to one-eighth and one-fourth part African ancestry, respectively, and were popular in the antebellum states of Louisiana, South Carolina, Maryland, and Virginia, where sexual relations across the color line were common, although not officially sanctioned or recognized (Dominguez 1986, 46; Davis 1991, 33–50). In 1870, the "mulatto" category was officially redefined to include "quadroons, octoroons, and all persons having any perceptible trace of African blood" (cited in Davis 1991, 11–12). The census was intent on keeping track of intermixtures between white and black, while also adopting the notion that these mixtures were really black. By 1890 the term "race" was added to the category "color," and by 1900 the mulatto category was dropped altogether, only to return in 1910. During this period, mixed-race persons encountered a rigid Jim Crow color bar. Politically, economically, and socially distinct from other Negroes, yet publicly stigmatized as Negro, mulattoes and other "mixed-race" persons were increasingly integrated into the Negro community as a whole, for often only "Negro" housing and economic advancement were open to them. By 1930, the census completely abandoned the mulatto category for good, making the one-drop rule the universal standard. It is significant that a sizable percentage of the urban Negroes identified in the 1930 census would have been classified as mixed-race in any previous census.

Between 1860 and 1930, then, "mulattoes" were socially and politically redefined as "Negroes." This transformation was solidified by the state through census classifications; moreover, the Supreme Court had already given its sanction to both Jim Crow segregation and the one-drop rule in its *Plessy v Ferguson* (163 U.S. 537) ruling in 1896 (Davis 1991, 8–12, 46). By 1920, then, with the help of state institutions, the racial order of the nation had been effectively redefined, reflecting the political climate of Jim Crow America. Scholars have recently noted that as many as four out of five African Americans today possess some European ancestry (Yinger 1995, 8).

As those with any known African ancestry were clearly defined as second-class citizens, new European immigrants increasingly sought to distance themselves from "coloreds." Fear of being tainted by any amount of "black African blood," along with increased industrial competition spurred by large-scale black migration from the South, led to increased racial discrimination and a solidification of the northern color line. Yonkers underwent a significant rise in Ku Klux Klan activity during the 1920s, even though the black population remained small and was largely excluded from local industry. The politics of ethnicity receded to a symbolic level and was supplanted by the politics of race.

Segregated together in employment and housing, persons with any visible "Negroid" traits or any known African ancestry were increasingly viewed, and viewed themselves, as one group. This phenomenon tended to minimize physiological, cultural, religious, and even class differences within the developing black community (Davis 1991, 58; Green and Wilson 1992, 118–123). Meanwhile, the Plessy decision had ushered in a new wave of exclusionary practices; even the lightest-skinned Negroes were barred from many restaurants, theaters, and public facilities and most educational institutions (Allen 1964, 28).

Osofsky (1971) observes that racial alienation and conflict intensified during the first years of the twentieth century. It was evident in the creation of segregated professional sports (the New York State Boxing Commission and the National Baseball League), in the formalization of segregation in churches, and in commentary published in the national media. Osofsky even notes an attempt in 1910 to reinstitute a New York State law barring intermarriage (Osofsky 1971, 41–42). In fact, Osofsky observes that the Negro community of San Juan Hill in mid-Manhattan got its name following a race riot, at the turn of the century, an allusion to the famous Spanish-American war battle. The media recorded small but frequent clashes between Irish immigrants and Negro migrants who resided in the area. The Irish were granted license to look with disdain upon Negroes; Negroes responded with their own brand of nativism and anti-immigrant sentiment (Osofsky 1971, 45).

Since the Draft Riots of 1863, there had been no major clashes between Irish and Negroes. A new era of urban racial conflict in New York City began in 1900. Under these conditions of heightened racial animosity the contemporary processes of urbanization, suburbanization, and the transatlantic migration of labor came together. Both West Indian immigrants and migrants from the American South headed toward urban areas like New York, only to find a rigid color bar in employment, housing, and civic life that would set the stage for the transformation of consciousness of a new people.

Harlem, Nepperhan, and the "New" Negro

Racial group consciousness was manifest as a crucial political axis so early in twentieth-century America because it evolved out of the newly structured racial communities that dotted the contemporary urban and suburban landscapes. By the time Nepperhan was founded, Jim Crow segregation, based on the one-drop rule, had polarized African and European descendants into two racialized groups. Black migration and residential discrimination continued to concentrate members of the African diaspora in urban racial communities like Harlem. Some would seek housing outside the overcrowded city, pushing north to suburban black belts in southern Westchester County. Some ventured even farther north, to form Negro communities in Tarrytown, Ossining, and Peekskill.

As racial communities developed, so did a sense among those with visible "Negroid" characteristics and those with any publicly known African ancestry that they were one people. Light skin no longer provided a significant advantage for blacks in the marketplace.[2] Soon the cultural renaissance was under way. Individuals of many hues, physical characteristics, and cultural backgrounds saw themselves as constituting a single new Negro people.

Accepting the logic of the one-drop rule, persons of mixed-race ancestry actively participated in forming a new Negro consciousness during the Harlem Renaissance (Davis 1991, 42). Paradoxically, many of the leaders of the Negro renaissance would have been officially recognized as mulatto in an earlier era, and could have participated in the elite mulatto societies of the South, like the Bon Ton Society of Washington, D.C. The descendants of people once classified as "mulattoes" or "free people of color" were now lumped together in urbanized areas with their darker brethren.

The term "colored," which had originally referred to all nonwhites, including Negroes, Japanese, Chinese, and "civilized Indians," was increasingly used to denote Negroes alone, including "light-skinned," "mixed blood," and "mulatto" persons. The term was adopted by the new Negro group to refer to all with known African ancestry, regardless of physical characteristics or nationality (Davis 1991, 6). Only in Louisiana and in parts of South Carolina, Virginia, and Washington, D.C., did people of mixed race intermarry and develop a racial consciousness distinct from that of Negroes. There, those of mixed African and European ancestry were able to segregate themselves economically and residentially from those of darker complexion. In these isolated pockets a clear mulatto or Creole identity took shape, only to fade in importance as urbanization and industrialization continued.[3] By the 1920s, the terms "colored" and "Negro" were used interchangeably in the Northeast to refer to anyone of any African ancestry. In Northern industrial suburban communities, as elsewhere, those who could not or did not wish to pass as "white" accepted the polarized definition and the "Negro" or "colored" label.[4]

The New Negro desire to be recognized as a people calls for a literature that reinforces and defines who "the people" are. The new Negro movement of the 1920s, usually referred to as the Harlem Renaissance, provided such a literature. Jamaican-born poet Claude McKay, District of Columbia–born novelist Eugene Toomer, and Missouri-born writer Langston Hughes joined such Harlem natives as the poet Countee Cullen in creating a renaissance in the Negro arts (Lewis 1981, 50–78). The consciousness that a new people was emerging seemed to demand a new name. References to the "new Negro" were prevalent in the literature, art, and journalism of this period.

Nepperhaners participated in the new Negro popular culture. Literature of the Harlem Renaissance can still be found in the homes of many community members. Again, the distinction between the middle and working classes is blurred in Nepperhan. Some residents supported the predominantly working-class United Negro Improvement Association headed by Garvey. Others subscribed to the more bourgeois *Crisis* magazine, published by the NAACP and edited by W. E. B. Du Bois.

Celebrated Negro weeklies such as the *Amsterdam News* and the *New York Age* also developed a strong following. These papers used the "colored" and "Negro" labels routinely to define the group, just as Southern Jim Crow politicians did. "Colored only" restrictions certainly signified "Negro" to white and black Americans in both the North and the South. The popular terms "Negro," "brown," and "colored" signified the inclusion of color differences within the group. The recognition and acceptance of the terms by both so-called pure Negroes (people of unmixed African descent) and mulattoes also signified acceptance of the one-drop rule in defining who was truly a Negro in twentieth-century America.

The new Negro popular culture which blossomed during the Harlem Renaissance also made reference to the new "brown Negro." The terms "colored" and "new Negro" were rife in the literature and art of the Renaissance, while the notion of "brown America" continued to gain popularity during the 1930s and 1940s (Davis 1991, 59). In fact, W. E. B. Du Bois used the terms "colored," "Negro," and "black" interchangeably in *The Philadelphia Negro* (1973), thereby foreshadowing future shifts in black political consciousness.

The Garveyite emphasis on dark skin as a mark of racial pride and strong identification with Africa was not generally accepted by Negro Americans. The image of the brown Negro was preferred until the political and social revolution of the Black Power and Black Arts movements of the 1960s. Garveyism did, however, provide a fundamental orientation for the new Negro who was entering the modern age of the industrial city. Garvey's famous parades through Harlem drew many sympathizers to the streets. The movement attracted crowds because it embodied the quest to be a people and the longing for a "black" nation. A modern city of black people was what the new Negro sought, and Harlem became both city and symbol, drawing people of African descent from across the nation and abroad. The new Negro was "new" both figuratively and literally. Cultural development and political mobilization brought about a change in racial consciousness, but the backdrop for this change was acceptance of the one-drop rule, as it came to define residential communities.

Given the mixed ancestry of many American Negroes, the Harlem Renaissance ultimately rejected Garvey's philosophy of "racial purity," which might have designated many notable Negro leaders, including W. E. B. Du Bois, James Weldon Johnson, A. Philip Randolph, and Walter White, as mulattoes and laid the basis for a mulatto politics of identity. The one-drop rule proved to be an effective strategy of inclusiveness that would define the racial boundaries of new Negro communities like Harlem and Nepperhan. Harlem became the cultural center where the articulation of the new consciousness was captured in the media. But in the move to the suburbs, the new consciousness would also find fertile ground.

As residents sought economic mobility in the suburban environment, psychological and physical ties to Harlem and its cultural politics were strong. One resident spoke of his Caribbean-born father: "He just didn't like white people. He liked Marcus Garvey. He talked about Marcus Garvey, and then he got all the black literature, the black books written by black authors. And that black bookstore down in Harlem somewhere, he used be down there all the time."

The pan-Africanist Garvey movement did contribute to the development of strong racial pride that swept through Harlem and Nepperhan during the 1920s and that continues to this day. Garvey, like the artists of the Negro renaissance, rearticulated a cultural link between Africa and the new Negro, providing a critical tie between West Indians and American blacks, who found common ground in the dream of a unified black Africa.

Osofsky (1971) describes America's fascination with Harlem during the 1920s and the symbolic significance of the Garvey movement: "The white world looked curiously at the success of Marcus Garvey, whose movement basically reflected a profound desire for racial pride and respect in a society that denied them, and concluded that Negroes in Harlem 'have parades every day.' . . . White audiences, like gluttons at a feast, vicariously tasted the 'high yallers,' 'tantalizin tans,' and 'hot chocolates' that strutted around in the Blackbird Revues, or in such plays as *Lulu Belle* (1926) and *Harlem* (1928)—and made them top box-office successes" (186). While whites looked for the exotic and the fantastic, Negroes viewed Harlem as a vast "black metropolis where the various strains of the race would be united" and where the new Negro would come of age (Kasinitz 1992, 43).

During the 1920s, the new Negro looked forward to economic progress and independence. This would be the birth of a new era. Harlem itself represented the future. The Great Depression, however, squelched many dreams of black autonomy and temporarily relegated black nationalism to the background of black politics and consciousness. Even the successful Colored Co-Operators in Yonkers, who were committed to "the development of the financial and other vital interests of the Negro race,"[5] were rendered ineffective by this time. Nevertheless, a new Negro consciousness was formed during this critical period of community development. The new consciousness lay not in any one intellectual philosophy or political movement but in the phenomenon of interlinked yet segregated Negro communities.

Gamson (1994) and Fein (1977) define the we-they characteristic of group inclusion and exclusion. They claim that within the "we" group, social obligations are allocated to members, and individuals can be held responsible to the group for their actions. They call this system a "universe of obligation" (Gamson 1994, 3). The structuring of U.S. residential suburbs by race had a direct influence on the universe of obligations that tied residents to one another and created their "linked fate." In Runyon Heights, the construction of a a set of mutual obligations was mediated by class interests. As racial obligations were formed that transcended class divisions and united the black working and middle classes in a racial melting pot, class interests were also developing that linked the material interests of black homeowners with those of their white middle-class neighbors.

The black community as a whole, and individual black communities, have been shaped by specific political and social concepts of who should be included within the "Negro" racial group, and by the political, economic, and social consequences of inclusion. In addition to urban centers like Harlem, the twentieth-century suburb was a place where race played a more prominent role in group consciousness than either ethnic culture or class interests. In Nepperhan–Runyon Heights, as in Harlem, cultural, religious, economic, national, and coloring differences were de-emphasized out of necessity, in order to encourage community cohesion along specifically racial lines. Rather than color or culture, race was perceived to be the dominant barrier to economic mobility. After initial signs of competition and friction, the West Indian–born population and the much larger native-born Southern population soon identified with each other in their common condition of racial subordination. Among residents of West Indian lineage, race would dominate their sense of identity; in relation to the outside world, they would increasingly identify themselves as Negro, rather than Jamaican or Trinidadian. Once immigration subsided, their children would assimilate further into an American Negro world.

Race and Place

The Yonkers real estate market, aided by government policy, provides representative evidence of the racialization of the suburban housing market in twentieth-century America. The experiences of black consumers contrast sharply with the model of the ideal market economy, in which neither the sellers' nor the buyers' racial identification would impinge on the cost of property or its availability. So-called coloreds were confronted with restrictive covenants, denied mortgages, and steered to specific areas like Harlem or further north, to the Westchester suburbs and Nepperhan. Not only did race determine access to property and housing, but residential areas like Nepperhan and Harlem came to be identified with the race of the inhabitants. As so-called Negroes moved into these areas, European Americans fled, and the areas became widely known as colored or Negro areas. Racial residential segregation threaded disparate social histories together along a rigid color line and gave rise to the organization of the Nepperhan community around "race" and race consciousness.

Distinction is usually made between a Southern form of segregation supported by state and local law and a de facto Northern style supported only by custom. Yet the term "de facto" obscures the key role of the federal government in bringing segregation to the suburban real estate market in Westchester County. Legal scholar Richard Thompson Ford (1995) argues that the actions of the state and individuals helped construct racially identified spaces, which ultimately provided a primary basis for political identity construction (pp. 450–451). Redlining, restrictive covenants, and FHA policy all contributed to defining residential space by race.

The implication is significant for conceptualizing the formation of community consciousness in Nepperhan. The segregation of communities by race provided a fundamental organizing principle within the polity. Social actors came to identify common political interests embedded within the geopolitical community. The community became the central locus for exercising political power and countering the practices of civil society and the state, as well as for protecting collective material interests; racial consciousness provided the glue for social solidarity and political mobilization.

In Nepperhan, differences in skin color, religion, nationality, regional identity, social status, and culture were minimized, as communal boundaries were drawn along racial lines. Racial consciousness-building was an active and creative response to residential segregation, political subordination, and the human need for communal ties. Through the organization of community institutions and clubs along the color line, community solidarity and racial identity were reinvented together.

Although a few local families that had migrated from Virginia and West Virginia did acknowledge European ancestry, most local residents claimed only Native American, Latino, or Caribbean ancestry, if indeed they recognized any nonblack identity.

Embedded in such segregated communities is the basis for both racial consciousness and nationalism; yet any tendencies toward racial nationalism are mediated by class interests. Nepperhan residents actively participated in building community solidarity around race, in order to foster their collective material interests. At the same time, they used their material, human, and social advantages to help fight racial oppression in the city of Yonkers. Although scholars have debated the significance of race for the black middle class, race, rather than declining in significance, remained a central organizing principle of civic and political life in Nepperhan. In the minds of both residents and outsiders, the community is defined in fundamental ways by both racial and class characteristics. Outsiders see it as a black middle-class community; residents see themselves as a black middle-class community. Both race and class, incorporated into the local social structure, influenced local conceptions of community and contributed to the definition of collective political interests.

5

Nepperhan
The Prewar Years

Although the influx to Runyon Heights has continued unabated for eight decades, two time periods capture distinct phases of community development. Chapter 5 describes the first period, from 1915 through the Depression years. These first two decades were a time in which the physical boundaries were delineated and Nepperhan was transformed from predominantly working-class to a predominantly middle-class community. Social, civic, and political organizations that emerged during this period reflected both the racial structuring of community life and the residents' material interests. A New Negro consciousness developed, with the support of local social organizations.

Socially, Nepperhan could be best described as hyperorganized; as numerous local social groups and associations evolved over the decades, most developed overlapping memberships and maintained multigenerational ties. High levels of social organization ultimately reinforced community cohesion and contradict conservative assumptions about black American cultural dysfunction. Much like other working- and middleclass suburbanites, Nepperhan residents were actively engaged in local civic life.

The establishment of racial boundaries affected every aspect of public life; schools, clubs, religious organizations, civic associations, friendships, and ultimately community consciousness all became segregated.

Although a small, predominantly Italian, white population had been in the area since its settlement in 1912, it and the black community remained socially segregated from one another; community political battles were often fought only by black Nepperhaners, because community itself was defined in racial terms.

During this early period, only children in the neighborhood regularly interacted across racial lines: they played baseball and football in the undeveloped woods and lots or bought ice cream in the local Italian-owned store. Adults were generally friendly toward one another, although lasting friendships only occasionally crossed institutionally maintained racial boundaries. This was equally true for the children; Boy Scout Troop #34 was virtually all black. Members of the largely Italian group were likely to frequent Catholic-based organizations. Black Nepperhaners were likely to attend School 1, Metropolitan AME Zion Church, and other all-black institutions, and to participate in racially homogeneous social organizations. While the two groups lived literally side by side in a demographically "integrated" area, segregation in civic life structured social interactions between groups. Still, the mutual respect between neighbors at times blossomed into true friendships, especially among the children. A woman resident of fifty-eight years gave her assessment of community race relations: "I think those that were here got along fine."

Tales of the community's founding, stories of the accomplishments of individual members, and sagas of community battles provided residents with a sense of historical continuity and collective memory that is passed down in the form of folklore. Older community members are regarded as the official keepers of this history and, in a sense, the living embodiment of the community's spirit. They ensure that the past is not forgotten by newcomers. A native-born resident of twenty-seven years explains the role of the community lore: "There is a legend here, if you will, of how this place evolved. And I think that makes us special. Kind of, you know, initially from people who were in a place where they kind of knew that they were not wanted, and, I think, worked even harder to make this place equal to the other neighborhoods because they knew they were not wanted. I think that's an ethic that still rings home today."

The community's founding was a common theme of the local folklore. One "old-timer" recalled: "Well, you see, you see, Runyon Heights, this used to be an estate. It used to be the Runyon Estate, and all this side and all on the other side . . . across the bridge. We used to say across the tracks. They broke it up and they made it into lots . . . in the twenties. And what the old-timers used to tell me is that the Jews wanted to buy it and use it for a cemetery. And so the guy in charge of the estate said that he would rather sell it to the niggers than sell it to the Jews."

Other residents told similar stories, a few adding that the preference was for "live niggers" over "dead Jews." This tale clearly situates the community's relationship to the outside world in a primarily racial context. Another resident, born and raised in Nepperhan, recounted his version of the community history: "My father built a house up here in 1929 on Chelsea Place. . . . It was one of the first houses up there. I guess everybody told you, there was a real estate broker and he was selling homes. And they opened this area up. At that time I think the city opened this area up, half of it was for Homefield—this was the white people—and this side was for blacks. And they had an imaginary line there drew up between the two of them: Homefield, and this was called Nepperhan Station, Runyon Heights."

Philip Pistone, Yonkers' Planning Director during the 1950s and 1960s, testified at the Yonkers desegregation suit that the neighborhood was founded on a tract of land owned by a state senator who brought busloads of Harlem residents to Runyon Heights for weekend picnics and auctions (Opinion 80 CIV. 6761: 48). Pistone recounted essentially the same story to me during an hour-long interview. Close examination of the historical record, however, reveals that these stories are part mythology and part fact. Charles Runyon was not a senator but an industrialist who married Isabel Randolph, daughter of a former New Jersey Governor.[1] Runyon died on October 13, 1903, in his home on Fifth Avenue in New York, long before his land was subdivided for sale to Hudson P. Rose in 1912.

The claim that Runyon had responded to local concerns about plans for a Jewish cemetery on his property and decided to sell the land to Negroes instead remains unsubstantiated. Many of the proposed subdivision plans developed by real estate agents were never officially submitted to the City Planning Bureau for approval, and today only scattered records of such proposals exist.[2]

Another dimension of the local folklore revolves around a large white home on Kenmore Street near Saw Mill River Road that was allegedly the onetime residence of the Runyon family. The stately structure, complete with Southern-style veranda and horseshoe driveway, was rumored to have housed a bootlegging operation and night club during Prohibition. The house itself left a considerable impression on residents. One early resident recalled: "When I was a kid, they say that used to be the big house. . . . They had an entranceway coming up to the house from Saw Mill River Road. And they had a big veranda porch all the way around it. And then, as you came up the entranceway, they had two great big pine trees. It reminded you of one of those old country estates."

Community folklore provided historical continuity to community life, and a framework for newcomers to interpret future community conflicts. It supplemented the intricate network of associations that came to dominate Nepperhan. The organizations themselves have come to be a part of local legend, while serving at the same time as a primary keeper of tradition. For all the many organizations that dotted the landscape, the foundation of Nepperhan community life lay in the family.

The Family

E. Franklin Frazier (1939; 1949) emphasized the primary role of the Negro family for the formation of stable social relationships and for "organized social adjustment to American life" (1949, 333). He and other scholars have argued that social disorganization was a characteristic of black family life following emancipation, but the families of Nepperhan provide striking evidence that material resources formed the undergirding for stable family life. Occupational security preceded home ownership; both greatly encouraged strong family organization and institutional stability in the community. The experience of Nepperhan suggests that occupational security and residential mobility are prerequisites for access to the middle class.

In Runyon Heights, family bonds have been central to the identity of individuals and the community. Although the scale of my project did not allow me to interview members of all the significant Nepperhan–Runyon Heights families, many of the same family names came up again and again during formal and informal interviews: Mingo, Smith, Downs, Perencheif, Keno, Moore, Fields, Colymore, Bray, Holst, Skinner, Jackson, Frances, Poe, Wilson, Joseph, Giddings, Booker, Ross, Grayson, Morgan, and several distinct Williams families. Members of many of these families still live in the community today; some are third- or fourth-generation Nepperhaners. Many families are mentioned here, yet dozens more contributed significantly to local history.

Families are central to the community's concept of itself. Family status, however, was based not on the status a family had had before settling in Nepperhan but on home ownership and the contribution the family made to collective life there. Leaders of local associations often made the greatest contributions to community life. Those who were publicly recognized as important residents had contributed to community stability through their active vigilance in protecting community interests. Small deeds did not go unnoticed. During the early days, the Women's Civic Club annually awarded a prize to the resident who had maintained the most beautiful front garden and lawn. Because family status was important, social institutions like the church and the local improvement association also came to be identified by reference to the family surnames of people involved in their establishment and maintenance. When residents talked about local organizations, the conversation often turned to influential families. Local homes were frequently described by the surnames of families who had once lived in them. As mentioned earlier, even streets took on the names of persons who had at one time had significance in the area. One street in particular took on symbolic meaning and connected Nepperhan with broader issues in the political discourse on race and political independence: Touissant Avenue was almost surely named after the Haitian freedom fighter Toussaint L'Ouverture.

Residents constructed a common history based on the notion that their family roots became historically intertwined in Nepperhan. Race and class were linked in time and space by a single common denominator, the community. The community, both real and imagined, fostered a local folk culture. Specific community members are regarded as the official keepers of the local history. These individuals, most of whom are the eldest generation in the families mentioned earlier, embody and symbolize the community.

The presence of multiple generations of families, in combination with frequent intermarriage, has created a tight kinship network of interconnected extended families, where children experienced neighborhood and community as truly integrated. Some people were so committed to the community that they maintained close ties with it even after they moved to Homefield, or other areas of Yonkers. One woman, whose parents left the community for a newly opened west side housing project when she was a baby, remembered: "My father was here every day of his life, every single day. . . . My mother was here five days out of the week." Her family maintained close ties to the area, because her father's mother, one of the earliest residents, still lived there. After she married, the woman bought a home on "the Hill," just a short walk from her grandmother's house across the tracks.

Nepperhan challenges the popular notion that suburbanization has brought only bland homogeneity, a loss of community, and isolation. One resident explained:

And it has a link, I think, through our morals and our values, again, because, you know, it was kind of a place where everybody knows everybody else as a child; everybody else, at least back when I was growing up, is your supervisor or guardian, and you were a little more restrained about doing things because you always kind of had eyes on you all the time. And I'd like to feel that, in other communities, that might not have been the case. You know, in other communities where maybe the first, some of the first and strongest, links are made through . . . schools and things like that, and being next-door neighbors and belonging to school organizations, a lot of the initial links—I mean, even as a child—is family links. I mean, people who I met later on through school or through participating in sports together, that was because again, my mother's sister-in-law, her cousin or sister-in-law, her kids, it's just family. Basically it kind of started as this large extended family. . . . There's always a family kind of thing. People out here identify themselves as being a part of such and such a family. They identify somebody's house, that's the so-and-so house, and that's the way you do normally with, let's say, a town or a larger area, but people out there still say that. They'll say, "Well, the car is parked out in front of the so-and-so house." That family could have been out of that [house] seventy years ago, but this person is going to say 'the so-and-so house.' . . . That's how we identify things. And we identify a lot of things here by people. I am Joe Jones's son. I am Carol Jones's son. Until I get to a certain point, and maybe when my generation dominates a little bit, then, and my kids will be, that's Pete Jones's son.

Unlike the parent-centered households that characterized many working-class American households, the child-centered pattern typical among the middle class was prevalent among the early Nepperhaners (Gans 1982, 54). Parents tended to organize households around their children; women tended to have primary responsibility for maintenance of the household, though many were employed outside the home. Making preparations for children's futures was a central preoccupation. Mothers' lives revolved around family, church, and work. Working mothers with children arranged for day care when their children were young. Many children stayed with relatives, who sometimes remained in the same household. Others stayed with neighbor women who did not work outside the home. Stay-at-home mothers gave one another moral and social support by forming groups such as the Idlers Club and the Mothers Club.

The African proverb popularized by First Lady Hillary Clinton, that "it takes a village to raise a child" was not a new concept to Nepperhaners. In many ways, the community functioned like an extended family network. Children were a primary concern for the community. Mischievous children could expect to be disciplined, and those in need of assistance found neighbors responsive. In addition, many children had grandparents, aunts, uncles, cousins, and assorted in-laws only a stone's throw away. As in other black communities, women were essential to the maintenance of this network and to community organization (Stack 1974). They provided critical community support through their active role in organizing community resources through the local Parent Teacher Association, the church, and local civic associations. They thus helped to draw residents into a web of local networks and associations.

While families linked individuals to a network of communal associations, local social organizations helped foster racial consciousness by laying the groundwork for local political mobilization. Social organizations gave residents a sense of having an interconnected history and future, without which individual families would have remained isolated and atomized. Without the associations, no central community identity, racial or otherwise, would have developed.

The Church

After the family, the church represents the second most important institution in the black community (Frazier 1948, 333). From the first days in Nepperhan, residents constructed a tight-knit community of associations through the development of religious institutions. Founded officially in 1914, before any officially recorded black presence in Nepperhan, the Metropolitan AME Zion Church played a particularly significant role in the lives of the early settlers, providing a central organizing force for community cohesion.

During the 1960s, the smaller Kings Highway Apostolic Church, led by Runyon resident Reverend Harrison, was also established in Nepperhan.[3] This church did not, however, play a significant role in the community's development. Only a handful of residents number among its congregants, yet the church has thrived, earning the respect of local residents.

The Metropolitan AME Zion Church stands on Belknap Avenue with its back to the railroad tracks. Metropolitan, as locals affectionately call it, is the oldest organization in the community. The cohesion provided by the church was crucial for the spiritual and even material survival of Nepperhaners. Church history not only parallels that of Nepperhan but also chronicles a chapter in the saga of this country's segregated religious life. In fact, the segregation of spiritual life in Nepperhan provided an institutional basis for reinforcing racial boundaries in civic life.

In his comprehensive study *The Negro Church in America* (1974), E. Franklin Frazier maintains that Christianity provided the basis for social cohesion among Africans' descendants in the United States during and after slavery (14). Baptists and Methodist missionaries evangelized among both free and unfree Negroes in the South and North during the 1700s. In 1784, the Methodist conference proclaimed that slavery opposed the laws of God (Frazier 1974, 14–29). Still, Negroes, frustrated by the discrimination and racial segregation typical of many congregations, formed an independent Negro organization within the Methodist church. Around 1787, after being removed from prayer at the St. George Methodist Episcopal Church in Philadelphia, Richard Allen and Absalom Jones organized the Free African Society with other Negro members of the St. George congregation. Allen, a former slave, believed that the Methodist form of worship was best suited to the needs of Negroes. Jones favored the Episcopalian model and ultimately founded the African Protestant Episcopal Church of St. Thomas. Allen, with the majority of the Negro congregants from St. George, formed the all-black Bethel Church in 1794.

These early organizations were the first attempts by Negroes to organize a mass movement around racial consciousness (521). Adopting Allen's idea of African societies, all-Negro churches began organizing in other cities, as well (Frazier 1949, 521). In New York City in 1796, Peter Williams, a sexton at the John Street Methodist Church, helped establish another all-Negro Methodist organization (Frazier 1974, 34). He was instrumental in drawing Negro congregants from the John Street church together to form the African Methodist Episcopal Zion Church in 1821. The church, officially founded by James Varick, was the first all-Negro congregation established in New York State. Varick was elected bishop in 1822 (Allen 1964, 19).

In 1816, representatives of many of the newly formed Negro Methodist churches convened in Philadelphia and established the African Methodist Episcopal Church; Richard Allen was selected as its first bishop (Frazier 1949, 346). Within the mainstream denominations, a rift arose just before the Civil War between the Southern and Northern sections of both the Baptist and Methodist organizations over the status of the Negro. Consequently, though Negroes joined both organizations in large numbers, they remained segregated in sections at "white" churches (Frazier 1974, 14–31). The racial rift in American religious life has never healed. Both the AME and the AME Zion churches have maintained racially separate organizations to this day (Frazier 1974, 32–34). Not surprisingly, most mainstream Methodist congregations remain all white.

A third Methodist organization, the Colored Methodist Episcopal Church, was established in Tennessee in 1870 by the remaining Negro members of the Methodist Episcopal Church South (Frazier 1974, 34). Today, the organization is known as the Christian Methodist Church, having dropped the term "Colored."

During the 1870s, several all-Negro churches were also formed in Yonkers. It is significant that the rise in racially segregated churches in Yonkers coincided with the formation of the nineteenth-century ghetto. The first to organize, in 1871, was the Institutional AME Zion Church.[4] Messiah Baptist Church, the first all-Negro Baptist congregation in the city, was established in 1872 and formally organized in 1879. Both groups rented Townsend Hall on North Broadway in Yonkers (Allison 1984, 289–291). Messiah Baptist was originally an extension of the Warburton Avenue Baptist Church, an all-white congregation. This relationship was akin to that at the segregated John Street Methodist Church just before its split into two racially distinct church organizations. Messiah Baptist and Institutional AME later raised enough money to build their own houses of worship. Founded by Reverend Jacob Thomas of New York City, Institutional AME was the first Negro church in Yonkers that was formally established from the outset; Metropolitan and Messiah had been local prayer groups before developing formal institutional ties (Allison 1984, 289).

One respondent, a presiding elder in the AME Zion Church, shows how the history of the Metropolitan congregation is intertwined with the larger history of segregated Negro churches in the North.

Maybe you want to know why we started with the two groups. The AMEs was led, they started because the first bishop, Richard Allen — he might have been a local preacher then — Richard Allen was praying downstairs in a white church in Philadelphia, and they came, some of the white people, pulled him up off his knees, and took him out. They didn't want him to pray down there. That was about 1787, or something like that. And then he decided, we are going to walk out, and we are going to establish our own church out of protest. Now the AME Zion, all the AME Zion belong to John Street Methodist Church in New York, white church. . . . They weren't AME Zion, they were just a group of black people. Well, they went to the bishop, who was Asbury, and to some white ministers, and they said, We would like to have our own church, so we can worship God the way we want. And the people in New York said, Well, we'll help you. . . . One minister by the name of Stillwell, he said, I'll get some of you ready, and we will ordain some of you preachers, and that's the way that started, way back when. . . . Now, the CMEs were started much later, when the white people still wanted to have some influence, but they wanted the black people to have a church, so they helped them people in the South to establish the CMEs. Now you have these three groups. All three are completely independent.

Race is a defining characteristic of these organizations. Reverend C. Guita McKinney, pastor of Metropolitan from 1973 to 1993, explained the church's hierarchical structure, which centers around Episcopal heads, or bishops: "[It] started off with a set of superintendents that were presiding elders, and in later years we called them bishops." Today, the organization has thirteen bishops, who preside over the thirteen Episcopal districts. Each Episcopal district is divided into conferences, which are further subdivided into smaller districts.[5]

As Negroes were increasingly unwelcome at established "white" churches and largely excluded from white neighborhoods, the Negro church continued to expand. The church not only ideologized racial segregation as a natural part of God's law, but represented itself as the embodiment of God's order, reflecting the natural divisions among man. Consequently, racially segregated churches influenced the boundaries of the social organizations that derived from them. Even though the neighborhood was in fact racially integrated, community life for Negro Nepperhaners remained largely self-contained in a Negro world.

Simplistic explanations that point to prior cultural and religious ties among Negroes do not explain the development and growth of an all-Negro church in Nepperhan, because such great diversity existed among the early settlers. In fact, many of the founders of the Metropolitan AME Zion Church came from other Christian denominations—only one of the original members of Metropolitan appears to have been an AME member before moving to the area; however, creating a safe place to worship took precedence over cultural, national, and even religious identification. The Metropolitan Sixty-Third Anniversary Souvenir Journal reports: "The original prayer band had long recognized the desirability of a church affiliation and though, on their own accord, [they] would not necessarily have chosen to come into the Zion Methodist fold, the members, feeling the need perhaps for the stability afforded by a denominational tie, acquiesced in the move by Mrs. Borden."

Though there were a number of white churches in the Nepperhan vicinity by the time blacks first arrived, church organization and membership continued to evolve along racial lines. In 1917, the church closest to Nepperhan was the Memorial Methodist Episcopal Church, on the corner of Tuckahoe Road and Altonwood Place, an ideal location for Negro Nepperhan residents. The cornerstone of the structure (which houses a small garden center today) is dated 1909. Allison's *History of Yonkers* (1896) reports that Wood Hill Methodist Episcopal Church stood at the corner of Saw Mill River Road and Tuckahoe Road (294), although maps of the period show no sign of it. It is interesting that the earliest black and white Methodist churches in Yonkers had nearly identical names: Memorial African Methodist Episcopal Zion Church and Memorial Methodist Episcopal Church. Like the early Messiah Baptist congregation, the first black Methodists in Nepperhan were merely tolerated by the local white Methodist congregation. One informant, a resident since 1924 and a long-time church member, reported that the group that founded Metropolitan AME met in the basement of Memorial Methodist Episcopal Church, on the edge of the community. Church records suggest that this occurred between 1928 and 1931, the period in which Nepperhan was expanding significantly.

A former pastor of Metropolitan AME Zion Church retold the story of the transition from the original small prayer group, first formed by the Negro Nepperhan settlers, to an established institution in the community. His account highlights the conflicts within the local AME organization that directly contributed to the prayer group's becoming a part of the AME organization. His account also stresses the strong links that existed between the AMEs in Yonkers and Harlem-based AME churches. His story makes it clear that Negroes had settled in Nepperhan before 1916.

But now this church was, I was thinking as I came down here, it was started with a prayer meeting that used to congregate and meet in the houses. A few people that moved into this section used to meet in houses. . . . That was around 1914. And we have a sister church across town called Institutional. I also pastored at Institutional. Institutional is a much larger church, much more prestigious church. We had a very brilliant man, whose name was Smile. I think Smile was a graduate of Harvard, I believe. Smile was pastoring over there, and when conference came in 1915, the AME Zion Annual Conference in 1915, it met at Institutional. This had nothing, so far, to do with the little group that you had having prayer meetin' out here. But this minister was a tremendous leader, and Bishop Hood, Bishop Hood started the educational system for the white people in the state of North Carolina, during the Reconstruction period. He was an extremely brilliant young man. He started out in New York. Our church was established in 1796. Varick was the first bishop, and Varick died in 1828, and the bishop that followed Varick (at that time there was only two—now we have thirteen), the bishop that followed Varick was Christopher Rush, a historian and a bishop. He was originally from North Carolina. . . .

Rush, who was the second bishop of the church, ordained Hood, and Hood lived to be the same man that I'm going to tell you about that moved this pastor to Institutional. He was a bishop for fifty years, and he covered a lot of territory: he was a writer, also a historian.[6] Also helped to establish Livingstone College, at Salisbury, North Carolina, and Hood Theological Seminary, along with two other very bright men. But Hood was the presiding bishop over the New York Conference in 1915. He was presiding bishop up until 1916. In 1915, he moved Smile . . . from Institutional. Smile decided he would pull out some of the members and set up his own church. Smile started working on setting up a church. Smile's sister was a member of this church that pulled out: they had to leave Institutional. Now, the reason he left, instead of the bishop promoting him, he thought the bishop had demoted him, because the bishop sent him to Port Chester, and he wouldn't go to Port Chester. . . . This precipitated a fight in the local church, Institutional. They had gas lights. They broke all the gas lights out with big bats and bottles. . . . Hood was an old man then, in his nineties and in a wheelchair. They had to take him out of the back of the church, put him in a big wagon, and take him away. But when it simmered down, Hood had moved two men. That caused trouble—the men at Mother Zion, that's the oldest church and the largest church in the connection in New York City. . . . Both of these men tried to establish new churches. Smile was trying to establish one, and he got a building on Main Street. And Smile went to the general conference and told the people he had been mistreated by Hood. He was a great orator, and Hood was not able to compete with him then. He was forty; Hood was ninety. So they retired Hood in 1916. Smile came back to try to push the church he had established the year before. And he was up on a ladder painting the church, and he fell off dead. So Millie Smile, his sister, came to this church, and she got together with that group of people who had been having prayer meetings. And when they went to the annual conference, she carried the church in to join the annual conference. And that's how this became an AME Zion Church. . . . They date this church, on our record, they date it for 1914. I really think it should be dated for 1916. The first minister of record for the church was Reverend Moore. And his stay was from 1928 to 1931.

The official church history printed in the souvenir journal tells a similar story but names Anna Borden as the central figure pushing for the AME designation. It seems possible that both accounts are true. The journal reports: "This group [the original volunteer prayer band] was later joined by a dissident faction which had followed Mrs. Anna Borden out of the Institutional A.M.E. Zion Church of Yonkers. The latter, being very active and influential in the New York Conference of the A.M.E. Zion Church, proceeded on her own initiative, but without the full consent of the members of the merged organization, to enroll it under the Zion Methodist jurisdiction."[7]

Both accounts highlight the seemingly arbitrary nature of the decision to join the AME fold. Frazier points out the tendency for the Northern black middle class to prefer the larger Baptist and Methodist churches (1949, 354). It seems possible that early residents of Nepperhan consciously chose the AME Zion denomination in order to establish a middle-class community character. The official community account differs from official church history in that it suggests some dissent over the AME designation. Watkins-Owens (1996) also documents a Caribbean preference, particularly among ministers, for the AME and AME Zion denominations, possibly because those churches existed in the Caribbean during the nineteenth century (59).

Metropolitan was literally built from the ground up by the new settlers, both foreign and native-born. By 1928, John B. Fields, one of the original prayer group members, with George Brown and Edward Smith, had purchased two adjoining lots on Runyon Avenue from Hudson P. Rose for $100. When they learned of the availability of a church in the Williamsburg section of the Bronx, Smith and Brown bought the structure for a reported $150. John B. Fields, Jr., and Warner M. Fields, sons of John B. Fields, dismantled the structure and moved it to the Runyon Avenue site. Master carpenter Norman Downs laid the foundation, Edward Smith did much of the reassembly of the structure, Ernest Query constructed a cesspool, and George Brown's wife financed the roof and raised funds. The construction of the church was truly a community affair. After a delay caused by the Depression, the cornerstone was finally laid in 1931.

Eric Lincoln, in *The Black Church Since Frazier* (1974), reevaluated the black church in light of the cultural and political changes of the civil rights and Black Power movements. He argues that the 1960s marked the dawning of the black church and the demise of the Negro church (Lincoln 1974, 106). The Negroes of yesterday have for the most part come to identify themselves as black today, and the change in identity is significant. According to Lincoln, with the coming of the black church, the church was transformed into a self-conscious, self-assertive, inner-directed institution, in contrast to the "otherworldly" orientation described by Frazier (Lincoln 1974, 109; Frazier 1974). Both Frazier and Lincoln claimed that although the Negro church provided a haven from white oppression and symbolized, by its very existence, the power of Negro self-determination, it also accepted and accommodated to an inferior status for Negroes (Frazier 1974, 50; Lincoln 1974, 107).

The black church in Nepperhan was never a direct source of social transformation or direct political mobilization, as was the Southern Christian Leadership Conference during the 1960s, but its presence in Nepperhan during the early years was critical. The church welcomed new members into the community, provided a basis for interlinked community social organizations, including the Nepperhan Community Center, and, most important, fostered a sense of unity, history, and identity for residents. Even those who are not congregants express great admiration and respect for the institution.

As early as 1899, W. E. B. Du Bois recognized the importance of the Methodist church in Negro community life in Philadelphia, even for the middle class. Nepperhaners placed spiritual life at the center of community consciousness and organization, a priority that promoted continued dialogue with other black congregations and renewed connections to the Harlem community. Thus the church in Nepperhan became another vehicle for the creation of racial consciousness, while reinforcing community and even class boundaries.

We can observe the institutional overlap between Metropolitan AME and other church organizations that linked the Nepperhan and Harlem communities. One longtime AME member, whose family shifted from Harlem's Mount Olivet Baptist Church[8] to Nepperhan's Methodist Metropolitan in the 1930s, recalled: "My parents at first continued to go back down, [from Nepperhan to Mt. Olivet], but we didn't have a car or anything, and transportation wasn't the greatest. So they became affiliated with the church right here, the Methodist church. At first my mother resisted: she was a Baptist and she wasn't gonna change, and all that. But eventually the whole family became members of this church."

For the dead as for the living, segregation was the norm in Yonkers. Burial of the dead in segregated areas was not uncommon, though cemetery segregation often seems to reflect the deeper issue of institutional segregation in religious life. Black residents were indeed buried at nearby St. Mary's Cemetery on occasion, although only a small number of the black Nepperhaners were Catholic. Often families have wished to bury their dead with other family members or with previously deceased members of their church or lodge (Kruger-Kahloula, 1994). Since 1929, many blacks in Nepperhan and the rest of Yonkers were buried through Brooks Funeral Home. According to Brooks representatives, a large portion of the black population is buried at Oakland Cemetery, the only large cemetery in the city apart from St. Mary's. Others are buried at Mount Hope Cemetery, which borders Hastings and Yonkers, and still others further north in Westchester. Burial in New York City, where friends, family, and even church affiliation often remained, was also common.

Preferences about burial sites have tended to follow patterns already established by family members, and this means that Nepperhan residents have a diverse burial history. Place of burial often depended on religious institutional affiliation. Some people were buried with their families in the South, others through their old churches in New York City, and still others in the local city cemetery.

One Nepperhaner, whose grandfather built the home in which his own children now live, recounted: "Yes, for example, my cousin died here, and he was born and raised here, but his life took him into the city, so he spent most of his time in the city. So when we buried him, we had to have two [services], his body was viewed in the village; then we had to bring him up here to Brooks . . . they had that many people who wanted to come up."

Informants report that racial discrimination occurred in subtle ways, even in so-called integrated cemeteries. One source reported that the Oakland burial site was spatially segregated by race; many blacks were buried in an area called "the Hill" (Esannason and Bagwell 1993, 30). A survey of the cemetery grounds undertaken with Nepperhan surnames as a guide revealed no clear pattern of racial segregation. Nevertheless, names of older black families were frequently found in the vicinity of the Hill.

Though burial associations were common in other Northern Negro communities, the economically stable Nepperhaners found little need for financial help in burying their dead. Other voluntary organizations, however, were pivotal for community stability and survival.

Civic Associations and Clubs

The principal civic organization throughout the history of Nepperhan–Runyon Heights has been the Runyon Heights Improvement Association (RHIA). Founded during the late 1920s, it provided recreational services and a meeting place for residents, as well as an organizational foundation for local clubs. Its first two presidents, George Brown and James Howell, were American-born. The third president, Norman Downs, was originally from Barbados. The RHIA published a newsletter, the *Nepperhan Civic Recorder,* which was a major source of information for Negro residents. The *Civic Recorder* was run largely by women. At least five women from the area were involved in its publication: Maud Jackson, editor; Lorraine Wilson, Julie Poe, Frances Frances, and Gertrude Skinner, reporters. The publication was discontinued as the Depression years wore on and community resources wore thin. In 1933, the *Recorder* ran a notice soliciting registrations in the RHIA from the various clubs and organizations in the community (Figure 5.1). Of the associations listed, some, like the Women's Civic Club and the Mothers Club, still exist, having slowly added new members over the years; others, like the Rod and Gun Club, fell into obscurity. Many residents belonged to more than one club; this connected individuals to a broader community network.

Figure 5.1. Notices from the *Nepperhan Civic Recorder*

Notices

The Runyon Heights Improvement Association is asking the various clubs of
Nepperhan if they would condescend to register their club and affairs with the
Civic Recorder so as to prevent a confliction of so many events happening in
one night, due to the fact that the Nepperhan Clubs are practically composed
of the same people and naturally carry the same followers. These clubs in
particular are: Westchester Junior League, Nepperhan Unit; Nepperhan
Republican Club; Runyon Heights Democratic Club; Runyon Heights Boys Club;
Rod and Gun Club; Runyon Heights Mothers Club; The Frivolities; The Blue
Monday; The Four Hundreds; The Unique; Les Jolies Coeurs; Club Thirteen;
Royal Boys; Studio Bachelors; Sewing Circle; Royal Athletic League, and
Womens C.C. If there are any clubs that are not mentioned here, that have been
formed and composed of the majority of Nepper haners, kindly send in your
names to the Editor of the pamphlet.

Source: The *Nepperhan Civic Recorder,* June 1933, vol. A., no. 4.

The middle-class aspirations of members of local associations are reflected in the activities they pursued. Even the names reflected the
groups' bourgeois preoccupations: the Four Hundreds, the Frivolities, and
Les Jolis Coeurs were purely social circles organized for leisure activities.
In fact, west side residents often called the Runyon area the Four Hundreds, a joking reference to the community's "upper-class" status. Other
associations sought to preserve the middle-class character of civic life.
Thus, the Women's Civic Club and the Runyon Heights Improvement Association were committed to beautifying the neighborhood and maintaining the quality of life. Some groups, like the Men's Club, a direct outgrowth
of the Metropolitan AME, were both socially and civically oriented. Over
the years, other clubs developed: the Royal Boys, the Studio Bachelors,
Club Thirteen, the Bridge Club, the San Tous, and the Chetocqua Debs
(Debutantes). Nepperhaners were also active in local politics. Early on,
they formed the Nepperhan Republican Club and the Runyon Heights
Democratic Club.[9]

In addition to publishing a newsletter, the RHIA built the Nepperhan
Community Center on Monroe Street. At the modest-sized community
house, youngsters could be found on afternoons gathered at the pool and
Ping-Pong tables. The center thrived until it was destroyed by fire in the
late 1930s. When the center was rebuilt, it was relocated to southwest

Yonkers, where the majority of blacks lived, in order to qualify for public funding and serve more of the black population of southwest Yonkers. For Nepperhan residents, however, the relocation meant a trip across town to use the facility. But Nepperhaners appear to have accepted a political identification and responsibility that transcended their material self-interest. Locked into a common fate with the working class, Nepperhaners maintained the identification with the tradition of Negro uplift. Just as residents supported the rebuilding of the Nepperhan Community Center on the west side,[10] they later became active participants and leaders in institutions like the NAACP and the YMCA, which served the black population of Yonkers.

Early Nepperhaners also established a community baseball team, the Runyon ACs. Local talent came together to compete, not in the local citywide league, but against other Negro communities in suburbs like Tuckahoe, Mt. Vernon, and even southwest Yonkers. The team survived until World War II.

A few Negro newcomers to Nepperhan established local businesses. A cooperative group based in Harlem, reportedly an offshoot of the Colored Merchants Association, opened a small grocery store on Monroe Street. Julius Smith and his family operated Smith's Nepperhan Model Market; the brick building that housed the store was built during the late 1920s by Norman Downs. The store enjoyed only moderate success and closed after a few years; this later became the first site of the Nepperhan Community Center. A second grocery store, a mom-and-pop venture, opened on Monroe Street during the late 1940s. The store was owned and operated between 1945 and 1952 by Adeline and Richard Williams and Tyler (Jackie) Jackson. This store too was only moderately successful and closed in 1952. These family enterprises competed with the A&P market on Tuckahoe Road, where most residents bought their staples.

Some of the more successful black-owned businesses in the area were those that served food and drink and doubled as local gathering places. The Roadside Inn, on Saw Mill River Road, served Southern cuisine and provided a place for dancing. The Cabin, just down the road, was another locally owned eatery.

Some residents, selling their skills directly to the public, advertised carpentry and electrical services in the *Civic Recorder.* Others started small businesses in their homes, like Paul Bray, who sold property in Nepperhan. Renting rooms to boarders was a common way of subsidizing rent or mortgage, although the extent of this practice is undocumented. Official records like the census rarely indicated the actual number of household members, and lodgers frequently went unreported. Renting rooms was a familiar survival strategy among Harlemites as well (Watkins-Owens 1996, 43).

In the years before the Depression, Negro settlers continued to arrive in Nepperhan. Like the original black settlers, the majority of newcomers were young couples with children. For them, the move to Nepperhan represented a move up the social ladder, as had been the case also for the early settlement of Harlem (Watkins-Owens 1996, 44).

By 1930, Nepperhan community boundaries had been clearly defined. The first black families in Nepperhan had opened local establishments and founded civic organizations, social and political clubs, and a church. Nepperhan became *the* place to live for the socially mobile Negro.

Politicizing "Race" in Early Nepperhan

Although institutional ties linked Nepperhaners to African-American communities in Yonkers and New York City, racial unity in the community did not spring from a natural attraction among Negroes but rather from political tensions between city government agencies and the community. When the actions of city government threatened residents' middle-class way of life, community sentiment became politicized along racial and class lines. As city officials afforded resources to areas like Homefield and Nepperhan differentially on the basis of race, race developed further as the source of collective identity for community residents as they asserted their right to the American Dream.

The first significant event that galvanized the community along explicitly racial lines involved the classic pattern of school district gerrymandering by race. This policy threatened the ability of black residents to use education as a ticket to economic mobility, yet its systematic nature also tended to unify a diverse population by providing a common framework for political action.

The event in question occurred just before the Depression. As parents and students prepared for the new school year in 1928, they learned that Nepperhan students were being denied the right to attend the newly constructed Roosevelt High School, located just half a mile down Tuckahoe Road, an easy walk from the community. School officials had decided that Roosevelt would remain all white.

After discovering that their children would be denied admittance and bussed across town to other schools, Nepperhan mothers organized community residents to petition the Yonkers School Board.[11] The matter was resolved when Nepperhan residents challenged the tax base that financed the construction of the school. Residents reported that taxes from the Nepperhan Valley region, which included the Nepperhan community, had gone toward school construction. Reluctantly, the school board permitted Nepperhan teens to attend the new school. The spouse of one activist mother explained simply, "The black mothers fought and got their children in the school."

Many residents today recall being among the first to racially integrate Roosevelt High. Although tolerated, they were not welcomed. They were often encouraged by teachers and counselors to attend Saunders Trade School rather than the more academically oriented Roosevelt. Unlike suburban schools today, many of which are eager to enroll black athletes, a number of Nepperhan men reported that Roosevelt had discouraged them from participating on the sports teams when they were students. One informant maintained that all the Nepperhan children had been required to attend summer school before enrolling at Roosevelt, but this assertion could not be verified.

Though institutional opposition was strong, white students were reportedly not openly hostile toward their new Negro classmates; however, as one female graduate from the 1930s stated, "There were times when you knew you were black." Tolerance for Negroes only occasionally resulted in close interracial friendships. Stories of positive memories of life at Roosevelt are interspersed with much less flattering tales of racism and exclusion. One early Roosevelt graduate reported being asked to play the role of a maid in a school theatrical production. "I was just so insulted," she said. "I thought this was about the worst thing that they could have done. I had a chip on my shoulder the whole time I was there." No one recalls any dating across the racial divide. Even when Negroes and whites became friends at school, they rarely visited one another's homes. This was in stark contrast to the relatively congenial racial atmosphere that had developed at community-based elementary School 1. After graduation, many cross-racial friendships that had begun during high school soon dissolved.[12]

The racialization of public education in the Roosevelt affair was the first outside event to trigger a political response based specifically on race from Nepperhan residents. Race shifted from an implicit to an explicit characteristic of community consciousness. The "we" of community was now unequivocally defined in racial terms. From this point forward, race would shape the community's interaction with local government as well as define its relationship to other residential spaces in Yonkers.

The Depression Years

During the 1920s, the economic character of Westchester shifted quickly from one of industrial production to one of suburban consumption. Prosperity came to Yonkers, as it did to the entire nation. But the rural tranquillity and material comforts that most Nepperhaners had come to expect would soon be shattered by the Great Depression.

The Depression hit Nepperhan hard, as it did other working-class American communities. It brought changes to the stable environment forged during those first years, including massive job layoffs, and threatened the community's very existence. Many of the small enterprises in the community were crippled. Creative strategies for survival had to be employed. Native- and foreign-born African-American families were brought closer together by the need to share the essentials: food, fuel, and the responsibility for raising children.

Many residents lost their homes as a result of bank foreclosures, layoffs, or work furloughs, but families and neighbors stuck together, pooling their resources to make ends meet. Some of those who lost their homes became renters in the area and were later able to purchase a home again when employment opportunities improved during the 1940s.

A coal bin next to the railroad tracks across from Dunbar Street became a source of fuel for struggling families. One male resident remembers:

And at that time when we was kids, it use to be a lumberyard there and a coal yard. And part of the lumberyard ran along here and up further on Runyon Avenue, we had a great big silo there, great big silo—and that was the coal silo. The trains would come there and deposit their coal there, and they would take it out of the coal cars and put it up in the silo. And on this side, when they come to sell the coal or come to get coal, a truck would come past and a guy would raise the shute, and all the coal comes down. . . . Well, it was a company called Baers Wood and Coal Company [that owned all the coal]. And that was way back in the early twenties. . . . During the bad times we used to go up there and steal all of the slats to burn the wood. They would steal the coal and all of that. That was during the Depression.

After World War II, the city warehoused salt for its streets in the old coal bin, a sign of the Nepperhan community's shift from a working-class industrial to a middle-class managerial suburb.

Many families took in foster children from the Westchester County Department of Child Welfare in order to supplement the family income and keep their dreams of suburban home ownership alive. This strategy was adopted by both Southern migrant families in Northern communities and Caribbean immigrants (Stack 1974). Apparently, no stigma was attached to the children or their adoptive parents. One woman whose father had been furloughed told of her experiences growing up during the Depression: "That's when my mother did take in the children to supplement the income. . . . You could board foster children and she did. And it was like one big happy family. They called her mom, and they were like our sisters. . . . She had two at a time. . . . They would come and stay maybe two years or six months."

A male Nepperhaner testified to having grown up as a foster child in the 1930s.

> I am a child of the family that was raised in this residence in the thirties, ah, I'm actually a foster child . . . and very appreciative of the fact that I was raised here in this environment. This was a special, particular environment, and I think at that time it may well have been called Nepperhan. You understand that now it is called Runyon Heights, but what's in a name? . . . What made it special was that I think a group of blacks, or Negroes—I'll use the terms of the day—a group of Negroes came up here and settled it and built houses, escaping from what they recognized as a ghetto situation that was prevailing in New York City at the time. I'm talkin' about in the twenties, now. The move was in the twenties, some clear-thinking Negroes felt they needed an out from the then-existing ghettos of New York City, so they came up here and they developed a community, and I can tell you, it was a godsend.

While the personal commitments and sacrifices of Nepperhaners who welcomed poor and homeless children into their homes cannot be minimized, we must also recognize the material advantages many stood to gain from becoming foster parents. In fact, many older residents addressed this issue during interviews. Social service agencies placed only Negro children in Nepperhan households, a practice that reinforced racial homogeneity and racial consciousness in the area by providing important links to the black working class and poor. There was, however, one exception. At least three Puerto Rican–born children were placed in a Negro Nepperhan home. The two youngest children assimilated into the community. One of the two eventually married a Negro neighbor she had met while attending School 1; the third and oldest child entered the military, never to return to Nepperhan.

During the Depression the practice of taking in boarders grew. Like fostering children, accepting lodgers was an attempt to maintain financial stability while preserving the integrity of family and community. Even women who had formerly been housewives resorted to creative forms of generating family income. A woman who moved to Nepperhan in 1929 at the age of nineteen recalled how her mother had to go to work during the 1930s: "She would go out and help people from time to time. She had a friend who was a maid and from time to time they would need somebody to waitress or something like that. My mother would go and help them out. Another time my mother did board children, as an income during the Depression time. We had just built this house in 1929, so you could imagine."

Many women held full-time day jobs as domestics. Often these jobs became the sole source of stable family income. At an average of four dollars a day, "day's work" proved to be the economic bottom line for many families. It is interesting to note that none of the respondents mentioned having received financial help from the Federal Housing Authority during this crucial period, though it is possible that some did. One longtime male resident described the importance of women's work during the Depression:

> During the Depression, if it wasn't for my mother working, because the factory jobs were down to nothing, so by my mother and her aunt and all of them doing domestic work helped to bridge the gap during those lean years. . . . Oh, they were working like one day a month, two days a month until things picked up. After Roosevelt got in and they started that New Deal, back in the late thirties, then things started picking up. But up from the time I was born, up until 1931 . . . until that time things were pretty rough. They were only paying like fifteen dollars a month rent and they could hardly pay that. And at that time, my mother, my father, my uncle, my aunt, and my sister, and myself, we were living in the same apartment.

So one week they would pay the rent and the next time my father would pay it. . . . For quite a few years there, they weren't working that much. But they held on to their jobs, they didn't quit their jobs and go to another job, which is good, because they were both able to get a pension and everything. In those days, not too many jobs that blacks could get had pensions.

Another woman recalled: "Bronxville—that was the place where most black people [women] worked from the area here. There was a lot of people working, doing domestic work, and I guess the pressure was on them, because there wasn't very much for men to do during those days with the Depression, but the women were more or less able to keep things going by this 'day's work,' which was four dollars a day."

Some enterprising teenage boys ventured to the publicly owned Sprain Lake Golf Course, where they could pick up work as caddies. One resident told of going when he was twelve to the golf course, where he could earn a dollar plus a twenty-five-cent tip for five hours of caddying a round of golf. Even there, they experienced racial discrimination. One caddie explained:

In those days it was really something . . . for a black caddie to even get a job, but since this was a new course, and they needed caddies, they weren't too particular about it, 'cause this was a public golf course. I play golf there now. Incidentally, I'm a golf buff now. If you want to play, I'll beat ya right now! [He chuckles] . . . But that wound up not all roses, because after a while more of us came up there, until we had about a dozen black caddies. . . . Sometimes when the caddy master would send you out on the tee, these white golfers would look at you and say to the caddy master, "Hey, you give us these black boys, we don't want these black boys for caddies." So the caddy master would say, "All right you kids come on back." . . . So when we come back, the white kids would look at us—"What happened, what happened?" We were ashamed, we wouldn't even say what happened, you know. And the caddy master would send somebody else out. Then, finally, he would send us out.

Also during the turbulent 1930s, a few local families became members of the controversial multiracial religious mission led by the charismatic spiritual leader Father Divine. At least three families along Bushey Avenue who joined Divine's Peace Mission Movement became an accepted part of black Nepperhan. Outside the community, however, the mission drew heated controversy in 1939 when it purchased a mansion at 357 Park Hill Avenue, in a section of Yonkers that was then all white. The mansion was to serve as a commune or "Heaven" for the mixed-race membership. Race was the clear reason for objections to the sect. Park Hill civic associations and political leaders condemned the Heaven. The front page of the May 1, 1939, issue of the *Herald Statesmen* carried the headline: "Park Hill Gasps at 'Heaven' Purchased by Father Divine . . . Former Valle Mansion on Lowerre Summit Acquired by Negroes—Association May Seek to Invoke Zoning Law—Stoltz Threatens to Leave Town." Alexander Stoltz was then director of the Yonkers Chamber of Commerce and a resident of the Park Hill area.

The Father Divine movement in Nepperhan was short-lived. Residents could not recall any members of Divine's Heaven still living in the community by the 1950s. Father Divine died in 1965, leaving behind a dwindling group of devotees in Philadelphia. In 1993, the still predominantly white Park Hill Residents Association, which had once protested the presence of the Negro religious leader, now favored the designation of the home as a landmark (Fitz-Gibbon 1993, 10A).

Among teenagers, scouting was a popular activity during the 1930s. Many who would later give their lives to the war effort were former Boy Scouts or scout leaders. And, as mentioned earlier, the Nepperhan Scout troop remained predominantly black. One resident recalled the period just before the war when scout masters were drafted into the army too quickly to be replaced: "When I got in, I was about eleven and a half, . . . and I stayed in there until, until they drafted me into the service. They were drafting our scout masters left and right. When one go, then we'd have another one, they'd draft them and then we'd have another one. And then when they drafted the last one, hey, we carried on. The older boys carried the troop. We used to meet every Friday down at the school, and then the war got so bad. Then they started drafting us, and that was it, that was the end of the troop."

The Runyon AC's also disbanded during the war as young men were called to arms. The Depression and later the war brought significant changes to Nepperhan. The war years ushered in a period of American prosperity that signaled a new era in domestic race relations. Nepperhaners were as determined as ever to hold on to their share of the American dream. As white Americans continued to migrate to the suburbs during the postwar years, however, suburban land increasingly became a battleground for race and class politics. White homeowners' resistance to accepting the poor and nonwhites in their Yonkers communities contributed to threats of ghettoization in Nepperhan. Community solidarity became essential for protecting the material interests of black residents. Contemporary debates have presented arguments for the ascendancy of either race or class to explain the forces shaping the life of the black middle class.[13] In fact, though, both race and class frame its existence.

6

Runyon Heights
The Postwar Years

After World War II, the community increasingly drew a more traditional white-collar Negro population. Runyon Heights became during this time the preferred name among many residents. Middle-class gentrification brought the revitalization of local community organizations. Race also played an increasing role in local political conflicts, as it became intertwined with the class interests of residents in conflicts over school gerrymandering, busing, low-income housing, land use, and absentee landlords. Segregation, which physically isolated the community and determined local institutional and political boundaries, had a direct impact on the political conscience of this middle-class suburb.

After the Depression, many of the numerous clubs and organizations that had developed absorbed new residents and continued to serve the entire community. Many new clubs also arose. After the community center was destroyed by fire, the Metropolitan Church and Elementary School 1 often provided a meeting place for other community groups.

The war years ushered in a period of economic prosperity that continued into the 1960s. In this era of expanded occupational opportunity, residents attempted to maintain and protect the middle-class character of their community. New residents came primarily because the area provided opportunity for home ownership, not necessarily because they were seeking a black neighborhood. Sample surveys of black attitudes were not conducted until the 1960s, but surveys of the black middle-class residents conducted during the 1980s indicate that most indeed prefer to live in racially mixed neighborhoods; whites, however, overwhelmingly prefer predominantly white areas (Farley and others 1978; Goldberg 1998; Massey and Denton 1993; Yingeer 1995). As members of the growing black middle class searched the suburbs for a place to build homes and raise their families, they were steered to this insulated enclave. Some had learned of Runyon Heights from friends, co-workers, and family who had already moved there; others were directed by local realtors and racist real estate practices.

Homefield, despite the invisible barrier created by the reserve strip, did not prove impenetrable. The first African American to live in Homefield was the wife of a European-American man. Just after the war, he purchased land in the area, to the frustration of some of his neighbors. The couple developed close ties with Nepperhaners. Other Negroes began to move into the all-white tract in 1947, the same year the Homefield Association purchased the reserve strip. Paradoxically, just when white homeowners committed their resources to maintaining the reserve strip, Negroes circumvented restrictive covenants on Homefield properties by purchasing land at auction from the city. One year later, the Supreme Court signaled a change in legal reasoning on equality by declaring, in the landmark *Shelley v Kraemer* decision (1948), that restrictive covenants were unenforceable by state action. These changes were, however, too little too late. Residential space in Yonkers had already been defined in racial terms.

Former Nepperhan residents Alfred and Ernestine Morgan took advantage of the public auctions, becoming one of the first black families to build a house in the Homefield area.[1] The Morgans were able to purchase six lots from the city, three of which they used to construct their home. In this context, state action worked in favor of Nepperhaners. Public auctions provided a degree of equity not found in the private market. Other lots, just across the road, were also available for sale by the city; nevertheless, Homefield would remain virtually all white into the 1990s.

The Color Line and the Postwar Suburb

Runyon Heights' public status as a place of middle-class respectability made the community attractive to those who held good jobs and middle-class aspirations. Though seemingly isolated in the suburbs, Nepperhaners maintained important links with other Negro communities, in Harlem and southwest Yonkers. One such link was a popular lounge that was founded just after the war.

Following the long tradition of Nepperhan food and drink establishments, a number of young men from the community, along with men from the west side of Yonkers, formed the Sportsmen's Club of Nepperhan. Under the leadership of local resident Leonard Morgan, the club was known for the creation of the Sportsmen's Lounge on Saw Mill River Road.[2] The lounge functioned like a local social club: people went there to hear music, dance, socialize, eat, and drink. Local organizations often held their social events there. The Polish Community Center, a large facility on Tuckahoe Road, was sometimes rented for large events. A good number of famous acts appeared at the Sportsmen's Lounge, including world-renowned African drummer Babatunde Olatunji. The lounge provided a way for working- and middle-class Negroes to meet, mingle, and form important ties. One resident met his wife at the Sportsmen's Lounge: "They used to have big-name bands up there such as Count Basie, Erskine Hawkins, and all them guys up there, you know, and that place used to jump—oh yeah, that place used to jump. So I met her there, and from then on I didn't forget her. I would call her from then on."

Until the late 1950s, the lounge provided entertainment, while also connecting Nepperhaners to a national Negro social scene. According to jazz historian Phil Schaap, the Sportsmen's Lounge closed around the same time as the Savoy. Famous jazz musicians had connections with Yonkers. Vocalist Ella Fitzgerald was raised on School Street in southwest Yonkers, and trumpeter W. C. Handy became an east side resident late in life.[3]

In addition to locally based organizations, fraternal lodges and national associations have found strong support in Runyon Heights. Both native- and foreign-born residents often joined racially exclusive national associations like the Masons and Elks. Women belonged to groups like the Eastern Stars, sometimes referred to as the women's auxiliary of the Masons. These societies were respected and popular in Runyon Heights.

At the turn of the century, Du Bois (1973, 224) described the secret societies as providing social intercourse, a realm of aspirations and intrigue, and insurance against misfortune.[4] The Masons drew much of their membership from the stable skilled working class and were Negro-organized precisely because whites resisted Negro membership in the original white Mason organization. As one member put it, "The white Mason, he's prejudiced." He added, using an expression common among Masons, "He didn't want to meet you on the level." These organizations, like Nepperhan civic associations, were attractive to both the professional and the nonprofessional middle class. Although they were "class-defining institutions," they fostered racial solidarity, self-help, and self-reliance while de-emphasizing the ethnic and national divisions among members (Watkins-Owens 1996, 71–72).

Prosperity during the postwar years brought changes to Nepperhan. Land was sold in the eastern section, the Hill, and new homes sprang up. Black and white real estate investors built ever more costly homes for sale in an expanding market. The newcomers differed from earlier settlers in that many were college-educated, as only a few of the children of the first settlers had been. Together, they constituted the first black workers to be employed in white-collar jobs as clerks, salesmen, teachers, and nurses. Overall, the socioeconomic status of newcomers tended to be higher than that of children of the original settlers, many of whom had had only a high school education. The working-class black residential suburb of Nepperhan was beginning to become gentrified by a more traditionally middle-class group.[5]

Gentrification would be the future trend for Runyon Heights. Like earlier residents, many newcomers had their homes built by hired contractors; others bought homes already built by independent developers. For many Nepperhan families the postwar era brought occupational mobility. Job opportunities for Negroes increased in Yonkers, a response to protests by Negro workers, the liberalization of employer attitudes, and an expanding industrial economy. Federal policies, which now barred discrimination in the awarding of government contracts and outlawed segregation in government facilities, also encouraged the new attitude. For the first time black workers were hired in the better-paying industrial and managerial jobs at companies like Otis Elevator, Phelps Dodge (Tarrytown), and Anaconda; a few were even hired at Alexander Smith Carpets. The occupational color line was becoming blurred. Occasionally, Nepperhaners found work in one of the more exclusive Fifth Avenue stores, like B. Altman and Company. Not surprisingly, the residents of this period experienced many firsts. One of the first black saleswomen at Gimbel's Department Store in New York, the first black nurse at Yonkers General Hospital, and the first black workers at the Alexander Smith Carpet factory were Nepperhan residents.

The modest gains in Negro employment opportunities did not come without hardship and confrontation. One of the first black sales workers in a New York department store recounted:

Oh yes, after a while there became more of us in the store, more sales, more black salespeople. And at one point (I have to tell you this little story), on the other side of the floor was a very stout black girl over there, with very short hair. I was a thin person—I've never been fat. I had long hair. She says to me, 'Oh, didn't you just wait on me over there?' The only thing she saw was black. . . . No, we didn't look anything alike. So, I knew the girl over there, so I went over, "Somebody thinks I'm you." And the girl said, "Oh, what happened now?" You know, something's always happenin'.

As historian Robin Kelly (1994) argues, working-class resistance often occurred in response to the subordinating circumstance of the workplace. For the homeowners of Nepperhan, the divide between the working class and the middle class was blurred. Resistance to subordination in the workplace was based as much on race as it was on class. My informant went on to explain, "We talked about it among ourselves, and you know. One time in the ladies' room, I went in and they [sales women] were talking about people, and I said, 'Oh, those white people all look alike to me,' because they always was saying how we looked alike, you know: 'They all look alike to me.' So of course all the whities looked around, you know: 'Is she for real?' you know." She laughed.

Another worker in the customer service department of a prestigious New York department store reported that black customers' files were flagged with a special code to indicate race. "They had a code that they put on black people's credit. You know, they could tell if this person was black. Of course, before I left there, I messed it all up! They never were able to get those files back together again."

Resistance occurred in the community as well. One woman who moved to Nepperhan in 1939 was later active in protesting black exclusion from Yonkers' industrial sector. She was also the first black nurse to work at Yonkers General Hospital at a time when local black doctors like Dr. John Alexander Morgan, a noted physician among local blacks, were denied the right to treat their patients there.[6] She remembers the employment situation for black workers during World War II: "There was nobody, there was nobody [black]. . . . There were black doctors here, but they did not have visiting privileges in Yonkers at that time. What could they do?

They couldn't treat their patients. They could send their patients into the hospital, and they could come around: some other, white doctor would take over that patient; they could come around, and they could read the chart, but they couldn't give orders, or they couldn't take care of their patients."

White doctors, who carried out the treatment or even surgery, received all the recognition. Even with the renewed vitality that the war brought to Yonkers industry, employment opportunities for Negroes remained marginal. Gains were not made in many industries until outspoken residents of both Nepperhan and the west side united across class lines to protest. Nondiscriminatory hiring practices would benefit all occupational classes, so the black classes organized during the 1940s, taking their message directly to employers. My informant went on:

> Not only community people, but they were people from out of the community who were interested in it. But they decided that the community should get busy, because in all of these plants and things, people were going to work for defense. And they weren't hiring black people here, you know. So they decided that they would make a survey and a visit to all of these plants. And Mr. McRae and Dr. Rivera, I think it was, and me, the three of us went to these various places like Alexander Smith down here. That was a big going factory then. And we went to Phelps Dodge, and we went to Anaconda Wire and Cable, and asked them why they didn't hire blacks. . . . I didn't go to Otis, but I think they went. I think they went, but I think Otis had one or two black people anyway. . . . And there was money around, and black people weren't getting any. And so that's why they went into it. We were being called to go fight, well, not really to go fight, but to go serve those fighters.

Retaining their high level of participation in the labor force, the women of Nepperhan were still employed largely in domestic service. Married black women have historically been more likely than their white counterparts to be employed outside the home. Sociologist Bart Landry (1987, 97–98) has argued that the additional economic contribution of women allowed black families to send their children to college. The marginal incomes of the black middle class have always required two wage earners in order to maintain middle-class status (Pinkney 1984, 103; Landry 1987). While the new black middle class has approached occupational and financial parity with whites, differences in total wealth between blacks and whites are pronounced. In 1984, the average white household with an income between $7,000 and $15,000 still had a greater net worth than middle-class black families earning between $45,000 and $60,000 (Sigelman and Welch 1994, 35).

During the 1950s, some Runyon Heights women sold Avon or Tupperware products part-time or worked for the school district in an attempt to balance work and household responsibilities. Others opened small businesses like hair salons. One second-generation woman used her experiences in retail sales and in a white real estate office to establish a local real estate business in the late 1950s. She had been inspired by the success of a local woman, Iris Hays, who had owned a beauty parlor on Saw Mill River Road since the 1940s.

> After I had worked for a couple of years, I decided, on the advice of a number of people, to, you know, open up my own [real estate] office. They kept saying, if you could put this much energy into someone else's business, why not put it in your own. A friend of mine who owned a beauty shop, I admired her a great deal. And it fascinated me, the fact that she was a woman and she was able to run a beauty shop and keep a house and car and travel, and so forth. And I felt that, if she could do it, why can't I? . . . I chose Runyon Heights because, as a black woman, I think I wanted to make a contribution.

While their efforts did not ensure mobility or stability for their families, postwar women in the workforce increased the likelihood that their children would continue their education and hold middle-class employment. Many working- and middle-class families of Nepperhan would not have survived, had it not been for the working women.

The first opportunities for black employment in both the public and private sectors occurred during this period, although opportunities for women were still limited. Improvements in the regional employment market, however, would be soon offset by the rapid decline in the manufacturing base of New York City and Westchester County within the decade following the war. Ultimately, community residents' economic marginality linked them to the broader black working community in Yonkers when it came to many political concerns.

The Rise of the Automobile Suburb

Runyon Heights residents developed consumer tastes much like those of their white counterparts, and the better incomes and opportunities resulting from the war enhanced their disposable income. Automobiles became commonplace, as community residents, like other suburbanites, took advantage of the extensive parkway and highway systems that crisscrossed the landscape.[7]

The creation of the postwar suburb was aided by the new government-sponsored highway system. Westchester County spent more than $62 million to purchase land for highway construction, which had the effect of raising property values by more than $1 million between 1921 and 1931 (Zukin 1991, 168). In fact, these first highways were designed as scenic routes to encourage suburbanites to take family drives on weekends, thus reinforcing the nuclear unit and, at the same time, boosting auto sales.

The popularity of public transportation diminished with the rise of the suburban detached home and the car. The dismantling of the last trolley system to operate in the county, Yonkers Trolley, in November of 1952, foreshadowed industrial decline in the region.[8] Buses, which still followed many of the old trolley routes, replaced the trolley system. The subway, however, remained a competitive means of commuting to New York for both the working and middle classes.

The creation of a national highway system favored the use of the automobile for both private and commercial conveyance and rendered public transportation nearly obsolete outside the central cities. The auto ushered in a new era in Westchester County and characterized the McDonaldization of the once rural landscape. The purchase of a house, a car, and domestic equipment integrated Runyon Heights residents and other suburbanites into a national culture of mass production and consumption (Zukin 1991, 140).

Runyon Heights was eventually surrounded by the new burgeoning highway and parkway systems that dotted the Westchester landscape. The Saw Mill River Parkway, which connects New York City to northern Westchester, passes just west of the community; the New York State Thruway (Interstate 87), which also provides transit north and south, passes just to the east. The Sprain Brook Parkway is less than a mile away, also to the east. Since the 1960s, the scenic parkways, first built for families on weekend drives, have become dominated by suburban commuters heading south to New York and north to White Plains and Stamford, Connecticut. Runyon Heights is also conveniently situated along Tuckahoe Road, providing access to the major shopping strip in lower Westchester County, Central Park Avenue. Early Nepperhan was attractive to working-class commuters taking mass transit; today Runyon Heights offers an ideal sub-urban location for middle-class automobile commuters.

As residents became more mobile, social life was increasingly centered outside the home. A couple of bars sprang up after the war on the outskirts of the community. One spot that became popular was a small smoke-filled joint on Tuckahoe Road called Club Shelton, where golfers and ten-nis players mingled with professionals and laborers before heading home to Runyon Heights. As older cohorts have aged, the "local" bar has played less of a role in bringing community residents together. One newcomer to the area, an engineer at a pharmaceutical company, characterized Club Shelton at the end of its heyday as a community-centered institution in the early 1980s:

I think it's deteriorated somewhat since I've come out here. The first time I came out here I really sopped it up like a sponge starving for water, when they had . . . Club Shelton. When I came out here, I found such a warmth and loving atmosphere in the Club Shelton from the older people. I was in my twenties at the time, but there were a lot of older residents here who knew [my wife's] parents. They knew who I was, that I was [her] suitor, new husband. You know, so they rolled out the red carpet for me. Whenever I would go into the Club Shelton they would say, you know, 'Get this guy a drink.' And they had a lot of professional people there. You had doctors. You had guys coming in from tennis games, you had golf-ers, you had all kinds of professional people stopping in at this little rinky-dink, smoke-filled bar called the Club Shelton. This was the Runyon Heights ethos, you know, this was the feel that you had up here.

Politicizing Race in the Postindustrial Suburb

While the occupational color line began to fade slowly after World War II, race took on added significance in local community conflicts. When school district lines were redrawn, Runyon Heights children were isolated in School 1, and community boundaries were aligned with school zone boundaries. Once again, residents' shared experiences with the Yonkers Board of Education helped reinforce racial solidarity as well as prompt community political involvement. Residents mobilized around what they perceived to be their material self-interest, defined in racial terms. Education, they believed, was the ticket to middle-class prosperity, and racial barriers prevented a free market from operating. They concluded that racial consciousness and political solidarity were prerequisites to their mobility, for race subordination linked them together in a community of fate.

Since the earliest days, School 1 had served elementary schoolchildren from Runyon Heights and neighboring areas. As in other suburban communities, the school was the heart of civic life. Children walked to the school on Dunbar Street; the parents knew the teachers, and the teachers knew the community. The Parent Teacher Association had even sponsored the reactivated Boy Scout Troop #34, which ran from the early 1950s through the early 1960s.

School 1 was the only truly integrated elementary school in Yonkers, drawing pupils from a broad geographic area. Black students constituted an estimated one-third to one-half of the student body. The majority of Runyon Heights senior residents had attended School 1, and strong and lasting bonds developed among classmates. Teachers at School 1 were highly respected. Good education seemed to matter far more to residents than race. Residents fondly remembered the good old days at their school.

> **B. H.:** What was the school like?
> **Resident:** Good school, good school, dedicated teachers, dedicated teachers.
> **B. H.:** Were they black, white?
> **Resident:** No, they were mostly white, mostly all white. I think that at the tail end of my career down in School 1, we had one black teacher there. I don't remember her name. Regardless of whether they were black or whether they were white, they taught.

School 1 retained its interracial character until 1938, when school district lines were first redrawn. White students who had previously attended School 1 were slowly relocated to the already predominantly white Schools 5 and 22. The rezoning made School 1 the smallest school zone in Yonkers and effectively isolated the Runyon Heights children (80 CIV. 6761 LBS.: 273). The four-foot reserve strip separating Runyon Heights and Homefield served as the northern border of the zone. The southern border was Tuckahoe Road, the western border Saw Mill River Road, and the eastern border Bushed Avenue.

During the 1950s, communities like Homefield continued to attract white homeowners. While Schools 5 and 22 became overcrowded, School 1 became underutilized and racially concentrated. By 1950, School 1 enrolled a mere 100 students in a facility designed to hold 240 and was 91 percent black (80 CIV. 6761 LBS.: 274). Underutilization resulted in mergers of the first- and second-grade classes and the third- and fourth-grade classes. According to informants, the assignment of the first three black Yonkers schoolteachers to School 1 during this period further emphasized the school's racial identity and marginal status.

By 1953, Runyon Heights formed a solid Negro community, having been cut off from adjoining, predominantly white communities in the religious, educational, and occupational spheres. In the hope of securing their children's educational and financial futures, parents in the community petitioned the Yonkers Board of Education to re-expand the School 1 district lines, thus reintegrating the school. One woman who served on the committee of concerned Runyon Heights residents remembers: "Number 1 had become a nothing. Number 1 had become just a place to put black children. Number 1 had become totally an all-black school. I think they had white teachers there that were pulling in a salary who really had no interest in our children. And they could draw and they could sing, you know, but don't ask them to add anything."

The NAACP joined the petition, but the board decided instead to close the school and assign Runyon Heights children to Schools 5 and 22. This decision immediately followed the May 1954 ruling by the Supreme Court in the case of *Brown v. Board of Education* of Topeka, Kansas, which declared racially separate schools unconstitutional. The board's decision solved the immediate problem created by the all-black School 1, while marginally improving the racial balance at Schools 5 and 22, but it also compounded the problem of overcrowding at those schools.

The closing of School 1 not only dispersed the Runyon Heights children to other schools and thus weakened community bonds but also undermined efforts to control deviant behavior among youths. Local Boy Scout troops had been typically sponsored by the local school. With the closing of the local school, the Men's Club began to sponsor the Runyon troop. By the 1960s, the local troop was disbanded, and Runyon children participated in troops based in their new schools. A community tradition had been lost.

Runyon Heights parents, who favored a community school and opposed busing their children, had challenged the board's decision legally. To their dismay, their challenge was rejected by the New York State commissioner of education. Even the local NAACP supported the commissioner's decision, in light of the Yonkers School Board's rejection of the parents' initial proposal to expand district lines (80 CIV. 6761 LBS.: 272–279). The parents, never satisfied with the busing solution, were obliged to comply with the state's decision. Runyon children would be bused.

Much of the history of School 1 is documented in the 1985 landmark decision linking school segregation and housing segregation in Yonkers and denouncing both the racial isolation of School District No. 1 and the Runyon residential community:[9]

> Other neutral justifications, if any, for this particular drawing of the School 1 attendance zone boundaries are absent from the record. Based upon the available evidence, the original drawing of School 1's attendance zone boundaries constituted deliberate, racially motivated gerrymandering, done in a manner which carefully incorporated privately created residential segregation (272–279).

Public education for Runyon children remains unresolved. Since the 1970s, the children have been shuffled from school to school in a vain attempt to create racial balance in the Yonkers school system. Prospects for racially balanced schools remain elusive, as the minority population in Yonkers has grown while the percentage of white school children has steadily declined. Efforts to create racial balance have annoyed parents and heightened racial tensions, but they have also inspired newer Nepperhan residents to become involved in local politics and community organization.

One recent event shows the negotiated nature of racial and class interests in the local community. The school issue in Yonkers again drew national attention during November 1995.[10] Runyon Heights resident and local NAACP President Ken Jenkins publicly challenged the national organization's forty-one-year-old policy supporting school busing as a means toward the integration of public schools. Jenkins questioned the relevance of the unwavering commitment to integration at all costs for the children of Runyon Heights. Although his public challenge resulted in his swift removal from office, his position echoed a sentiment expressed by community members since the closing of School 1. At the root of this sentiment is not an objection to the philosophy of racial integration but a concern for quality education and community control. Yet public discourse has suggested that the black middle class has shifted away from its traditional civil rights commitment to integration. As one male resident who is active in local civic activities stated nearly two years before Ken Jenkins' infamous declaration: "The NAACP just closed the school. They got up there and raised hell and just closed the school. I had agreed with them at that time because I said, if they wasn't getting the teaching and they wasn't getting the learning, well, let's close the school up. Now I look back and I think maybe we should have just kept the doggone thing open. But that was beyond us. That was between the Yonkers Board of Education and the NAACP."

Integration, while socially desirable for many middle-class blacks, was never the primary goal of Runyon Heights residents. For them, integration was a strategy for achieving equal opportunity for their children. But desegregation policies diminished their direct influence over their children's education. It also weakened ties among the children themselves, who were now dispersed among numerous schools. As the quality of public education declined, many residents removed their children from the system and enrolled them in parochial institutions.

Negotiating Race and Class: Dilemmas of Public Housing

Although restrictive covenants had been deemed unconstitutional by the Supreme Court in the *Shelley v Kraemer* (1948) decision, black residents of Yonkers and Westchester County during the postwar period still experienced racial steering practices from realtors, a reluctance on the part of lending institutions to give them loans, and resistance by many white homeowners to selling or living next to them. Today, some of Westchester's more exclusive suburban towns and villages are home to fewer than 100 blacks. Owing to the way federal housing policy was implemented during the 1960s and 1970s, the majority of Westchester's 119,000 blacks are now concentrated in the older cities of New Rochelle, Mount Vernon, Port Chester, Tarrytown, White Plains, and Yonkers (Berger 1993, 6).

The role of the Runyon Heights Improvement Association in the community had declined significantly following World War II and the loss of the community house. The city's proposal for a public housing complex acted as a wake-up call for residents. In 1956, community members mobilized to challenge the city council's plan to build 335 rental units of low-income public housing on the southern end of Ridgeview Avenue. The reborn Runyon Heights Improvement Association was called into action to organize residents. A project of this scale would have radically transformed the economic composition of the community, by housing more families than were currently living in the entire area. Residents wished to maintain the low population density as well as the level of city services available to their middle-class single- and two-family housing. The addition of 335 units would have overwhelmed the area and transformed it into a ghetto. As one former president of the association commented, "This is the reason why you see a community house. This is the reason why you see us organized now—because we had to get organized. That was it."

Their common concerns also brought Runyon Heights residents into alliance with the neighboring Homefield community, which believed that the proposed low-income development was too close to home. Both groups protested to the city government. Paradoxically, after having created and maintained the four-foot reserve strip as an artificial border separating them from black Nepperhaners, the Homefield community now made common cause with their black neighbors. Both groups of residents wanted to maintain the middle-class character of the area. The paradox of this class alignment was that the initial fight for low-income housing in Yonkers had been championed by the local NAACP, an organization widely supported by Runyon Heights residents. In fact, numerous leaders of the Yonkers Branch of the NAACP have been community residents. Initiatives for low-income housing would disproportionately benefit the poor and working-class black populations of Yonkers, and the middle-class of Runyon Heights, in taking on the fight against racial oppression, supported local NAACP activities with both financial and intellectual resources. But residents also sought to protect their own class interests by resisting the placement of low-income housing in or near their community. They hoped to prevent the ghettoization of their neighborhood.

Davidoff and Brooks (1976) note that predominantly white suburban communities have resisted low- and moderate-income housing. At first glance, the reactions they cite closely resemble those of Runyon Heights residents. Davidoff lists: "(1) a reaction to the families that are believed to be moving into those units; (2) a reaction to the type of dwellings that is associated with low- and moderate-income housing; (3) a fear of the fiscal impact on the community; and (4) the "why us?" syndrome" (Davidoff 1976, 139). The "why us" syndrome is a concern with the impact of housing density on quality of life and a fear of loss of community. Even though Runyon Heights residents expressed these same concerns, they expressed them in reverse order, emphasizing the why us syndrome in particular and the type of dwelling proposed. Unlike the white suburban-

ites, Runyon Heights residents were obviously not troubled by the presumed race of prospective low-income residents. Their concern focused
on the class position of the newcomers and the impact a multiple-dwelling
unit might have on community life.

The "why us?" syndrome was manifested in the way Nepperhaners interpreted events. They believed race to be the motivating factor behind
the site selection. "Why us?" became "Why us blacks in Runyon Heights?"
Their motivation for resistance was material and not specifically racial:
avoid ghettoization at all costs.

An attorney for the RHIA told the city council that the national trend
was "away from putting housing sites in minority areas, as it has a tendency to create slums" and that the placement of a public housing project
in Runyon Heights would have similar consequences (80 CIV. 6761 LBS.:
19). Speaking to the city council, representatives of the Yonkers branch
of the NAACP and the Urban League of Westchester County voiced similar apprehension about black residential concentration, segregation, and
community deterioration (80 CIV. 6761 LBS.: 19).[11]

The initial housing proposal was defeated, but another, much smaller
proposal was put forth in 1958. After vociferous debates and numerous
city council meetings, the community won the battle but lost the war.
Nepperhan succeeded in blocking the original proposal for 335 units, but
a 48-unit housing project was slated for Dunbar and Kenmore Streets. The
Hall Court Housing Complex (called the Dunbar Housing Project by local
residents) was finally completed in 1962. The bitter irony for residents
was that the project was constructed on the old School 1 site. Hall Court
was the only public housing built before the 1980 federal desegregation
suit that served families in east Yonkers.

Like the school-segregation issue, the construction of low-income
housing in Runyon Heights was connected to broader issues that the black
population of Yonkers would soon be facing. Where would the remaining
public housing be located? White middle-class neighborhoods resisted.
The opinion of the Supreme Court makes it clear that the concentration
of low-income housing in already predominantly African-American areas
of the city was a calculated decision aimed at isolating the black population. Between 1940 and 1980, 98 percent (6,644 of the city's 6,800 units)
of low- and moderate-income housing would be constructed in southwest
Yonkers (Sheingold 1993, 5A). The court also noted that the only exception to this pattern of black ghettoization in Yonkers was the community
of Runyon Heights:

According to the 1980 census figures, Southwest Yonkers accounts for 37.5% of the City's total population, but contains 80.7% of the City's minority population. . . . In contrast, only two of the thirty-two census tracts outside of the Southwest have a minority population greater than 6%. One is census tract 7, whose 28.6% minority population is clustered in the southern end of the tract, where it abuts Southwest Yonkers and the Hudson Division Railroad on the western edge of the tract. The second is census tract 18 in East Yonkers, which contains Runyon Heights, a longstanding enclave of black home owners, and the site of Hall Court, the only subsidized housing project for families that is located outside Southwest Yonkers (Opinion 80 CIV. 6761 (LBS): 3–4).

The Dunbar Houses at first had little noticeable impact on the community. In fact, a number of current homeowners were some of the original tenants. The project merely reflected the loss of community control and the beginning of changing land use and housing density in the area. Whereas residents would have preferred to have single-family housing continue to develop in the area, to their dismay, the Holiday Inn Company purchased land in 1959 and constructed a 103-room hotel on the site of the originally proposed 335-unit construction.

Reviving the Community House

In 1961, after more than twenty years of operating without a community center, the reactivated RHIA made plans to construct a new center to provide residents with locally based services and with a meeting place for community activities. The new center, on Runyon Avenue, was dedicated in 1963 as the Runyon Heights Community House. A number of residents participated in the new center's fund-raising and organization.[12]

The community house was born in an era of increased government sponsorship of community service programs. Its expanded programs and services would help to maintain active participation in the RHIA by residents old and new. This was particularly significant given the demise of School 1, which had served a critical role in drawing residents and their children together, and the decline in church attendance. The community house and its array of youth-oriented programs became the major focal point for integrating both children and parents into the community, as well as for mobilizing residents when the collective faced critical issues.

Fliers were sent out, phone calls made, and the community quickly mobilized for a "town meeting" at the community house.

The Defended Community

In 1960, when the new community center was being planned and constructed, the Carvel Inn opened on the southeastern boundary of the community, at the intersection of Sprain Road, Tuckahoe Road, and Bushey Avenue. Along with the Holiday Inn, this motel was an early threat to the area's suburban tranquillity.

The 1960s brought other changes to Nepperhan that threatened the character of the area. Other business establishments appeared along the Tuckahoe and Saw Mill River Roads. After Conrail closed passenger service on the Put in the late 1950s, parcels of land were sold along Runyon Avenue. Businesses took advantage of earlier zoning designations and began moving in. This brought congestion, air pollution, and noise to the community, as well as a transient population with little commitment to quality of life in Runyon Heights.

Residents lamented the loss of their noisy railroad. Railroad consultant Phil Pepe claimed that a personal relationship had existed between residents who lived along the line and the railroad. This characterized Nepperhaners' relationship to the Put as well. Children used to jump on the back of the train as it weaved past their backyards on its way south or north. Adults noted the passage of the time by the train's predictable schedule. Railroad historian Dan Gallo recounted that passenger service was discontinued on May 28, 1958; freight service continued to decline throughout the 1960s and 1970s, until the line was finally terminated. On August 16, 1982, the 5:47 left New York on its final trip to Brewster.[13]

During the 1960s, residents, led by the RHIA, began a long fight with city hall and the City Planning Bureau to ensure that land use in the area would retain a suburban character. They then realized that zoning could be used to restrict businesses and protect the neighborhood quality of life. This is a curious turn of events, since zoning had traditionally been used to restrict Negro infiltration into the suburbs. Although Runyon Avenue was originally zoned for industrial use in 1920, in 1928 local zoning codes were modified and the area was designated an "I" district, which allowed for continued industrial use. According to the director of Yonkers City Planning, Lee Ellman, "The 'I' zone is the most permissive in terms of what kind of business you can put there."

In 1920, the land west of the tracks, with the exception of Runyon Avenue, was designated a "B" district, with medium population density and a sixty-foot height limitation. According to Ellman, "B" districts permitted "lodging or boarding houses, hotels, churches, schools, libraries, museums, clubs, railroad passenger stations, farming and accessory uses, customarily incidental to the principal use. In other words, your basic garage, stable, whatever." It encouraged neighborhood businesses and apartment buildings by stipulating a population density of 175 persons per acre. Housing officials maintained that the "B" and "A" population designations were typical for land contiguous to local arteries. The relatively high population density assumed in zoning of the area would also have contributed to the undesirable qualities of the land. Another factor contributing to neighborhood population density was that early building lots were only twenty-five by a hundred feet, considerably smaller than the typical fifty-five-by-a-hundred-foot lots that are common today.

In 1928, the portion of land east of the railroad was designated a "T" district by the city, thereby allowing maintenance of low population density, thirty-five-foot-high structures, and the erection of only single- and two-family dwellings on a minimum frontage of fifty feet. The area was typical of suburban neighborhoods in Yonkers.

In 1953, the Runyon Avenue strip as well as the land west of the tracks and north of Dunbar Street were designated "C" districts, a decision that permitted wholesale businesses and storage warehouses as well as single- and multiple-family dwellings. The city also designated the small area south of Dunbar Street and west of the railroad a "T" district, thus permitting single- and two-family homes to be built.

Although the property bordering Runyon Avenue was available at the time, the community was unable to afford the cost of the larger parcels offered by the railroad. Consequently, the RHIA purchased two fifty-foot lots directly across the street from the railroad from a local resident for $1,500. Today, the community house sits opposite a row of commercial enterprises. The paving company was one of the first businesses in the area. It soon left but was quickly replaced by a number of businesses, some of which still remain.[14]

With the growing encroachment of local businesses, the neighborhood experienced deterioration in its quality of life. Businesses split the original west-side area in two by cutting off access between Runyon Avenue and Moultrie and Touissant Avenues. Soon the RHIA exerted pressure on government agencies to use zoning to limit land use to single- and two-family residences. In 1968, it succeeded in having the Runyon Avenue strip upgraded to a "CM" zone, a less permissible category than the "I" or "C" designations. While the "C" district allows for wholesale businesses and storage as well as residences, the "CM" district allows for commercial storage and light manufacturing and excludes residences.[15] The zoning change was actually a compromise solution. Although it insured that the Runyon Avenue strip could never become a site for low-income public housing or even a private apartment complex, businesses relegitimated their right to operate in the area.

After numerous battles with local businesses over parking, trucks, and noise, the RHIA urged the city to upgrade the area east of Hunt Avenue and Belknap Avenue, including a small part of "Old Nepperhan" as well as the Hill area, to an S-50 district in 1968. The S-50 classification restricts land use to allow only detached single-family units on fifty-foot lots. A large portion of east-side residential real estate in Yonkers is currently in this category. The remaining Runyon Heights area west of the railroad, excluding the Runyon Avenue strip, was also upgraded to a "T" district in 1968. From the standpoint of preserving the suburban character of the community, the "T" district designation was an improvement over the old "B" designation, which had permitted apartment buildings and neighborhood businesses. Through active negotiations with city government, the RHIA helped ensure the middle-class, detached, single-home character of much of the community.

Many of the businesses in Runyon Heights have been distributors: Miracle Plywood distributed wood; Gerassi and Otto Brehm both distribute baking goods; Tristate distributes automotive parts; Badia distributes spices. Distribution-type businesses, which are dependent upon truck or rail transportation, have taken their toll on the community's quality of life. Between traffic congestion and the parking problems created by company employees and delivery trucks, community patience on the west side of Runyon Avenue runs thin.

Some businesses, like Otto Brehm, Miracle Plywood, and Gerassi, have managed to develop a mutually beneficial coexistence with the community, supporting local events and respecting residents' desires for tranquillity. Other companies have proved more intrusive. Problems of congestion were created by the MediCab transportation service for the disabled and the Pecora Construction Company during the late 1970s. Pecora owned the building that MediCab used. By bringing more than thirty passenger vans to the area, as well as the private vehicles of van drivers, MediCab added to the tractor trailers, delivery vans, and passenger cars already flooding the area. Particularly affected were the two small residential blocks of Potomac and Dunbar Streets. The flow of commercial traffic embittered residents and helped to transform Runyon Heights into a community on the defensive.

The local newspaper, the *Herald Statesmen,* took note of the conflict. In the May 29, 1977, edition, community leaders were quoted as saying, "The residents here are being charged Scarsdale taxes and receiving ghetto services." According to the paper, business representatives countered that these leaders did not speak for the entire community. In recalling the incident, however, residents emphasized the disruptive impact of the business activities on community life. Steven Jones, vice president of MediCab, was quoted as saying, "Thank God Milton Holst hasn't incited the neighborhood against me or we'd have been burned down." Milton Holst, longtime resident and past president of the RHIA, was for many years action chairperson of the organization. When things need to get done, residents often call on "Milty" Holst.

Whereas Pecora has made peace with the local RHIA, MediCab left the community in the late 1980s, amid rumors of federal and local criminal investigations. Tristate, which depends on tractor-trailers for the movement of goods, still battles with Runyon Heights residents. Large diesel trucks drive along Potomac and Dunbar Streets to get to Runyon Avenue. Meanwhile, residents can often be heard complaining of idling diesel engines and parking problems along the strip. In an attempt to appease residents, the city erected signs regulating both truck parking and engine idling. The battle seems to have reached an impasse. The control of business activity in the area has remained a central issue for many residents, one that has grown in importance since the mid-1980s. For residents and the RHIA, community solidarity and the vigilant enforcement of zoning regulations remain the major source of hope for limiting business activity and expansion in the area.

Land-development projects have been cited as a primary cause of the formation of neighborhood associations in other northeastern suburban communities after 1980 (Logan and Rabrenovic 1990, 77–78); however, land-development issues hit the community early and involved not only industrial and commercial encroachment but also challenges to the character of local housing stock and the racial and class composition of the area. While business encroachment in the area remains a community concern, it is secondary to that of low-income housing projects, a recurring community issue. Originally an organization to promote neighbor-hood upkeep, social activities, and children's recreation, the RHIA now also serves as a quasi-political instrument to protect community interests.

Despite the infiltration of businesses into the community during the 1960s, 1970s, and 1980s, industry in Yonkers continued to decline, owing to the forces of deindustrialization sweeping the region. Industrial de-cline in the city of Yonkers began with plant closings during the 1950s and escalated by 1970 (Zukin 1991, 145), and it reversed many of the em-ployment gains black workers had made in regional industry after the war. Combined with rising housing costs and racial steering, it limited further suburbanization of working-class homeowners. Industrial decline would limit even middle-class job opportunities for the children of Run-yon Heights, as it fueled middle-class occupational stagnation and helped to break the widespread pattern of families' upward occupational mobility that had characterized the community until the 1980s.

Middle-Class Stagnation

The community cohort that entered the job market after 1970, con-sisting of baby boomers raised during the mid-1950s and early 1960s, was most affected by industrial decline. Real efforts to integrate industry in Yonkers, even by the relatively liberal Otis Elevator Company, were not made until the 1970s, when government-backed affirmative action came to the city (Zukin 1991, 148). Unfortunately, this change provided little benefit to black workers, for the overall number of manufacturing jobs had declined significantly, beginning with the closing of Alexander Smith Carpets in 1954. Otis Elevator, which still employed 1,300 local residents in 1968, was purchased by United Technologies in 1975, just when affirmative action was beginning to benefit black movement into managerial positions. Only 375 workers were employed when the plant closed in 1982. Neither the union nor the city government was notified before the shutdown. Consequently, by the 1980s, the black middle class was left with few local employment opportunities apart from affirma-tive action–backed government jobs. By 1988, the largest employers in Yonkers were the Yonkers School District (with 2,484 employees) and the city of Yonkers itself (with 2,000 employees). Yonkers exported much of its labor force to service-sector jobs in other areas of the county (Zukin 1991, 154).

The change in local employment opportunities is reflected in the occu-pational distribution in Runyon Heights. Like other middle-class African

113

Americans, Nepperhaners are most likely to be employed in the public sector; the community today boasts a good number of teachers, social workers, and other city workers (Collins 1997). The few holding high-level administrative positions in the private sector often work in specialized fields and include lawyers, computer consultants, realtors, entrepreneurs, a senior referee for the National Basketball Association, and two senior security experts who work for national sports organizations.

After 1960, the black and Hispanic populations increased in lower Westchester County, as industrial jobs dwindled. New public housing was built only in areas already dominated by minority residents. By the 1980s, corporate office relocations had converted central and northern Westchester into affluent commercial suburbs (Zukin 1991, 145). Except for the small enclave in Runyon Heights, the black population of Yonkers was largely excluded from the suburban prosperity of the Reagan-Bush years. Although most residents have acquired at least as much education as their parents and many hold college degrees, occupational mobility remains uncertain for the current generation, owing to industrial decline, white-collar downsizing, and government cutbacks.

Occupational and educational mobility for native-born (third-generation) Runyon Heights residents after the 1960s tended to take three distinct trajectories. Interviews revealed that one group experienced continued upward mobility: it acquired advanced education and secured professional and managerial positions. Success for many meant relocating to other cities and regions, although a few of the more successful children of Runyon Heights have either remained in the community or returned with their families, sometimes purchasing property on the Hill. A second group experienced downward mobility: it achieved moderate levels of education but failed to find stable employment. A third group experienced lateral mobility: its members secured low- and mid-level white-collar positions like their parents before them, in the service sector, despite the fact that many had attended college. The most successful among this group were able to purchase modest homes; others continued to live with their parents.

Those who graduated in 1967 don't recall drugs in the local high schools, but by 1969 things in Yonkers had changed. As societal pressures mounted, a minority turned to drugs or alcohol. Reliance on those represented a significant deviation from community norms, and it is an indication of the direct influence that the larger society exerted on this once-isolated enclave and of the weakening of community institutional controls on behavior. The impact of growing up without the benefits of community-based School 1 is most evident in cohorts who graduated after the 1960s.

In spite of occupational stagnation and even downward mobility, rising real estate prices after 1970 contributed to the continuing gentrification of the overall area. During the 1980s land values skyrocketed and building costs soared throughout Westchester County. By 1990, new home construction was costing builders upwards of $125,000 and home buyers as much as $250,000 per house. Homes built for $14,000 in the 1960s were selling for more than $180,000 by the 1980s. The $2,000 bungalows of yesteryear have become the $250,000 two-car-garage homes of today. In spite of the stagnant economy and the fact that many of the older residents are retired and living off savings, pensions, and social security, the Runyon Heights community experienced a 38 percent gain in real household income between 1980 and 1990 (Table 1.1).

The recent influx of residents indicates that the community is still evolving. Most newcomers hold managerial or professional occupations. The majority are college-educated, many with advanced degrees. This group includes both the West Indian– and native-born who benefited from government enforcement of antidiscrimination policy during the 1970s (Landry 1987). They represent what Bart Landry calls the "new black middle class." The newcomers also included a smattering of families of European descent. Several professionals from both Latin and West Indian backgrounds have moved in, infusing the community with Afro-Caribbean culture. This seems to have bolstered the centrality of Africa and African culture in the consciousness of residents. By 1993, Kwanza celebrations had become an annual event for many residents, often existing side by side with Christmas festivities.

The newest members of the area also tend to be the least involved in community activities and organizations. This is due to a number of factors. First, adults have traditionally become involved in the community, directly and indirectly, through their children, since school issues have often provided a focal point for political mobilization. The disappearance of School 1 has meant that parental concerns are not centralized through the community-based Parent Teacher Association (PTA). Second, the web of interlocking community volunteer organizations, institutions, and clubs allowed past cohorts to organize quickly in response to forces from outside the area. Many of the newer residents have yet to be drawn into this network of extended families. The RHIA will most likely play a central role in fostering future community cohesion and political consensus, for the conditions that created the hyperorganized community have changed.

The newest residents also tend to be young baby-boomer professionals. Because of the tight housing market, skyrocketing real estate prices, and high interest rates in Yonkers during the 1980s, interest in the area from nonblacks has heightened. According to local realtors, one reason for the increase in interest among white homeowners was the artificially low prices of Runyon Heights homes. Since most white homeowners would not venture into a black area, and whites dominate market demands, homes in predominantly black areas are undervalued. In the short run, this factor benefited many newcomers, who were able to secure housing in the area more cheaply than in many predominantly white areas of comparable socioeconomic and aesthetic characteristics. In the long run, however, since home ownership constitutes a major source of family wealth, the devaluation of Runyon Heights homes hinders the ability of community residents to acquire capital and pass it on to their children (Oliver and Shapiro 1995). Residents are aware of the link between home ownership and wealth for the middle class. As one male resident put it: "The Caucasian race, they've always been able to pass on something to their children—a home or whatever finances they had. Whereas blacks weren't able to do that too much. But a community like this, most of these people, now they are gonna turn their homes over to their children and their children are gonna benefit from it one way or another."

Though the western section has older housing stock and a more working-class population than the east-side Hill section, social status and even class distinctions among residents have been minimized in order to foster a sense of community. Residents include both old Nepperhan and the more recently developed Hill area in their definition of the Runyon Heights community. Although they recognize distinctions in occupational status, residents' common situation as black homeowners has reinforced shared class interests. As they defended their group interests, they articulated race consciousness.

Contemporary Community Life

Through the years, families, schools, churches, and civic and social associations provided the basis for the development of sentimental ties and feelings of community cohesion. The racial basis of these institutions was strengthened both implicitly and explicitly by governmental policies, segregating social practices, discriminatory housing and labor practices, and threats to the community from outside forces.

Race shaped community boundaries and group interests in ways that transcended religious, occupational, and ethnic differences among residents. As in the early days, Runyon Heights today is a diverse community. Members practice a variety of religious faiths and attend many different churches and temples in Yonkers and in New York City. Catholics, Baptists, Episcopalians, Methodists, Apostolics, and Muslims are all represented in the area. A few residents still maintain affiliation with the churches and mosques they attended before moving to the area, many of which are in Harlem. Some newcomers have become a part of the local AME congregation, often sending their children to Bible school there, although to a lesser extent than in past eras.

The AME Zion Church remains the central religious institution in Runyon Heights, although attendance has declined. Metropolitan does, however, play an important symbolic role for many community members, in part because of its historic importance as a founding community institution and its connection to the legacy of black institution building.

At the same time, the community is religiously tolerant and diverse. Members affiliated with various religious denominations have often supported one another's events. In fact, the black congregations in Yonkers, particularly the Baptists and Methodist Gospel choirs, communicate regularly, although a strained relationship sometimes exists between the west-side churches and the central religious institution of the Runyon community. A minister from Yonkers challenges the view held by some west-siders that Runyon Heights folks are too snobbish, sophisticated, and preoccupied with their middle-class status: "But the whole thing is, they [the west-siders] have false conceptions. These people are down to earth, they're fine people. I don't see any sophistication in them, you know. They are friendly, they like other people to come, they're emotional like other people, when they have an emotional preacher. [He laughs]. They like good preaching, good singing. . . . We have one group of singers over there called the Metrolites, and they sing these gospel numbers, and my members are just crazy about them."

The AME Zion Church in Runyon Heights remains an institution that links the community to other black communities in the region, thereby providing a basis for interaction and communication between distant populations. At one event I attended, held at the Metropolitan AME Church, choirs from across Yonkers, the Bronx, and the lower Hudson

Valley participated. It was a joyous and song-filled celebration. The congregation was enthusiastic and emotional. Events like this draw church members and nonmembers alike from the community.

Politically, the Runyon Heights Improvement Association is by far the most significant organization. Some issues shouldered by the association have been relatively peripheral to community life, like ensuring that the city decorates a Christmas tree or plants flowers along Chelsea Place. Other issues have been crucial to maintaining the quality of life in the area. The association monitors the maintenance of such community services as snow removal, garbage pickup, dealing with abandoned cars, and traffic flow. Its emphasis on neighborhood upkeep and recreational activities during the 1920s and 1930s was supplanted in the 1950s by a focus on community defense and neighborhood preservation. Like the RHIA of yesteryear, the new organization publishes a quarterly newsletter, the *Runyon Heights Voice,* an instrument often used to announce upcoming community meetings and events.

The community house has played a central role in organizing children's activities since the 1960s. Parents have taken advantage of the athletic and social programs offered year round to their children. The focus on children reflects the child-centered middle-class attitude prevalent in the community. One resident whose son and daughter grew up during the era of the community house recalled: "When they were young, the parents with young kids used to take turns going over. With Mr. Wilson they used to have, on weekends, little socials . . . as long as the parents, someone could be there to supervise. . . . Before that they were in the day camps and things over there. They played on the basketball teams. That was very instrumental in their development too. The center over there, that was sort of a focal point for them and their activities."

The construction of the community house by the RHIA represents an early example of a suburban community's response to suburban growth, urban renewal, and business encroachment. During the 1990s, many services and programs were delivered to community members, as well as to a number of people who traveled from other parts of the city to participate. At its largest, in 1992, the volunteer staff of the community house boasted twenty-five individuals. Mary L. Tynes, former director of the rebuilt Nepperhan Community Center, was hired as executive director of the community house, along with four other staff members: an administrative assistant, an after-school instructor, a crisis-intervention supervisor, and a recreation director.

The board of directors of the Runyon Heights Improvement Association oversees the community house. The board is elected by member-residents who wish to be active in local affairs. Although board members have traditionally been drawn from the older generations, younger residents have become more actively involved over the past ten years. During the 1990s, a forty-three-year-old president was elected, and the board came to include two members under thirty-five years of age. The arrival of younger members on the RHIA board provides the basis for the future maintenance of this vital community organization.

The variety of services and programs reflects the community's needs and concerns. The mainstay of the community center through the years has been its sports program. This program was made popular by the late Hudean (Boo) Wilson, who for years was athletic director and coach of the Runyon Heights Colts basketball teams. The Colts have been a part of the seventy-one-team citywide Recreation Basketball League since the late 1950s. Since 1967, the RHIA has also sponsored the popular Runyon Heights Summer Basketball League, founded by Boo Wilson. The league has attracted some of the best players in the city. Teams start in the Pee Wee Division (8–10 years old) and progress to the Open Division for adults twenty years and older.

The second most active program is the Senior Citizens Program, which is organized through the Yonkers Department of Parks, Recreation, and Conservation. The "Seniors," officially called Group 8, meet every Wednesday at the community house. Many members join in competitive games like bridge and pickino. Others sew or practice crafts. The room is abuzz with activity when the seniors meet. In addition to the Wednesday meetings, Group 8 is active in the Senior Bowling League in Yonkers. These individuals make up a unique group. Though mostly retired, they have active lives and are involved in community affairs. Many volunteer at the community house, keeping track of everyday affairs and events; a number are hobby enthusiasts who enjoy reading, painting, golf, travel, gardening, fishing, or walking.

Other community house programs have included an office skills program, which offered instruction in typing and clerical skills to those experiencing work transitions or unemployment, a computer training program, and a community advocacy program, which provided workshops and seminars on community preservation, conflict resolution, crime, and other environmental concerns. The alcohol and drug abuse program and the parent advocacy program have provided guidance, education and workshops for children and teenagers. The alcohol and sports programs have been most widely used by both residents and those from outside the community. In addition to a host of services, the community house holds an annual New Year's Eve party for adults, and Christmas, Kwanza, and Easter parties for local residents of all ages. At times the community house has been host to weddings, ethnic craft and gift fairs, raffles, art shows, social nights, and, of course, the Nepperhan Reunion.

The reunion is the community's largest formal celebration and represents an active attempt to preserve its past. On Saturday, September 25, 1993, the community house hosted the Second Nepperhan Reunion Day. Although the luncheon and ceremony were not scheduled to begin until 2:00 P.M., current and former residents began arriving before noon, eager for a chance to greet old friends and mingle with people who for them were associated with the word "home." The home-cooked meal and the chance to reminisce over common experiences growing up in Nepperhan seemed well worth the twenty-dollar donation. Earlier that week, members of the RHIA had been busy sprucing up the community house and preparing the feast. The seniors were most active, but younger members were busy helping out. Some five hundred fliers were mailed weeks in advance, including one to every household in Runyon Heights. The community house was filled to capacity. Seventy-five hot lunches were served, and close to two hundred people attended the ceremony. A few European Americans were also represented among the attendees. Twenty-four former Nepperhaners came from out of state, including from North Carolina, Florida, Delaware, Connecticut, Maryland, Virginia, and New Jersey. According to residents, the turnout rivaled that of the First Nepperhan Community Reunion, held in September 1981.

Over the years, the operating budget of the community house gradually increased from a few hundred dollars donated by local residents, until it reached a peak of more than $50,000 a year in 1993. Before 1994, the community house had received as much as $45,000 from the federal government's Community Development Program. Budget cuts reduced that figure to $30,000 in fiscal year 1994–1995. The difference, however, was more than made up by Youth Services, which contributed an additional $25,000 to community house programs.

Public funding brought consequences to the community. Federal and local guidelines regulated community house activities and restricted the institution's autonomy. Not all RHIA members were happy with these constraints. Some felt that with the trend toward the delivery of citywide services, many needs in the community ran the risk of being neglected. Those people preferred more autonomy from government control and more isolation from outsiders who use community programs.

Voices opposing public funding of the center prevailed. In March 1996, the board of the RHIA voted to end the majority of programs and services. One might interpret this move as an attempt to close ranks and limit westside access to the area. Today, the sports and senior programs remain the primary activities at the community house. It once again subsists primarily on neighborhood contributions. Plans are being made to raise funds to rehabilitate the facility and add wheelchair-accessible ramps. The popular sports program merely borrows the community house facility and is actually a distinct entity funded by the Community Development Agency; the senior's group remain part of the city's Division of Parks and Recreation.

In contrast to widely held beliefs about the richness of middle-class social organization and working-class disorganization, Runyon Heights has become less organized in some ways as it has become more middle class. The number of interlocking groups and organizations has declined, while organizational life has become more centralized through the RHIA. Group solidarity has actually increased, and residents have become more politically proactive as they defend their turf. The future of community solidarity and political influence may depend upon the ability of newer cohorts to establish and participate in local community clubs and associations, particularly the Runyon Heights Improvement Association.

Currently active clubs and organizations include the Men's Club, the Mothers' Club, The Women's Civic Club, the Monte Carloites,[16] the Bridge Club, the Idlers, and a group of women who refuse to call themselves a "club" although they meet regularly on Mondays to play cards. Many of these clubs draw only older community residents. At one time the Men's Club had thirty members; today its numbers have dwindled to fifteen. The Women's Civic Club no longer functions as a civic beautification committee. Since the 1970s, its activities have been largely reduced to awarding scholarships to community youths. Members hold theater parties as one way of raising funds; however, since some members have come to reside in other areas of the city over the years, scholarships are not limited to Runyon Heights residents but are awarded to Yonkers students through the Board of Education. Student scholarships are also supported by the James H. Farrell Lodge of the Masons, by the Eastern Stars, and by the Beth Omega Chapter of Gamma Phi Delta.

A few new clubs have sprung directly from the church. Two of the largest are the Calendar Club, which organizes trips to plays and other events, and the Missionary Society, which is divided into four age groups and works to help people in Africa. One of the oldest church-based clubs is the Men's Club, originally founded by the first male settlers around 1930. A second Men's Club grew out of the church around World War II and supplanted the first group. The Men's Club holds a prestigious role in the community, for it claims some of the oldest and most respected community residents as members. Its main role is to provide scholarships for youth in the community. Beyond that, the club functions as a peer group, drawing members into trips, card games, afternoon chats at the community house, and neighborhood chores. The popular gospel choir, the Metrolites, continues to link Nepperhaners to other black communities across the region.

On the surface, the generation currently coming of age seems less connected to the traditional value system of the community, yet it faces dilemmas similar to those that past generations faced. Hard work and education are still operative values, although the current generation seems to be more influenced by American popular culture. Old institutions and agents of socialization like the church, family, and school have less legitimacy and influence over the current generation of teens. The Protestant work ethic exemplified by the "old heads"[17] has been challenged by the easy, fast money of pop stars, sports legends, and street hustlers. Even in isolated Runyon Heights, the impact of national trends is felt.

The roots of many community problems are external to the community and therefore largely outside its control. At school and on television, teens are exposed to a different set of standards than those that are common in the community. Most recently, issues of drug use, teen supervision, and community policing have been discussed in local community meetings. While past generations developed a strong racial identity based in the local community, today's youth are increasingly removed from local institutions and exposed to the popular cultural styles of working-class and poor black urban youth. Community institutions, which were once central to the hyperorganized community, play a less significant role as agents of community socialization. The church has less influence in the lives of most teens, by comparison with past generations, and the stabilizing influence of School 1 no longer exists. Even the local Boy Scout troop has vanished.

Societal forces, particularly the post-1980 drug epidemic, have had an impact on the atmosphere in Runyon Heights and in its institutions. Even the old community-based bar, the Club Shelton, has been replaced by Charlie's, a bar that carries a dubious reputation among residents. One former patron of the Club Shelton speculated about why older residents no longer go to Charlie's:

> You have a lot of the local drug addicts and the good-for-nothings. You have some good people that still go to Charlie's, but really, the atmosphere has changed a lot. It's more or less, watch your hip, watch your money, don't go into the bathroom unless you take your money with you, whereas in the Shelton, you could leave the change of a twenty or a fifty or whatever up on the bar. . . . There's just a perception, you know, that anybody can come into the bar now. And these kids come in and they just want to buy a beer. They're not gonna sit at the bar like the old-timers who come in and buy a round on the house for everybody.

Ever since crack vials turned up in Boo Wilson Park during the 1990s, teen-age drug use has headed the list of local concerns. With the decline in community institutions, only the RHIA remains in a position to address local discontent with the changing character of the neighborhood, its institutions, and its teenagers.

Surviving Against the Odds

During the period between 1980 and 1990, the first sustained decline in the city's total population of the century took place. The trend has continued, compounding the effect of the continued growth of the black population. Blacks came to represent more than 14 percent of the total population of Yonkers between 1980 and 1990. The Hispanic population grew even more quickly and now constitutes 16 percent of the city population. Like the blacks of an earlier era, most of the new nonwhites can find housing only on the southwest side of the city, where affordable public housing is available. Nearly 26,000 black residents have inherited the oldest housing stock, located near the commercial core of the city. Some white residents refer to this area in a derogatory way as Ghetto Square. Today, black Yonkers residents remain segregated and largely excluded from a now declining industrial infrastructure. Growth in the low-skill service economy has not made up the employment gap.

The 1980s and 1990s have brought changes that threaten the way of life of Runyon Heights and are likely to draw community members together along both racial and class lines. For the entire century, real estate in Yonkers has been defined in racial terms. This has created economic opportunity for a few. Over the years, both black and white individuals have become involved in real estate speculation in Nepperhan; both residents and nonresidents have profited. Today, few sizable parcels of land are available for development in the western section of the neighborhood. The Hill area is still undergoing residential development and middle-class gentrification. Nearly a dozen homes have been constructed in the past decade, and a number of private developers have purchased lots in recent years. Along the southern end of Ridgeview and Patmor Avenues and the eastern portion of Drake Place, new construction is visible.

One Runyon Heights resident from the West Indies recently built some highly valued homes in the Hill area and placed them on the market. Residents believe this to be a positive trend. White gentrification is an ever-present concern as young middle-class white families seek cheaper suburban homes in the inflated real estate market of Westchester County. As Runyon Heights has become attractive to white home seekers as well as to white real estate speculators, residents fear the loss of their community to whites. Though racial exclusivity has historically been a matter of white privilege, black residents have increasingly encouraged local homeowners to sell only to other blacks. Their concern does not reflect racial separatism so much as ambivalence toward whites, created by frustration with their own limited opportunities. Nonresident builders, many of them white, tend to raise community suspicions because residents perceive them to have little personal commitment to the area. Rumors that one local white business owner on Runyon Avenue owns a number of properties in the area have exacerbated fears. Residents, who report that federally subsidized Section 8 tenants occupy two of his properties, are concerned about the increasing number of absentee landlords. Some residents believe that renters, especially those with low incomes, are less likely than owners to maintain their homes, yards, and community.

Neighborhood fears of absentee landlords are not unfounded. One local entrepreneur owns at least two houses, as well as other properties in the area. Although he would not disclose exactly how many he owns, he reported paying more than $20,000 a year in property taxes. He indicated that the biggest problem facing the area was caused not by absentee landlords but by school desegregation, busing, and the laziness of the younger generation. Meanwhile, he reported that placing publicly subsidized (Section 8) tenants in his properties was the most effective way of renting. Expansion of this practice could unsettle the class homogeneity of the area, lower property values, and lead to the ghettoization of Runyon Heights. The fear of losing Runyon Heights to whites has been fed by white realtors who have gone door to door offering to purchase local homes. Residents assume that white realtor interests will bring white home buyers.

That many absentee landlords and realtors are nonblacks interjects race into the equation. One of the first black women to graduate from Roosevelt High School described her nephew's recent futile search for housing in a predominantly white neighborhood in Westchester and conveyed her ambivalence toward further integration of Runyon Heights at the expense of her community's future. Her comments also reflect the desegregation controversy and residents' perceptions that their way of life and their property values are imperiled by the continued threat that economically marginal and less committed residents will infiltrate the area. Local concerns encourage racial solidarity, even at the cost of short-term material gains.

Somebody has recently bought the house and remodeled it. Another family took it over, and they apparently lost it, and now it's a white owner. And that's something I would like to talk about, how people now are letting the whites come in. They don't want us anywhere, you've seen Yonkers has spent millions of dollars so they wouldn't have to integrate schools and the housing. And for whatever reason, they don't want us, so I don't want them either. We have a nice neighborhood here now. Across the street from me now is a white man, he's a very nice man, I have no problem with the man, it's just the idea that he's white and he's in our neighborhood. . . . I just hate to see the area infiltrated with other people. I feel that this is what black people kind of look up to as a place to be. And if we let everybody, if we let them into the area, after a while we're gonna be pushed out. I mean our young people need a place to live, too. My nephew recently got married, last August, and he tried to buy a home, and they put him through hell, and he didn't get it anyway. . . . By the time he filled all the requirements to buy the house, of course he didn't have anything left in the bank, so then they said he had no backup. So I mean, they make it so hard for us, and our young people need to have a place to go. They want something nice out of life too. He's a working young man. He has a business on the side, and his new wife is also working. . . . There was no place here that was for sale that he wanted. They make it very hard, and we in turn, I think, when we get ready to sell our property, should not be so hungry for the money that we sell it to the highest bidder. We should be able to encourage our youth to stay in the neighborhood, and, you know, give them a break. We have a man in the community now who is buying up property. He's white, and he's renting it. So that's an absentee landlord, right? He's not gonna really care, after a while, how the place is kept. He's not gonna really care for anything except his money. . . . It's the person more so, really, than the black and white, but the whites that we are attracting may not be the kind that wants to keep their place nice. . . . Absentee landlords, two-family houses, tenants.

One thirty-six-year-old resident of six years expressed the dilemma between his racial commitment and his economic interests: "I remember when I first bought into the area I used to hear from the old-timers, when you sell, don't sell to whites—sell to blacks, you know. And I can understand what they're saying, you know, kind of preserve the neighborhood. But I guess if we were placed in that situation, we'll see who'll have the money, ha ha."

A common resolution to community concerns is that many homes are not sold on the formal real estate market. Family networks and personal contacts still remain the central recruitment mechanisms, helping to maintain the racial composition of the area. While residents fear an influx of white residents, the Detroit-Area Survey suggests that most middle-class white Americans will tend to avoid predominantly black residential neighborhoods. Seventy-three percent of white Americans would be unwilling to move into a neighborhood that contained a black population greater than 36 percent (Massey and Denton 1993, 93; Farley et al. 1978, 335; Yinger 1995, 118). When blacks bought property in white areas, like Homefield, they often did so outside the traditional market. One local realtor had reported to the State Attorney General's office several incidents of racial discrimination by lending institutions during the seventies and eighties. The realtor told a number of interesting stories about negotiating the racial terrain as a local broker. On one occasion, he reported how he came by a Homefield property during the mid-sixties:

The reason I got the house, it's the funniest thing. This man who owned it was mad with his neighbor. They were fighting and he was gonna fix her, and so he came to my office and told me he had the house and he wanted me to sell it to some "colored" people. I think we were "black" by then, but he hadn't gotten the message. . . . And every time she made him angry, and I had no intention of getting involved in this at all, he'd come into my office and lower the price maybe five thousand dollars. "Find somebody, find somebody, I'm gonna fix her!" and so on. And finally I just said, this is mine! . . . You know, he wanted me to get a "colored family with a lot of children" (laughs).

The realtor went on to describe other experiences with Homefield residents: "Funny thing, I had a couple of white families who came to me and that asked me not to sell to blacks. That I could sell their houses, but please not to sell them to blacks. . . . I told them that I had to sell to anybody who came to me. I could not discriminate against anybody."

Today, it is the Runyon Heights residents who fear that the racial balance in the area has been shifting, although census data reveal a surprisingly stable ratio of blacks to whites since the 1940s (Table 6.1). In fact the percentage of white residents has slowly declined. Residents may, however, have misjudged the recent influx of Latino residents, believing that their lighter skin signified "whiteness."

Battles that began in 1956 over public housing in Runyon Heights have persisted into the 1990s. A city-owned section of land on Sprain Road became the center of controversy during the summer of 1992, when the city proposed building low-income townhouses on the site. Yonkers soon abandoned its plan after the community petitioned, arguing that the land had already been designated a public park. Subsequently the area was officially named Carter Ash Park. Once again, residents unified and raised their voices to defend community interests.

Meanwhile, the black population in Homefield has slowly grown. According to the 1990 U.S. Census, though Homefield remains 92 percent white, there are 109 blacks (7 percent) among the community's residents. Should the black population of Homefield continue to increase, white homeowners may seek housing elsewhere, even though the middle-class residential character of Homefield is ensured by housing costs, real estate values, and zoning regulations. In other words, should the area become "too black," white flight may occur, and middle-class blacks and other non-whites may come to dominate the area. Generations of forced segregation and inhospitable reception in predominantly white areas of Westchester

Table 6.1. Population of Runyon Heights, N.Y. (Census Tract 18) by Race, 1925–1990

Year	Total Pop.	Black Pop.	White Pop.	Hispanic Pop.
1920[a]	56	0 (0%)	56 (100%)	NA
1925[b]	369	195 (53%)	174 (47%)	NA
1940	1,015	736 (72%)	279 (28%)	NA
1950	1,109	836 (75%)	272 (25%)	NA
1960	1,367	1,100 (80%)	263 (19%)	NA
1970	1,485	1,068 (72%)	397 (27%)	18[c]
1980	1,270	987 (78%)	238 (19%)	26[d]
1990	1,378	1,085 (79%)	214 (16%)	96 (7%)

Source: Data from U.S. Census of Population unless otherwise noted.

[a] U.S. Census Manuscripts

[b] New York State census manuscripts

[c] Hispanic origin or descent

[d] Total Hispanic

County have led a number of middle-class blacks to choose areas like Runyon Heights, which thus gains a steady stream of new recruits. In the final analysis, the four-foot reserve strip may prove to be only a temporary barrier to a nonwhite presence in Homefield. The historical evidence suggests that Homefield will become a middle-class black area before Runyon Heights comes to be dominated by whites.

In addition to helping to segregate racially defined groups within specific neighborhoods, state institutions helped strengthen a racially defined group identity through political exclusion, which had an impact on community relations. We see this phenomenon occurring at the points when the FHA restricted loans to racially homogeneous areas, when restrictive covenants were used to exclude black homeowners, when the school board denied Nepperhan children access to Roosevelt High School, when School 1 district lines were redrawn, and when Runyon Heights was targeted for low-income housing. Rather than declining in significance, race has remained an important determinant of the character of black middle-class life.

The political, economic, and social subordination of racial communities encourages political mobilization along racial lines. This is what occurred among residents of Runyon Heights. These political communities may be organized around local territory, as in the case of the Runyon Heights Improvement Association, around a more general concept of "racial uplift," as in the case of the NAACP, or around local issues, as was the case for the mothers who fought against the inferior education imposed on their children. In Runyon Heights, community-based political and social organizations emerged to challenge the existing racial order. Their challenge was racial uplift in the pursuit of class mobility; this is the essential paradox embodied in the lives of the black middle class.

Eisenhower Republicans
and Republican Democrats

The formation of the Nepperhan–Runyon Heights community was predicated on residents' having stable jobs and access to suburban real estate
that was isolated from poorer populations. The survival of the community, however, depended on strong community solidarity, including active participation in local politics. Though physically isolated, Nepperhaners had considerable leverage in local politics. In this chapter I shall
examine the environment in which Nepperhan residents articulated their
common concerns and exerted influence in the political process. Through
a review of both national and local elections, this analysis demonstrates
how race and class interests were reflected in residents' political loyalties
and voting behavior.

Negotiating the Ward System

At the time Nepperhan came into existence, the city of Yonkers was
divided into twelve wards, each electing a representative to the city council. Nepperhan was originally designated as a small portion of the large
Third Election District in the Tenth Ward. In 1930, Nepperhan was re-
assigned to the Sixth Election District of the Tenth Ward, and as a result the political boundaries of the district closely approximated those of

the community. The change had only symbolic importance with regard to political power in Runyon Heights because the community remained within the same ward. Aligning the district with community boundaries did, however, make it easier for local politicians to assess voting behavior in Nepperhan and helped to carve out the area as a Negro space. Redistricting, coincidentally, occurred during the same period that the Nepperhan children met with resistance at the newly opened Roosevelt High School.

From the outset, residents of Nepperhan were involved in local government and politics. The highly organized nature of the community ensured that they would quickly learn about issues facing them and their neighbors. While residents believed that contributing their financial and intellectual resources to civic and community organizations was essential to fostering and preserving the Nepperhan enclave, they also believed that active participation in local ward politics was a critical factor in community preservation.

Active participation in local affairs became a community norm. High levels of community organization led directly to high levels of political involvement. The Runyon Heights Democratic Club was formed in June 1933. By that time, the Republican Club of Nepperhan and the Phillis Wheatley Republican Club had already been established. Historically, the Tenth Ward Republican Club was a center of political influence in local politics; Nepperhan residents supported club activities.

Between the 1940s and the 1970s, even a trip to the barber or the hairdresser could be a catalyst for political action in Nepperhan. Two Nepperhan-owned beauty salons along Saw Mill River and Tuckahoe Roads catered to local women. Men often frequented Trent's Place, a makeshift barbershop in the basement of a local resident's home. These establishments not only provided practical cosmetic services but also served as gathering places for locals. One resident recalled: "Trent's, it was a very political atmosphere. You know, when you went in, they talked about what was going on in the community."

Like other residential suburban populations, Nepperhaners made full use of the electoral system. An early characteristic of Nepperhan voting was that residents were issue-driven and tended to cross traditional party lines in casting their ballots. Locally, such independence gave them leverage in closely contended mayoral and ward races. Successful involvement in local politics meant more than voting, though; it meant getting involved in ward and club activities. Early Nepperhaners established a tradition of active involvement that has been continued by succeeding generations. Many residents are aware of the multiple strategies that have been employed to wield political influence in Yonkers and continue to socialize new community members into the practice. One resident of eight years, a thirty-one-year-old male, shared his understanding of the local political scene:

> What happens is politicians count every vote, no matter which one it is, and fortunately for us, because of the education of the folks in the neighborhood, this is something that's been there way before my time. So people are smart enough to be on both sides of the playing field. We have a Republican leader of the Tenth Ward . . . and he has a lot of networks. And a lot of the folks that live in Runyon Heights either work for the city as employees . . . so they have a lot of political savvy. They know that you have to show up at the fund-raisers, and all that other kind of stuff, and that's how that works, that people are able to make phone calls and do that. . . . And now it hits them twice, because is this going to be a problem with people of color, is this going to be a problem for the NAACP, . . . or is this a problem in the neighborhood, is this a problem for Runyon Heights? And we know how to use our leverage appropriately to get the things done.

He then explained his understanding of the community's political philosophy.

> The community would survive without the different organizational levels, but they [community members] wouldn't survive if they did not participate politically. If they didn't participate politically, they would get left out, as everyone does when you don't participate politically. That's been the general problem for our folks is that they vote and they vote one line. They vote Democratic, but they don't look at issues. I try to educate people: you don't have to vote Democratic. You vote for the person that does, that handles your issues best, that supports the things you're looking to support. And if that person is from the New Zimbabwe party, then you vote for them. . . . Political support doesn't mean you voted for somebody. It meant who you worked for. Because they need foot soldiers, and all that stuff, going out there, priming the pump, talking to people, delivering whatever percentage of votes, because one vote, Nicholas Wascizco can tell you, he won by twelve votes.

Informal channels were equally important in addressing community concerns. As one resident explained: "You network, you work for the city, you know the right people, you talk to the right people. And if you do that properly, you'll get things done, because you'll be able to pick up the phone and talk to the right person. You see, the appropriate person is not always the one that's in charge. The one that's appropriate may be the one that's sitting on the truck."

Yonkers has developed its own system of political patronage, which is closely linked to residential life and interpersonal ties in the city. Many of the early Nepperhaners attended school with whites whose families became important players in local government and city administration. These ties have proved useful in navigating the bureaucracy at city hall. Milton Holst, one of the most active members of the RHIA, is often called the "mayor" of Runyon Heights by local residents and public officials. Holst, a member of the Parks, Recreation, and Conservation board and president of the Tenth Ward Republican Club from 1990 to 1992, explained how he first got involved during the 1960s by attending city hall meetings and planning board seminars, and by participating in the clubhouses and party politics. He maintains that the local district leaders are the "first line of offense" in local political battles. Holst was honored by local Republicans at a dinner-dance at the Italian Unity Club in April 1993.

One woman, a former district leader, explained why she got involved: "By this time, I was beginning to get a little involved into politics. I had become the district leader, but prior to that I was attending a lot of political meetings. I was interested in Malcolm X—was who I knew—and his words were the words that I felt, and I felt that I could make a contribution in Runyon Heights."

These leaders, who have resided in the community since the late 1920s, represent an aging cohort of extremely active residents. Old-timers have expressed concern over the aging of its organizational base.

Eisenhower Republicans

Though early residents supported both Democratic and Republican political clubs, Nepperhaners were predominantly Republican. This may reflect the traditional commitment to the GOP that many black Americans held following the Civil War, or it may have reflected a typically conservative suburban insularity. As we shall see, however, Nepperhan voting behavior is explained neither by Republican traditionalism nor by blind allegiance to post–New Deal Democratic party liberalism.

Table 7.1: Political Party Registration: Sixth Election District 6, Tenth Ward, Yonkers

Year of Party Affil	1930	1940	1950	1960	1970	1980	1992
Republican	189	223	237	292	260	147	99
	(77%)	(57%)	(54%)	(60%)	(41%)	(27%)	(16%)
Democrat	42	136	179	188	360	333	429
	(17%)	(35%)	(41%)	(38%)	(57%)	(61%)	(71%)
Socialist	1	0	0	0	0	0	0
	(.41%)						
Amer Labor	0	9	5	0	0	0	0
			(1%)				
Liberal	0	0	3	3	3	23	1
			(1%)	(1%)	(.47%)	(4%)	
Conservative	0	0	0	0	1	2	13
					(.16%)	(.36%)	(2%)
Right to Life	0	0	0	0	0	0	0
Void Blank missing non affil	11	22	16	6	10	38	64
	(5%)	(6%)	(4%)	(1%)	(2%)	(7%)	(11%)
Total	243	390	440	489	634	543	606
	(100%)	(100%)	(100%)	(100%)	(100%)	(100%)	(100%)

Source: Registration rolls, political party registration, Westchester County Board of Elections.

Note: Registration rolls were acquired for the years 1930 through 1970. Between 1930 and 1960, political party affiliation was calculated by including only streets within the boundaries of Runyon Heights. These numbers, therefore, do not represent the entire district. After 1960, community boundaries were completely in line with the district boundary, such that the Sixth Election District comprised only streets within the boundaries of Runyon Heights. For the years 1970 through 1992, the entire Sixth Election District is used. In 1993, however, the southern portion of Bushy Avenue was gerrymandered into another election district in the Sixth Council District.

Voter registration records reveal the early Republican leanings of the black population in Nepperhan.[1] In 1930, 77 percent of the Nepperhan residents were registered Republicans (Table 7.1). Although this pattern is typical of white suburban communities, it is an anomaly among predominantly black communities; ever since President Truman solidified the black vote through his civil rights campaign of 1948, black Americans have maintained a predominantly Democratic affiliation and have voted overwhelmingly for Democratic candidates both locally and nationally, save for a few local Republican enclaves (Schuman, Steeh, and Bobo 1985, 17; Jaynes and Williams 1989, 216).

While the total number of registered Republicans in Nepperhan grew from 189 in 1930 to 223 in 1940, the percentage of Republicans actually fell, from 77 to 57 percent. Democrats entered the community at a rate of more than two to one. Nevertheless, the community remained predominantly Republican into the mid-1960s, a period when many black Americans had become solid supporters of the Democratic party. In fact, in contrast to national trends in black voting behavior, the largest aggregate increase in the number of registered Republicans in Runyon Heights occurred between 1950 and 1960; 57 registered Republican, whereas only 9 joined the Democrats. One woman explained, "When I registered to vote Republican, it was back in the Eisenhower years." Her comment echoes those of a number of older residents who claimed that they were "Eisenhower Republicans."

Within a decade the racial climate of the nation was reflected in local community registration patterns. Residents slowly began to turn away from the GOP; newer voters increasingly registered Democrat. Between 1960 and 1970, the percentage of Republicans declined by 11 percent, while Democratic registration grew by 91 percent. Despite this trend, 41 percent of the voters remained Republican in 1970. During the 1970s, a retreat from the GOP is evident; some older residents began shifting party affiliation. The total number of voters declined by 14 percent, and Republican registration declined by 44 percent; the Democratic ranks dipped only slightly, by 8 percent. For the first time, the majority of voters were now registered Democrats.

The 1980s witnessed further erosion in Republican support. As of this writing there are only ninety-nine registered Republicans, a meager 16 percent of the voters, the weakest Republican registration in the history of Nepperhan. Significantly, 11 percent of the voters are not currently affiliated with any party, whereas the Conservative party has seen a small growth of 2 percent.

The early pattern of heavy Republican registration begs the question: "Did Nepperhaners vote for Republican candidates?" Would residents follow the post–World War II middle-class pattern of Republican patronage typical of white suburbs, or would they support the Democratic party, as much of black America has done since the 1930s? Our analysis suggests that Runyon Heights residents did both: they voted to protect their material interests as well as their racial group interests.

National Voting Behavior

Republican sympathies reflected in party affiliation were also extended to residents' support for early GOP presidential candidates. Although Republican registration reached a peak of 60 percent in 1960, 69 percent of the district actually voted for the Republican Eisenhower-Nixon ticket in 1956. In 1960, the Republican Nixon-Lodge ticket received 51 percent of the community's vote.

Until 1964, the election district supported the GOP at roughly the same rate as the rest of the Tenth Ward and the city of Yonkers. The 1964 presidential election brought an abrupt change in this pattern. Debates over the passage of the Civil Rights Act, the liberalization of the Democratic party, and Republican intolerance on the question of race shifted Nepperhan voters' political support away from GOP candidates. Voters concluded overwhelmingly that the liberal agenda was in their interest. The conservative Goldwater and Miller, running on the GOP ticket, received 39 percent of the city vote but only a meager 9 percent of the community vote. Johnson and Humphrey, running on the Liberal party–Democratic party ticket, received 92 percent of the Nepperhan vote, but only 62 percent of the city's patronage. For the first time, the voting behavior of Runyon Heights residents deviated significantly from that of Yonkers residents in a national election.

This trend toward support of Democratic presidential candidates continued. In 1968, the Republican team of Nixon and Agnew did gain ground, capturing 17 percent of the Sixth District's vote, although this was a far cry from the 51 percent Nixon had marshaled in 1960. The Liberal-Democratic team of Humphrey and Muskie still claimed 82 percent of the vote. During this period there was an observable gap between party affiliation and voter preference. Although at least 41 percent of the community was still registered Republican, many supported Liberal-Democratic candidates. Republicans continued to receive appreciable support in the Tenth Ward and in Yonkers, 49 percent and 48 percent respectively.

The 1980 presidential election continued the pattern. The Reagan/ Bush team, running on both the Conservative and Republican tickets, received only 15 percent of the district vote, while Democrats Carter and

Mondale received 83 percent. For Nepperhan–Runyon Heights voters, middle-class suburban issues like crime, schools, taxes, and the quality of life were overshadowed by concern with trends in national policy on race. Despite the material interest of this middle-class suburb, residents have become increasingly liberal in their voting behavior since Goldwater transformed the GOP in 1964.

During the 1990s, race became a central issue in American politics, as conservatives attacked both social welfare policy and affirmative action and charged that the liberalism of the 1960s had created today's problems of unemployment, teen pregnancy, drug abuse, and youth violence. The conservative agenda, led by Speaker of the House Newt Gingrich and Senate Majority Leader Bob Dole, ushered in a new wave of attacks on liberal policies aimed at ending racial discrimination. Insisting that racial discrimination in America had been eradicated, the GOP proclaimed America a color-blind society. Continued decline in GOP support by Runyon Heights residents suggests, however, that the black middle class did not buy into conservative rhetoric on race. In 1992, the Bush-Quayle ticket received just 13 percent of the vote in the Sixth District, the smallest percentage since Goldwater. Democratic support dipped slightly as well, as Clinton and Gore took 80 percent of the vote. Perot and his third-party ticket picked up 5 percent of the district, and Fulani and the New Alliance party mustered another percentage point. Republican support in Yonkers also slipped, from 58 percent in 1980 to 42 percent in 1992. In 1996, the incumbent Democrats secured an impressive 90 percent of the Runyon Heights vote but only 56 percent of the city vote. Republicans claimed only 7 percent of Sixth District votes, the smallest percentage in Runyon Heights history.

A comparison of residents' voting behavior and their political affiliation reveals an interesting paradox. The two roughly coincided until Goldwater's bid in 1964. The candidate's position on civil rights shifted the traditional platform of the GOP on race in America and polarized national party politics. Although more Republicans than Democrats actually supported the Kennedy-Johnson Civil Rights Act in 1964, Goldwater was one of only six Republican senators to vote against the bill. With this act, Republicans were no longer viewed by many blacks as the party of Lincoln and the free Negro. Goldwater's politics on the question of race actually pushed black suburban voters out of the GOP. Meanwhile, the conservative, racist Southern wing of the Democratic party gave way to a more liberal leadership and a concomitant social agenda. Democratic presidential patronage in Runyon Heights quickly followed (Jaynes and Williams 1985, 216).

Scholars have observed that Democratic support among the educated professional middle-class voters increased between 1972 and 1992, owing to liberal views on social issues such as abortion, civil rights, and women's roles (Brooks and Manza 1997, 204). Yet abandonment of the GOP began early in Runyon Heights. The shift can be attributed only partly to professionalization and liberalism. In a more important way, it has been a response to the discourse on race in national politics. Black Nepperhaners responded to the GOP attack on the civil rights agenda by withdrawing their support.

Voter Participation

In addition to this shift in support from Republican to Democratic candidates, residents were extremely active voters in both national and local elections. Voter turnout in the community for the 1968 election can be calculated by comparing the number of registered voters in 1969 with the number of ballots cast during the 1968 presidential election. Nearly 90 percent (579/644) of the registered voters in the Sixth Election District cast votes during the national election. If we calculate voter turnout using the 1961 voter registration rolls, 92 percent voted in the 1960 presidential election (489/529), and 82 percent (498/606) in the 1992 presidential election.

Traditionally, voter turnout has also been large in local elections. If we use the 1970 registration rolls to calculate voter turnout in the 1969 mayoral campaign, 85 percent (539/634) of the registered voters cast ballots. Local voter turnout declined in the 1990s, however. Only 43 percent (262/606) of registered voters cast ballots in the 1993 city council election, and an estimated 46 percent (277/606) voted in the 1995 mayoral contest.

Although racial interests dominated voter preference in national elections after 1964, in local contests community interests clearly reflected both race and class. Before turning to a discussion of anomalies in local voting behavior, I shall set the stage with a brief discussion of political organization in Yonkers.

The Political Overview

At the turn of the century, Yonkers was organized into a ward system characterized by a strong mayoral form of government. Under this system, the mayor controlled the budget and all administrative appointments; the approval of the city council was not required (Steigman 1967, 69). After a controversy involving the former mayor, this system was abandoned in 1940 in favor of the council manager style of government (sometimes known as the weak-mayor system), which remained in effect until 1991. (Steigman 1967, 11). The city was still divided into twelve wards, each of which elected, by majority vote, a representative to the city council. Both the mayor and the twelve ward representatives were elected for two-year terms. The only citywide election was for the mayor, who served on the council as member-at-large. The mayor's primary responsibilities were to appoint members of the board of education, vote in the city council, and act as official head of the city. The city manager was the chief executive and administrative officer and was appointed by the council to oversee the budget and the appointment of administrative heads. The tenure of the city manager was decided by a majority vote of the council. The new system shifted political power to the wards and ultimately to the city council representatives; the mayor maintained control of only the school system.

Though the Runyon Heights community was first established during the era of the strong mayor, it evolved primarily during the period of political organization characterized by strong wards and weak mayors. Even under the earlier system, political patronage through the wards was an integral part of Yonkers politics.

Until the 1980s, Yonkers continued the twelve-ward weak-mayor system. Following the release of the 1980 federal census, a plan was adopted in 1983 to redistrict and switch to a seven-member city council. Under this proposal, the city would be divided into four council districts, each comprising three wards and each electing a council member. Three additional members would be elected at large, of whom the two who received the most votes would become the mayor and vice mayor. This plan was challenged by the local NAACP on the grounds that it virtually excluded minority representation on the city council. The plan received widespread criticism from other local groups because it gerrymandered the large black area of southwest Yonkers into a predominantly white council district, thereby weakening black working-class influence on the council. The plan also designated Runyon Heights as a small component of a district much larger than the old ward. In response to criticism, a new redistricting plan was ordered by the courts, and in 1985 elections were held temporarily using the old twelve-member ward system. The first black council person, Joseph E. Burgess, Jr., was elected to represent the First Ward, the area encompassing Getty Square. In 1987, the ward system was finally abandoned in favor of the seven-member city council system. Unlike the 1983 proposal, which created only four council districts, the 1987 plan created six districts.

Under the six-district plan, each district elected a representative to the city council, and the mayor was elected at large. Although this new plan maintained the homogeneity of the first predominantly "minority" council district in the southwest downtown area, it also placed Runyon Heights in the predominantly white and Republican Sixth Council District. In fact, the majority of the Tenth Ward and all of the Fifth Ward became part of the Sixth Council District. By comparison with the old ward system, the council district system divided the political geography into larger areas, thereby increasing the relative power of each council member but diminishing the impact of the Runyon Heights vote.

Solutions proposed by city government to aid the black working class on the west side have often failed to benefit east-side Nepperhaners. In this case, a working-class minority district was salvaged at the expense of a weakened Runyon Heights voter block. We have observed how the underutilization of School 1 and racial imbalance in the city schools in the past were remedied by the busing of Runyon children; we observed that desperately needed public housing was targeted in Nepperhan, the only black area in east Yonkers. In many ways, black working-class needs in Yonkers have often been met in the context of a political trade-off with middle-class Runyon Heights residents.

One political insider revealed how favoritism determined the political composition of the Sixth District. The Republican-controlled city council helped maintain the political constituency of longtime Tenth Ward Republican incumbent Ed J. Fagan, Jr. When district lines were redrawn, rather than including a balance of Republicans and Democrats in the Sixth District, the district was weighted toward Republicans. The Republican-majority city council ensured Fagan's political future. As it currently exists, the Sixth District is more white and more conservative than the Tenth Ward was. Consequently, Fagan has remained in office.

The new system curtailed the influence of the Runyon vote in local elections. During the earlier ward system, Nepperhan had carried critical swing votes in elections that were closely contested, particularly since Nepperhaners supported both Democrats and Republicans. A balance between Republicans and Democrats would have secured Runyon Heights' swing-vote status. Owing to the closeness of recent races, however, the Runyon vote remains a factor in local contests. The recent trend in declining voter turnout could eventually jeopardize this leverage. Residents are placed at a further disadvantage because council districts overlap with the old ward political divisions, thereby diminishing the influence of local ward leaders in local politics. Shifts in the political landscape could have consequences for Runyon Heights if the system of personal contacts in the old political machine is disrupted.

Race came to dominate the Yonkers political scene during the 1980s. The housing and schooling discrimination lawsuit, filed in the U.S District Court in Manhattan in 1980 by the NAACP and the Justice Department against the city of Yonkers, was the spark that ignited local racial tensions. Conservative city council members nearly bankrupted the city by ignoring the federally mandated housing desegregation plan handed down by Judge Sand. Council member Fagan at first supported compliance but soon became an outspoken opponent of the federal proposal. Council members finally conceded to the court order after hefty fines were levied against the city. The incident, which nearly crippled city finances, helped to shift the political winds in Yonkers. Voters moved to transfer real power back to the mayor. In 1991, the strong-mayor form of government, abandoned in 1940, was revived. The new city government reinvested power in the mayor's office and weakened the influence of the city council over administrative decisions. Under the new system, both the mayor and the president of the city council were elected at large; the remaining six districts elected representatives to the council.

The 1993 redistricting plan, which had been based on the 1990 census reports, created another "minority" council district. The Second Council District included a portion of the former First District but contained a predominantly Latino population.

The 1993 redistricting plan raised troubling issues for Runyon Heights. An initial proposal by the Puerto Rican Legal Defense Fund, in a bid to create the second minority district, elicited strong opposition from the Runyon Heights community. The proposal suggested collapsing the Runyon community and the predominantly black First District on the west side into a single minority district. This plan would have politically segregated virtually the entire black population of Yonkers. The plan was strongly opposed by community members; as a result, Runyon Heights remained a part of the Sixth District. Residents feared that becoming part of a single minority district would not be in their best interests. The class interests of Nepperhaners would have been overshadowed by the needs of the much larger and poorer west-side community. In political terms, their swing vote would no longer count in a predominantly Democratic area. The hoopla surrounding the proposal to subsume Runyon Heights voters within the First District hindered close scrutiny of the Sixth District plan. Seeking to protect their political autonomy and class interests, residents resisted racial homogenization but ultimately lost critical leverage in the local political landscape.

Local Voting Behavior

We have seen that the political influence Runyon Heights wielded in local elections was strengthened by their support for both major parties. From the 1930s to the mid-1960s, residents often split their votes in local council and mayoral contests. Until 1981, Nepperhan voting patterns were indistinguishable from those of their neighbors. In a sample of mayoral and council elections from 1935, 1939, 1945, 1957, 1965, 1969, and 1979, Nepperhaners supported both Republican and Democratic candidates at levels roughly equal to those in the Tenth Ward. Support was strong for GOP Tenth Ward candidates until the mid-1960s, when the moderate Democrat Alfred Del Bello claimed 57 percent of the election district. By 1969, Democratic support had solidified. Del Bello claimed 63 percent of the Sixth Election District in his successful bid for mayor, and Dominick Cuccia claimed 60 percent of the district in his successful bid for councilman of the Tenth Ward. Even with Democratic support slowly increasing throughout the 1960s and 1970s, GOP candidates still collected a respectable 30 percent of the vote in the Sixth District.

Although the 1980s brought a renewal of racial discourse in national politics, local politics also took on a decidedly racial cast. The local crisis over school and housing desegregation during the 1980s exacerbated local racial divisions. As the GOP again became associated with an anti–civil rights agenda, support in Runyon Heights for local Republicans eroded. Judge Sand's decision linking school and housing segregation in Yonkers ignited widespread white opposition, and the conservative interests of white homeowners were reflected in the political positions of local politicians.

Runyon Heights voting patterns reflected local community concerns. During the 1980s, residents increasingly supported policies that challenged racial discrimination and segregation in Yonkers. As minorities and the poor squared off with white homeowners over the court-ordered desegregation plan, Runyon Heights residents reacted to the racial and class polarization taking place in the city. Though efforts to desegregate the schools had already been undertaken by the more moderate school board, Republicans generally opposed compliance with Judge Sand's order to construct low-income housing in predominantly white areas; Democrats generally supported compliance.

Former Republican mayor Angelo Martinelli (1973–1977) had developed a reputation for supporting and encouraging the segregationist policies of the city and the school board during his tenure, to the point of leading marches and demonstrations against desegregation in the late 1970s. He narrowly lost the mayoral bid in 1979 to liberal Gerald Loehr, who won 51 percent of the city vote. Martinelli had a modest showing of 30 percent in the Sixth District. He ran again in 1981, just as Yonkers' landmark desegregation lawsuit got under way. During this campaign, Martinelli shifted dramatically toward a less provincial political outlook. Claiming that his earlier position had been an error, he now encouraged settling the federal desegregation lawsuit and ultimately desegregating low-income housing and public schools in Yonkers. Whether desegregation was his aim or whether he simply assessed the city's slim chance of victory in the lawsuit, the voters in the Sixth District were unconvinced of his change of heart. Martinelli gained only one percentage point over the previous election, by securing 31 percent of the vote. Even this modest showing is a curiosity, given his former opposition to the desegregation plan.[2]

In 1985, now positioned as a moderate, Martinelli was again elected mayor, having gained an astounding 66 percent of the vote in the Sixth District. This was the strongest showing for a local Republican candidate since John Flynn received 51 percent of the vote in 1965. It is actually not a surprising figure, because Martinelli's opponent, Bernie Spreckman, was a stark opponent of desegregation. In 1987, Martinelli lost the mayoral race to the late Nicholas Wascisko, another Democratic candidate who flirted with the segregationist idea of challenging the court's decision. This time the vote was split, and Martinelli won a narrow majority of the Sixth Election District, with nearly 53 percent of the vote.

After the court's 1986 ruling, the school board quickly moved to develop a magnet program to desegregate the schools; the school plan proceeded unencumbered. White homeowners, however, opposed the court's proposal to place predominantly black and Latino families in two hundred units of low-income rental housing and eight hundred units of subsidized middle-income housing across the city. Local politician Jack O'Toole organized the Save Yonkers Federation, a group of white, largely middle-class homeowners from around the city who adamantly opposed public housing in their communities. Although group members often claimed to be protecting their housing values and communities, public discussions often centered on the implied race of potential occupants. Community opposition to Negroes had a long tradition in Yonkers; in this case, class acted as a mask for underlying racial animosities.

Before long, however, Yonkers' stubborn resistance to the court-ordered housing plan would come to an end. After the city council refused to develop a desegregation plan in 1988, council representatives Ed Fagan, Jr., Nicholas V. Longo, Henry Spallone, and Pete Chema were found in contempt of court. In September of that year, under threat of state intervention and fiscal bankruptcy, the council reluctantly voted to comply with the court order, though some members still vowed to oppose the judge. By 1989, Democratic mayoral candidate Nicholas Wascisko had shifted positions, as had Martinelli, and wanted the council to settle. Henry Spallone angered Runyon Heights residents during the campaign with his controversial rhetoric. Ironically, Spallone and the "Gang of Four" successfully challenged the contempt fines levied against the individual representatives by Judge Sand. With renewed vigor they swore to fight on. In 1991, Pete Chema ran for mayor on the GOP ticket, still vowing to direct, if not resist, the court order. In an unusual three-way race, Terence M. Zaleski won on the Democratic ticket with merely 36 percent of the vote. Martinelli, running on the Independent ticket, became the spoiler candidate, capturing 28 percent of the vote and crushing Chema's bid in the process. Still, Chema received a respectable 34 percent of the city vote. In the Sixth District, he mustered only 9 percent, while Zaleski and Martinelli received 48 percent and 42 percent, respectively.

After the 1991 elections and the shift to the strong-mayor form of government, the city council finally decided in April of 1992 to comply with the housing mandate. The judge ultimately rejected their proposal, however. Since then, the council has sought to comply with the judge's order, without upsetting the members' respective constituencies, in the hope of reclaiming the city's autonomy and future. In 1993, city officials finally complied with Sand's initial order to construct two hundred units of scatter-site low-income rental housing, which has been built on seven sites around the city. By 1996, city officials had regained more control over the housing program, and plans were made to assist predominantly black and Latino middle-income families with buying houses, while another

140 units of subsidized middle-income housing were constructed on four sites. In February 1998, Judge Sand ruled that New York State was partly responsible for housing segregation patterns in southwest Yonkers, and the state agreed to pay Yonkers $16.4 million to finish the desegregation plan.

Runyon Heights residents have managed to resist housing in their area. Local residents hold paradoxical attitudes toward low-income housing, at times lending support through organizations like the NAACP and at times resisting through organizations like the RHIA. One resident explains: "I think we kind of felt that look, we've done our responsibility, and we've made it work. A lot of people in the community were initially members of the projects [Hall Court]. I think we kind of divorced ourselves from the issue in a sense. We realized that this was something the city should do, but in terms of pressing for it, I don't think we pressed very hard."

The dramatic impact of race on voting patterns in Runyon Heights is demonstrated by the eighteen-year career of Councilman Ed Fagan Jr., most recently of Council District 6. In his early years as Tenth Ward representative, Fagan enjoyed a fair share of the votes in the Sixth Election District. As he became more opposed to Judge Sand's housing desegregation order, voting patterns became polarized along racial lines. In 1979, as a newcomer to the political scene, Fagan received 58 percent of the votes in the Tenth Ward, but only 20 percent of the votes in the Sixth Election District. By 1981, support for Ed Fagan in the Sixth Election District had grown to 29 percent, as compared with 64 percent in the entire ward. His support had gradually risen among Runyon Heights residents, probably a result of his having provided city services to the community. As one resident proclaimed, "Issues come and issues go, but services always stay. People always say, 'What have you done for me?'" Fagan clearly recognized his constituency; he made regular visits to the community and appeared at community events. By 1985, he had regained 37 percent of the election district, in opposition to future supporter of the Save Yonkers Federation O'Toole, who ran on the Democratic ticket. Over time, Fagan's extremely conservative position began to chip away at his local support. In 1987, while he was running for council representative of the newly formed Sixth Council District, and just as he was approaching a standoff with Judge Sand, his support slid to 32 percent in the district. In the 1989 council race, his support dropped still further, to 18 percent, where it remained in 1991. The desegregation battle exacerbated racial divisions in Yonkers and polarized the Runyon Heights vote. With the passing of the crisis, Fagan has slowly reestablished respectable support in the Sixth District. In 1993 and 1995, maintaining his stronghold on the council district, he won the elections with 55 percent and 50 percent; in the Sixth District, he received a modest 21 percent and 34 percent of the votes, respectively.

Scholars have noted that African-American political behavior is influenced by national politics and perceptions of group interests, yet little attention has been paid to how segregation and local policies have informed the formation of group interests (Dawson 1994). Voting behavior in Nepperhan is motivated by neither knee-jerk racial nationalism nor blind adherence to Democratic liberalism. Residents have been careful to select the candidates who have best represented their multifaceted interests. Until the late 1960s, residents were strong supporters of Republican candidates in national elections, but they split their vote between the major parties in local elections. After the racial polarization in national political discourse in 1964, support for the GOP in presidential elections shifted. Race became a central concern to Runyon Heights voters. During the 1980s, a similar shift in the local political discourse placed race at the center of local contests. In general, support for the Democratic party has paralleled the GOP's retreat from supporting antidiscrimination policy. Consequently, voting patterns in Runyon Heights have become more homogeneous as residents have articulated their collective racial and material interests.

8

Defining Black Space

A number of residents referred to a symbolic wall that allegedly sat along the four-foot reserve strip separating Nepperhan from Homefield. Many perceived the strip as symbolic of the racial intolerance of many Homefield residents. The "fence" or "strip" was mentioned whenever the Homefield community was brought up in conversation.

The September 29, 1988, edition of *48 Hours* presented a segment entitled "Not in My Backyard," hosted by Dan Rather. The program, which covered the 1980 federal housing discrimination suit in Yonkers[1] and featured a segment on Runyon Heights, focused on the fence that allegedly divides Nepperhan from Homefield. Although the reserve strip is a prominent feature shaping community boundaries, a number of Nepperhan residents were disappointed that the community they had struggled to build was reduced to this symbol of racial intolerance and exclusion.

One longtime resident reflected the community's concern with media representations in his retelling of the history:

> When I was a kid, they used to separate Runyon Heights from Homefield. They used to have a chicken-wire fence up there. . . . The white

people used to come through our neighborhood to take the shortcut. We never had no problem, never had no problem. But you know a lot of people blew it up. A lot of people blows things up. Somebody had mentioned to a reporter about a chicken-wire fence, and all of a sudden the newspaper reporters started harping about the chicken-wire fence and all of that stuff. I said, yeah, it's always been there. . . . It just rotted away, it just rotted away.

Evidence suggests that a chicken-wire fence did exist along the strip, but that it was a feature left over from the estate's previous life as a farm. After World War II, many Homefield owners built homes bordering the strip and erected high fences, shielding the view of their homes from their Runyon Heights neighbors. Although high fences are commonplace throughout Homefield, they are unusual in Runyon Heights.

In fact, it was not the chicken-wire fence that symbolized segregation from Homefield but rather the existence of the reserve strip, which resulted in dead-end streets in Runyon Heights. This buffer zone, though invisible to the uninformed, nonetheless symbolized Homefield's racial exclusivity and rejection of its black neighbors. During my interviews, these dead-end streets were pointed out on numerous occasions. Paradoxically, Runyon residents today see these streets as a blessing in disguise. With the increase in vehicular traffic, community members are thankful that the streets do not allow Homefield residents a shortcut through Runyon Heights to Tuckahoe Road. In fact, access to Runyon Heights from Tuckahoe Road has virtually ended. Over the past fifteen years, the RHIA has succeeded in petitioning the city to block access to the community streets from Tuckahoe Road; Runyon Avenue was closed to two-way traffic from Tuckahoe Road, and a barrier was erected at the intersection of Altonwood Place and Tuckahoe Road. As a result, the isolation and relative seclusion of community streets allows children to play in their neighborhood with little fear. Once a symbol of racial exclusion and rejection, these streets have now become a symbol of community exclusivity and self-preservation.

The very labels of Nepperhan and Runyon Heights symbolize changing class aspirations in the community through the years. The two names adopted by residents for their community correspond to two distinct periods of land development in the area. The name Nepperhan, which meant "rapidly running water" to the indigenous Nappeckamack inhabitants, came to signify the rapid movement of people and freight in the modern era. When the area was home to a primarily working-class population, it took on the name of the local railroad; as middle-class gentrification began after World War II, the Runyon Heights name became more common.

The name Runyon Heights was actually used by residents as early as 1933 and has always included the "Old Nepperhan" area. The Runyon Heights Improvement Association and the Runyon Heights Democratic Club both adopted the name Runyon early in the community's formation. Other community groups used the Nepperhan name. Over the years, the two names have been used more or less interchangeably; however, today they sometimes carry distinct connotations of time and place. "Old-timers" tend to live on and be associated with the west side or old Nepperhan, newcomers with the east side, Runyon Heights, or "the Hill."

This shift in community characterization embodied in the changing nomenclature is even apparent in the way local roads were designed before and after World War II. The older western Nepperhan area is laid out in a classic grid pattern, typical of urban areas. Street names were similarly urban: First Street, Second Street, Wilson Avenue. At the same time, the Hill area has characteristically suburban winding streets with names like Chelsea, Lamar, and Drake Place. It is no coincidence that after World War II, the term of choice for the entire area was increasingly Runyon Heights, a name that evokes images of the wealthy industrialists whose exclusive estates once dotted the Westchester landscape. Though stratified by class and status, the entire area was nevertheless defined as a racial community. In the minds of residents as well as outsiders, Runyon Heights included all black residents in the area. Still, residents recognize, within this racially based definition of the Runyon Heights community, local status distinctions that embody real difference in material wealth. Inferences are often made on the basis of east-west geographic references.

One older woman spoke of the distinction between residents on the west side of Runyon Avenue and the railroad, on the one hand, and those on the Hill in the east, on the other. She was careful to make clear that these class divisions do not transcend the solidarity of the racial community. While positing race as superseding social status, her response reflects the significance of class in shaping status distinctions within the group. In a real sense, this resident appears to appreciate the social benefits gained from the recent gentrification of the area.

From the group we first had, I think we had a very ambitious group that made this community. They all moved from Harlem to this place because they wanted more, better, and freedom. . . . It looks like the tracks has divided, and mainly this side more business, you understand. That side is more residential. But like I said, we have judges, lawyers, doctors, and we have plenty of teachers, and we have plenty of social workers across the tracks. Because it's all Runyon Heights, 'cause when I say across the tracks, that area is more recently built up, so we have a very advanced community, I think. To me, now it's more professional.

The physical area in which the community of associations has developed in Runyon Heights is defined as "black space,"[2] by those both inside and outside the community. While local labels make distinctions that incorporate status, tenure, and locality, the racially segregated social life makes racial identity an integral part of community identity. The area is also imbued with a particular suburban, middle-class character. While residents recognize that financial, educational, and occupational status differences exist between those from Old Nepperhan and the Hill, the two groups characterize the entire Runyon Heights area as both middle-class and black. This generalization is based on the belief that home ownership in the community represents entry into middle-class society, while racial membership is determined by acceptance of the "one-drop rule." Part of what makes the community distinct in the minds of its residents is their perception of both racial and class homogeneity in Runyon Heights. In fact, Runyon Heights symbolizes the *black middle class* in Yonkers.

Early on, the Nepperhan–Runyon Heights community came to resemble what sociologist Gerald Suttles (1972) describes as a defended community. Community cohesion had been determined by the structural constraints placed on local residents by the larger environment. Residents who shared local territory also came to share a common fate (Suttles 1972, 35). The common fate of Runyon Heights residents was, however, shaped by race and class. Residential segregation encouraged social solidarity and fostered a community identity and a common history that tied Nepperhan residents to the belief in a shared fate.

By the 1920s, the community found it necessary to organize to oppose outside forces that threatened its way of life. School and labor issues came first. By the mid-1960s, business development and low-income housing challenged the area's suburban character. These issues continue to shape community politics in the 1990s. Community issues have been further compounded by solutions that have often brought unforeseen negative consequences. Although it is the socioeconomic character of the area that is threatened by outside forces, the mechanism for the production of social, economic, and political inequality has been explicitly racial.

As we saw in Chapter 7, there is a local and natural context that shapes feeling of common fate among residents in Runyon Heights, what Michael Dawson calls linked fate (61). Runyon Heights residents reacted independently to the racialized environments of national and local politics in the 1980s and 1990s. The Reagan years ushered in a period that included a reorganization of welfare policy, an abandonment of affirmative action policy, and the embracing of a "color-blind" model of government. The Reagan policies were overtly hostile toward the interests of Runyon Heights residents who were feeling the pinch of an economic recession. These factors combined to drive middle-class blacks in Runyon Heights toward liberal Democratic candidates in national elections. At the local level, racial polarization over housing and school desegration led to a shift to the Democratic ticket in the late 1980s.

The "black utility heuristic"[3] and the feeling of "linked fate" observed by Dawson are a product of changes in the relation of black communities to local and national political environments. In Runyon Heights, class interests were temporarily muted as race came to dominate political consciousness. In short, local and national racialized issues converged on the local community, leaving Democrats the clear preference for the 1990s electorate. In the 2000 presidential election, Republicans received a mere 10 percent of the black vote.

The social-class characteristics of the community are linked to race, and together race and class provide the sentiments necessary for community solidarity and defense. The invocation of racial sentimentality, which has often mistakenly been labeled primordial, takes place amid the structural forces that push and pull individuals into specific residential localities. Racialization has been a major force in shaping suburban development. Thus, in Runyon Heights, race makes place. Opposition from outside forces rather than "primordial" sentiments gives the defended community its solidarity. Racial consciousness is informed by the physical boundaries that define the community. Consequently, the reverse is also true: place makes race. The need for common history links race and place across time and space. Race becomes reified, disembodied, and ahistorical. Racial affinities and residential segregation seem natural.

The Runyon Heights community differs fundamentally from its white suburban counterpart because of racial subordination and the politicization of racial identity that subordination generates. While predominantly white communities use race as an exclusionary strategy, race becomes a major defining characteristic of any sense of community for blacks. Rather than declining in significance, race remains the focal point for community cohesion. When the community encountered the strongest threat to the local ecology and possibly its very existence, residents increasingly used race as a way to articulate community interests through local associations. Meanwhile, ardent support for social policies that specifically target black Americans reflects not only a trend toward liberalism but also the preeminence of race in the everyday lives of African Americans. Through the organization of segregated community life, race has come to shape the political identity of middle-class suburban residents.

Neither the racial homogeneity of the area nor the significance of race for the developing community identity was a natural phenomenon. Individuals came together not because of primordial attachments but because of the common experience of racial oppression and subordination. Objectively, the community contains both American-born and foreign-born individuals; people with pale skin, thin lips, and straight hair, and those with dark skin, thick lips and curly hair; those born in cities and those born on farms; and Protestants, Catholics, Muslims, and agnostics.

Although many Americans adopted the view that equality meant moving "across the tracks" to white areas, where better schools, homes, and services were available, in Yonkers moving to the "good" area often meant moving to Runyon Heights. Most black middle-class home seekers who ventured into predominantly white areas encountered strong resistance; when they did "integrate" white neighborhoods in Westchester, they often met with inhospitable neighbors. The continued middle-class black gentrification of Runyon Heights has been a direct result of these exclusionary practices.

In 1957, when E. Franklin Frazier wrote *Black Bourgeoisie,* race consciousness was seemingly on the decline, as the black middle class struggled to take advantage of a more open America. However, Frazier failed to see the resurgence of racial antagonisms and race consciousness in the 1960s. The period of cross-class Civil Rights agitation ended, ushering in a period of new opportunity for the black middle class in the 1970s. Following Frazier's lead, William J. Wilson (1978) again raised the question concerning the relative importance of race and class in predicting the life chances of black Americans. Like Frazier before him, Wilson made an argument consistent with the Chicago School model that maintained that class was increasing in significance in contemporary society and that the rational basis of group affiliations was breaking down. Although Wilson never argued that race was unimportant, he has often underemphasized race in his analysis of inequality, and his work has touched off a debate on the relative importance of race and class in the lives of middle-class black Americans (Wilson 1980, 1987, 1996).

But again during the 1980s and 1990s, racial antagonisms resurfaced, at both the local and the national levels, and were reflected on college campuses across the nation (Feagin and Vera 1995, 34–44). Racism has remained a fixture of American life, so race has remained significant to middle-class black Americans (Feagin and Vera 1995). Race comes to shape the most basic issues in the lives of many middle-class black Americans. When American troops were stationed in the Persian Gulf during Operation Desert Storm, the response by Runyon Heights residents was qualitatively different from that of other middle-class communities in Yonkers. While numerous Homefield residents adorned their front doors and yards with American flags in support of the nation and a scattering of yellow ribbons in support of the troops, Runyon Heights residents had blanketed their community with only yellow ribbons. There was not a single flag to be seen. With this gesture residents, while expressing their hope for the return of the U.S. troops, many of whom were black, made a clear statement that they saw the war itself as an unjust and unnecessary risk of black lives.

Similarly, the decision by blacks to seek out a predominantly black residential area has often been driven by parents' desire for a supportive psychological environment for their children. This is the reason traditionally given for other groups' selection of suburban neighborhoods (Suttles 1972, 38). Today, however, most Runyon Heights resident are not eager to live in predominantly white areas, nor would they be happy to see their neighborhood transformed. Rather than understanding the consequences of decades of black suburban exclusion, some tend to highlight the recent reluctance of the black middle class to pioneer in all-white neighborhoods. This has led many to conclude falsely that the black middle class has abandoned its liberal commitment to social integration.

Recent scholarship has indeed shown that blacks have become hesitant to be the first to desegregate all-white neighborhoods (Yinger 1995, 118).[4] One local black real estate agent did not even direct black home seekers to Runyon Heights. "But I really wasn't that interested in Runyon Heights per se: I was more interested in finding beautiful homes for black people in predominantly white areas."

Today, reluctance among blacks to live in predominantly white areas has been taken as a sign of their growing militancy or separatism and of a waning commitment to integration, but this analysis overlooks the fact that much of white middle-class suburban America has not accepted black neighbors, regardless of their class. This is blatantly obvious in many sections of Yonkers. What the black middle class has found is not the color-blind society envisioned by Martin Luther King, Jr., and proclaimed by the GOP but, rather, suspicion and resistance. Many Runyon Heights residents who once lived in predominantly white areas found only alienation there; the black middle-class enclave of Runyon Heights provides the institutional support and suburban environment that eluded them elsewhere. The self-conscious search for a black community by members of the middle class can be understood only in the context of ongoing white resistance.

Racial steering remains a critical factor now in the peopling of Runyon Heights, as it was yesteryear. A resident of seven years stated that realtors had directed him to Runyon Heights, although he was actually seeking housing in the predominantly white Colonial Heights section of Yonkers: "We didn't look for a house in Runyon Heights. We didn't do that. We were steered towards there by real estate folks, white real estate agents." They had been looking for a house that suited their needs, not a black or white area. Another current resident, born in Nepperhan in 1929, summed up the relationship between white real estate agents and blacks in Yonkers: "Discrimination was open, blatant, and customary."

The history of Nepperhan–Runyon Heights reveals how an aspiring homeowner class established and maintained a stable suburban community. Many characteristics of community success lay beyond the direct control of the local community, while other aspects were dependent upon community participation. First and foremost, residents acquired stable employment, which provided the necessary backbone for community life. Second, they had access to land that was zoned primarily for residential use. Third, they secured home mortgages from lending institutions. Fourth, ongoing resistance to black homeowners in other suburban areas provided Runyon Heights with a constant supply of new prospective homeowners, as well as fresh financial and intellectual resources. Fifth, active participation in both formal and informal political forums provided residents with considerable leverage in local elections. Sixth, a strong sense of racial identity evolved in reaction to racial subordination and provided the glue for community organization and mobilization. The relatively homogeneous class background of the area's residents aided in the creation of this race-centered group consciousness.

The dynamic interaction among these characteristics allowed the anomalous suburban black community of Runyon Heights to grow and even prosper. The same forces that led many foreign-born and native-born blacks to Harlem, channeled them into service and menial jobs, and opened limited opportunities in the suburban housing market were also the forces that impressed upon those residents the need for minimizing cultural, religious, and national differences. The history of the community also reveals the tensions between racial subordination and American democracy. While members of the black middle-class community pursued the dream of self-sufficient individualism, racial antagonism and discrimination prevented them from abandoning a racialized worldview. Runyon Heights residents have, as yet, been unable to "afford" to give up race and simply be individuals. As scholars from the left and right champion the notion of a raceless society, Runyon Heights is a testament to the enduring legacy of racialization.

Notes

Introduction

1. The Dutch later renamed the river De Zaag Kill, which translates as "the Saw Creek"; the English translation became "the Sawmill" (Allison 1984, 14–15, 128). Today the river is referred to as both the Nepperhan and the Saw Mill.

2. The terms "Negro," "black," and "African American" refer to the same populations of African descent in the United States. Occasionally, I use the historically appropriate terms, in an effort to convey the social and cultural context. See Chapter 4 for further discussion of racial classifications in the United States.

3. Racialization has been defined as a historically specific ideological process that extends racial meaning to a previously unclassified relationship, social practice, or group (Omi and Winant 1986, 64; Winant 1994, 59).

4. See the decision of United States District Court Southern District of New York State: *USA and Yonkers Branch of NAACP et al. v Yonkers Board of Education, City of Yonkers, and Yonkers Community Development Agency*, 80 CIV 6761 (LBS), 1985.

5. U.S. Census of Population, 1990.

6. Median family income in current dollars from *1996 Statistical Abstract*, Table 732, p. 474.

7. Even Williams's (1987) study of industrial workers focuses on the work environment and pays little attention to black suburban community development.

8. Historian Kenneth Jackson's classic study of American suburbanization, *Crabgrass Frontier: The Suburbanization of the United States* (1985) is a notable exception. See his chapter 11, "Federal Subsidy and the American Dream: How Washington Changed the American Housing Market," for a thorough discussion of race and federal housing policy.

9. Two principal sources of data were used in this study. Ethnographic information was gathered through field research, using the observer-as-participant model (Gold 1969, 30–39). Thirty-five residents, selected through a snowball sample, described their personal, family, and community histories in in-depth interviews. Lofland and Lofland (1995) have called this technique "intensive interviewing," but it is generally referred to as "unstructured interviewing." A majority of the residents with the longest tenure in the community are a part of the sample. Interviews with residents have been supplemented by interviews with former residents, community leaders, city officials, and local historians.

    The thirty-five residents interviewed in depth possessed the following characteristics: the sample is 46 percent male and 54 percent female; 97 percent own their own homes. They average 13.8 years of education and 39 years of residency in Runyon Heights. Ages range from twenty-seven to ninety-seven, and the average age is sixty-one. Twenty-five percent possessed some Caribbean ancestry, and 29 percent were born and reared in the community.

    The second source of information is historical records, including census data, local newspapers, deed records, land records, voter-registration and election records.

10. For one exception, see Irma Watkins-Owens, *Blood Relations: Caribbean Immigrants and the Harlem Community, 1900–1930.*

Chapter 1: Race and Place in Industrial Yonkers

1. Getty Square, a Yonkers landmark, is at the intersection of five streets in the downtown section of the city: Palisades Avenue, North Broadway, South Broadway, Main Street, and New Main Street.

2. In 1928, Habirshaw consolidated with Phelps Dodge Copper Products Corporation, taking on the latter's name.

3. Winner of the Organization of American Historians' Merle Curti Prize for U.S. Social History 1990–91.

4. (Galenson 1986, 44–57). Although not one major union has had a black president since the founding of the labor movement in the 1880s, a number of black vice presidents appeared after World War II. A. Philip Randolph and Willard Townsend became vice presidents following the AFL-CIO merger (Raskin 1986, 16).

5. Bogart (1898) Table 7, Nationality of Families.

6. Bogart (1898) Table 8, Occupations of Adults.

7. Bogart failed to obtain data on John Street, which, interestingly, is the street with the highest Negro concentration. One can only surmise that wages on

this street were relatively low. Vineyard is excluded because only one family of 173 is identified as colored.

8. For a discussion of the cumulative economic impact of racialization, see Melvin L. Oliver and Thomas M. Shapiro's *Black Wealth, White Wealth: A New Perspective on Racial Inequality,* and Dalton Conley's *Being Black, Living in the Red.*

9. Moultrie (Merril) Avenue in Runyon Heights was named after Francis J. Moultrie.

10. The 1920 U.S. Census manuscripts and the New York State Census manuscripts for 1925 show no listing of these occupations for black workers. The first Negro policeman was Thomas Brooks, who was appointed in 1925. The first Negro firemen was Curtis G. Giddings, appointed in 1942, by which time Yonkers still had only two black police officers (see *Herald Statesman,* "Curtis Giddings to Become Yonkers' First Negro Fireman," Feb. 18, 1942). It was not until the 1940s that the first Negro nurse to work in Yonkers General Hospital (interview manuscripts; see also Bogart, 1898).

11. See also microfilm no. scmicro R-3700 ("28 Miscellaneous Schomburg Titles"), "Hudson-Fulton Souvenir Celebration, 1909," the Schomburg Collection, New York City Public Library.

Chapter 2: The Peopling of Nepperhan

1. Libre of Deeds 791, p. 302. Libre of Deeds and Libre of Mortgages are filed with the Westchester County Department of Land Records, 110 Court Street, White Plains, New York.

2. See Libre of Deeds 802, p. 315, and no. 895, p. 233, for sale to Reuben Van Pelt. See Libre of Deeds 811, p. 65, for sale to School District No. 1, Yonkers.

3. Westchester County Department of Land Records.

4. Libre of Deeds 1902, p. 208.

5. See Libre of Deeds 1764, p. 13. See also the "Second Amended Map of Part of the Runyon Estate," filed with the county in 1912, as well as the "Map of Nepperhan Gardens, Nepperhan Station, City of Yonkers, N.Y.," filed in 1927 by the Nepperhan Home Building Corporation. Land Subdivision Maps are filed with the Westchester County Department of Land Records, White Plains, New York.

6. The then newly constructed Croton Aqueduct Easement provides a convenient landmark, because it was cut through the community close to the Fowler-Runyon estate borders—to observe this, compare the Planning Bureau maps of 1907 with the subdivision maps mentioned earlier.

7. The Sarah E. Baxter School for Girls, located on Tuckahoe Road between Altonwood Place and Runyon Avenue, also owned a few lots on the corner of Saw Mill River Road and Kenmore Street (formerly Third Street). Although they are shown on city planning department maps of 1907, neither the school nor the Baxter land was in existence by 1914. On maps dated 1931, the Mary E. Johnson Boarding School for Girls appeared where the Baxter School had once stood.

8. The church took possession of the small one-and-a-half acre parcel in the late 1800s. The land was eventually converted into an extension of the cemetery, where the first burial took place in 1946.

9. See Libre of Deeds 1971, pp. 154, 158.

10. Libre of Deeds 2019, p. 419.

11. Advertising brochures for lots in Homefield, published by the Homeland Corporation, depicted the landscape of the surrounding area. The drawing excluded the Nepperhan community, while clearly showing School 1.

12. Reference librarians at the New York Public Library's Schomburg Center for Research in Black Culture informed me that the earliest issue available anywhere in the country—including at the Library of Congress or the archives of the *Amsterdam News*—was for November 29, 1922.

13. Libre of Deeds 1764, pp. 13–15.

14. Libre of Mortgage 1412, pp. 388–89.

15. Libre of Deeds 2144, p. 460. Libre of Deeds 2159, p. 192.

16. Libre of Deeds 4457, p. 162.

17. Libre of Deeds 1980, p. 9.

18. Rose's son, an eighty-year-old resident of Florida when I interviewed him in 1996, stated that he had little knowledge of his father's real estate ventures, although, as late as the mid-1960s, he was still selling parcels of Runyon land he had inherited.

19. See Libre of Deeds 2170, p. 233.

20. See Libre of Deeds 2072, p. 150.

21. On September 25, 1993, the matriarch of the Perencheif family was recognized publicly at the Second Nepperhan Reunion Day for having resided in the community for the longest time.

22. For a general discussion of residents' resistance toward Negroes in Westchester County, see David Johnson's "Working for Fair Housing," *Herald Statesman*, March 4, 1990, p. J1; and "In Accord, Black and Hispanic Families Would Be Offered Westchester Homes," *New York Times*, April 1, 1993, p. B6. For a discussion of resistance to Negroes in the Park Hill section of Yonkers, see *Herald Statesmen*, May 5, 1939, p. 1, May 22, 1939, p. 1, and May 19, 1939, pp. 1 and 2. For a discussion of resistance to Negro employment see *Amsterdam News*, July 29, 1925, p. 1. For a discussion of residential barriers and resistance encountered by Negroes in the city of Yonkers, see the U.S. District Court Southern District of New York State ruling in USA and Yonkers Branch of NAACP et al. v. Yonkers Board of Education, City of Yonkers, and Yonkers Community Development Agency, 80 CIV 6761 (LBS), 1985.

23. See Monte Williams, "Blast Hits Car After Man Sells to Blacks," *New York Times*, May 15, 1997, p. B12.

24. *New York Age*, July 3, 1926, 1.

25. "Mortgage Lending Bias Clear as Black and White." *New York Daily News*, October 27, 1994, p. 61. (See also Oliver and Shapiro 1995, pp. 19–20.)

26. Libre of Deeds 3459, pp. 390–93.

27. Toussaint-Louverture, born François-Dominique Toussaint (1743?–1803), led Haiti to independence from French rule.
28. See map 267, filed with the Westchester County Bureau of Land Records.

Chapter 3: Working-Class Roots

1. There were two other hospitals in the Tenth Ward on Sprain Road. The municipal hospital housed fifty-six persons, and the Scarlet Fever Hospital 35, none of them black.
2. Although "Negro" was the category used in the compilation of federal census reports, census enumerators actually used the symbols "W" (white) and "B" (black or brown) on the manuscript tables they filed for racial designation. The category on the manuscripts was "Color or race." We can conclude that "B" and "Negro" were treated as interchangeable terms by census enumerators.
3. For the number of residents see Table 4, "Population of Wards of Cities and Villages Having 5,000 Inhabitants or More: 1920, U.S. Federal Census."
4. Federal census manuscripts, 1920, Tenth Ward, Third District.
5. In the 1920 census manuscripts, occupational data on two heads of household were either missing or destroyed, although other information was available on those individuals.
6. Because federal census data for 1930 through 1960 were recorded only at the ward level and not at the census-tract level, occupation and ancestry for those years are currently unavailable. Federal census manuscripts remain confidential for a period of seventy- two years; the 1930 manuscripts will not become public until the year 2002.
7. Bronxville was a particularly popular area.
8. Bray wrote an article called "Progress of the Negroes of Yonkers," published in the *Souvenir History of Yonkers,* issued by the Fiftieth Anniversary Celebration Committee, 1872–1922 (Yonkers, N.Y.: Fernhead and Bleakley, 1922).
9. Reynolds Farley, "West Indian Success: Myth or Fact," unpublished manuscript (Ann Arbor, MI: Population Studies Center, University of Michigan, 1987); Nancy Foner, "West Indians in New York City and London: A Comparative Analysis," in Constance R. Sutton and Elsa M. Chaney, eds.,*Caribbean Life in New York City* (New York: Center for Migration Studies of New York, 1987); Roy Simon Bryce-Laporte, "New York City and the New Caribbean Immigration: A Contextual Statement," *International Migration Review* 13:2 (1979).

Chapter 4: E Pluribus Unum

1. "Hypo-descent" was used by the Nazis to determine who was Jewish. According a 1933 decree, having a Jewish parent or grandparent made one Jewish (Johnson, 1987: 486–87). Yet this rule proved flexible, and an intermediary category between Jew and German was created that paralleled the mulatto category in the United States. Some *Mischlings,* or part Jews, were eventually incorporated into the Nazi state bureaucracy in a way similar to the way in which American mulattoes passed as whites. The racist logic of racial descent

under Nazi rule, which led to the death camps, paralleled ideas about race that had already found acceptance in the United States.

2. Evidence does suggest that light skin and other physical features can be correlated with economic advantage (Keith and Herring, 1991).

3. Frazier 1962, 99, 164–65. It is interesting that early studies of Negroes by W. E. B. Du Bois, Charles Johnson, George Haynes, and others emphasized the racial hybridization of the new Negro.

4. Some scholars estimate that as many as a quarter of so-called white Americans possess at least one African ancestor (Yinger 1995, 8).

5. From the prospectus of the Invincible Order of Colored Co-Operators of America, Schomburg Library, scmicro R-3700.

Chapter 5: The Prewar Years

1. Runyon's obituary in the October 14, 1903, edition of the *New York Times* helps clarify the record:

> During the last forty-five years he [Charles Runyon] had been in business in this city, his start having been made with the Union Rubber Company, of which he was Secretary and Treasurer. Later he was with the firm of Randolph Brothers, which firm he left to become Secretary and Treasurer to the Superior Mountain Coal Company.
>
> Mr. Runyon was instrumental in organizing the Hoboken Coal Company, of which he became the head. The Communipaw Coal Company was his next venture, and since its organization (until his death) he had been the President. Mr. Runyon married Isabel E. Randolph, a niece of former Gov. Randolph of New Jersey. A wife, a daughter, and three sons survive him.

2. Interestingly, the City of Yonkers Planning Bureau did in fact receive proposals for subdivisions in the eastern section of Runyon Heights modeled after the grid pattern typical of the early metropolis, and typical of the streets on the west side of the community. Instead of the grid layout, the more rustic pattern of curving streets, common in many post–World War II suburbs, was adopted in the east as well as in the neighboring Homefield community.

3. The original structure on Kenmore Street has recently undergone renovation and expansion, reflecting the growth of the congregation over the years.

4. Allison (1984) reports the founding as May 1870, although church records indicate a date of May 1871. Institutional AME Zion was originally named Memorial AME Zion. The name had changed by the time the cornerstone was laid for its second building, in 1924.

5. Each district is headed by a presiding elder. The fourth Episcopal district includes the New York, New England, Western New York, and Bahamas Conferences. The New York Conference includes the Hudson River, Long Island, and Brooklyn Districts. The Hudson River District encompasses the lower Hudson River Valley, including Yonkers. Metropolitan is a part of the Hudson River

District of the New York Conference, which is a part of the fourth Episcopal district.

6. Frazier reports that Bishop James W. Hood was elected president of a convention of Negroes in North Carolina, which may have been the first such convention for newly freed Negroes after the Civil War. In addition, Hood served as local magistrate and later as deputy collector of internal revenue for the United States (Frazier 1974, 48).

7. It seems possible that Anna Borden and Millie Smile were related by marriage. It was reported that Charles Borden was the brother-in-law of Rev. Smile. Assuming that Anna and Charles were husband and wife, we may conclude either that Anna was Rev. Smile's sister or that Charles Borden had a sister who married a brother of Rev. Smile; however, no other Borden or Smiles family members are recorded as ever having been involved in Nepperhan.

8. Mount Olivet was known as a "shouting" church and had established the first all-Negro YMCA in the nation in 1899.

9. Note that even during this early period, both the Nepperhan and Runyon Heights names were used by area residents.

10. Today the community center, still called the Nepperhan Community Center, is located on Warburton Avenue near Point Street, a short walk from the nineteenth-century west side Negro settlement discussed in Chapter 1.

11. Mrs. Downs, Mrs. Bookman, Mrs. Jackson, Mr. and Mrs. Bonner, and Mr. and Mrs. John Fields led the battle.

12. Italian Americans interviewed in Nepperhan seemed completely outside community politics until a few joined the community center in the 1980s.

13. See William Julius Wilson, *The Declining Significance of Race: Blacks and Changing American Institutions* (1980), and the subsequent debates that the book generated when it was first published in 1978.

Chapter 6: The Postwar Years

1. Rev. Wyatt T. Walker, civil rights leader and Harlem minister, was also an early resident of Homefield.

2. That Leonard Morgan was also an early president of the RHIA is an indication of the highly integrated nature of community organizations.

3. Information obtained from an interview with Phil Schaap, fall 1998.

4. The Grand United Order of Odd Fellows Hero Lodge No. 1520, was instituted in 1872 in Yonkers. In August 1884, the order called Queen of the North, No. 330, of the Household of Ruth branched away from the Odd Fellows. None of the residents interviewed recalled having any family members with connections to these two groups. Membership was drawn primarily from West Yonkers. These branches of the Masons and the Odd Fellows were black counterparts of the white fraternal organizations.

5. The availability from 1930 to 1970 of census data on the community only at the level of wards makes demographic changes difficult to assess. In my analysis of this period, I rely heavily on interview material.

6. Esannason and Bagwell (1993, 28) report that Dr. Morgan, the second black physician in Harlem, moved his successful practice to Yonkers in 1905, becoming Yonkers' first black doctor.

7. A system of highways was built, beginning in the early 1920s, which helped to usher in a new era of consumption and suburban growth. Parkways, designed to capture the bucolic feel of rural landscapes, often followed the course of rivers, winding through the hilly terrain of the lower Hudson Valley. The first roadway built exclusively for cars was the Bronx River Parkway, completed in 1923. The Hutchinson River Parkway was completed in 1928, and the Saw Mill River Parkway in 1929. All three parkways increased automobile access southward to New York and northward to upper Westchester. The Cross County Parkway, dedicated in 1931, supplied access from the east and west through Yonkers. After World War II, the New York State Throughway and the Sprain Brook Parkway expanded access even farther north.

8. Westchester County Historical Society vertical files, Yonkers Trolley.

9. *United States of America and Yonkers Branch-National Association for the Advancement of Colored People et al. v Yonkers Board of Education, City of Yonkers, and Yonkers Community Development Agency,* Opinion 80 CIV 6761 (LBS).

10. See Raymond Hernandez, "N.A.A.C.P. Suspends Yonkers Head: Doubts over Usefulness of School Busing Cited," *New York Times,* November 1, 1995, p. B1; *Reporter Despatch* October 29, 1995, Metro Section, p. 11, "NAACP Retreats from Criticism of School Busing," and October 31, 1995, Metro Section, p. 2, "Yonkers NAACP President Suspended for Busing Stand."

11. Both the Urban League and the NAACP have supported the Runyon Heights community and have often rallied to its defense. This support may be attributed to the fact that both associations are linked to the community. The congregations of both Baptist and Methodist churches in Yonkers back the local civil rights organizations. Thus, strong organizational links have been formed through dual membership or affiliation. In addition, the active leadership roles a number of Runyon Heights residents have held in the local NAACP and Urban League interlock the community further with these traditional civil rights organizations.

12. Organizers: Adele Mingo, Mr. and Mrs. Edward B. Smith, Norman Downs, Ora Curtain, George W. Bonner, Thomas Keno, Frank Hurley, Jack Moore, Milton Holst, Fred Taylor, Eugene W. Smith, Elise Williamson, and John Bryant. Penny socials and tea parties were held to raise funds for the construction and operation of the center.

13. Since that time, the county of Westchester has purchased the railroad right of way from Conrail to preserve the land as a hiking and bicycle path. The 175 acres of land were reportedly acquired for $2.1 million.

14. In 1965, Herbert G. Martin, Inc., an electrical contractor, was one of the first to set up shop at 60 Runyon Avenue. In 1974, Otto Brehm, Inc., a bakery supply company, relocated from downtown Yonkers to 75 Tuckahoe Road, near the Tuckahoe Road Bridge and the old Nepperhan Station. Pecora Construction Company moved into the area around 1978, taking over the site at 76 Runyon

Avenue. Mase Electric, Inc., which began operation around 1979, was located at 24 Runyon Avenue. Other businesses came but did not stay. Miracle Plywood, one of the last to use the railroad for freight, moved to 44 Runyon Avenue in 1980 but left in 1993. Both Medicab and Gerrasi Bros., Inc., came and left during the 1970s and 1980s. Badia Spices, Inc., taking over the former location of Gerrasi, came to the strip during the summer of 1994. Tristate Warehouse Distributors took over the Miracle Plywood site in 1993.

15. Article 3, sections 107–11 of *The Code of the City of Yonkers* (Rochester, New York: General Code Publishers Corporation, 1993).

16. The women's club the Monte Carloites was originally named the Monte Carloite Debs. After most members married, they dropped "debs" from their name.

17. For a discussion of "old heads," see Elijah Anderson's *Streetwise* (1990).

Chapter 7: Eisenhower Republicans and Republican Democrats

1. Westchester County Archive has maintained voter registration data, beginning in 1929. No earlier records exist in the county.

2. In May of 2000, the U.S. Supreme Court let stand an appellate court ruling that the state must pay nearly $85 million per year to offset the cost of busing and magnet schools. Still at issue is another $1.1 billion to remedy damage from the "vestiges of segregation." See David W. Chen (2000).

Chapter 8: Defining Black Space

1. United States District Court Southern District of New York. United States of America and Yonkers Branch National Association for the Advancement of *Colored People et al. v Yonkers Board of Education;* city of Yonkers; and Yonkers Community Development Agency. Opinion 80 CIV 6761 (LBS).

2. Sigelman and Welch (1991) report that blacks prefer the term "black" over "African-American" 66 percent to 22 percent. Indeed, in Runyon Heights, "black" is the term most often used in conversation.

3. The black utility heuristic "simply states that as long as African Americans' life choices are powerfully shaped by race, it is efficient for individual African Americans to use their perceptions of the interests of African Americans as a group as a proxy for their own interests" (Dawson, 1994, 61).

4. In Brooklyn, New York, for example, a small but growing middle-class black population can be found in the working-class communities of Flatbush, Jamaica, and Brooklyn Heights.

References

Alba, Richard D., and John Logan. "Minority Proximity to Whites in Suburbs: An Individual Level Analysis." *American Journal of Sociology* vol. 98, no. 2 (May 1993), 1388–1427.

Allen, James E. *The Negro in New York: A Historical-Biographical Evaluation from 1626.* New York: Exposition Press, 1964.

Allison, Charles E. *History of Yonkers.* Harrison, N.Y.: Harbor Hill Books, [1896] 1984.

Anderson, Elijah. *Streetwise: Race, Class, and Change in and Urban Community.* Chicago: University of Chicago Press, 1990.

———. *A Place on the Corner.* Chicago: University of Chicago Press, 1976.

Barlow, Anthony. Unpublished manuscript "The Put: Story of the Putnam Railroad." Westchester Historical Society, Yonkers, N.Y., call number HOB 420, pamphlet no. 2, 1980.

Barnes, Annie S. *The Black Middle-Class Family.* Briston, Ind.: Wyndham Hill Press, 1985.

Bell, Michael J. *The World from Brown's Lounge.* Chicago: University of Illinois Press, 1983.

Berger, Bennett. *Working-Class Suburb.* Los Angeles: University California Press, 1968.

Berger, Joseph. "In Accord Black and Hispanic Families Would Be Offered Westchester Homes." *New York Times,* Apr. 1, 1993, B6.

Beveridge, Andrew, and Jeannie D'Amico. "Black and White Homeowner Cost: An Analysis." Unpublished paper. Department of Sociology, Queens College, New York, 1994.

Bittle, William E., and Gilbert L. Geis. "Racial Self-Fulfillment and the Rise of the All-Negro Community in Oklahoma." In *The Making of Black America: Essays in Negro Life and History,* August Meier and Elliott Rudwick, eds. New York: Atheneum, 1969.

Blalock, Hubert M., Jr. *Toward a Theory of Minority-Group Relations.* New York: Wiley, 1967.

Blassingame, John W. *The Slave Community: Plantation Life in the Antebellum South.* New York: Oxford University Press, 1972.

Bogart, Ernest Ludlow. *The History of the Working People in Yonkers.* American Economic Association Economic Studies, vol. 3, no. 5 (1898). Available at Butler Library, Columbia University.

Brooks, Clem, and Jeff Manza. "The Social and Ideological Bases of Middle-Class Political Realignment in the United States, 1972–1992." *American Sociological Review* 62(2), 191–208 (1997).

"Charles Runyon." *New York Times* (Obituaries), Oct. 14, 1903, 9.

Chen, David W. "State Remains Liable for Half of Yonkers' Integration Costs." *New York Times,* May 23, 2000, B8.

Clark, Kenneth. *Dark Ghetto: Dilemmas of Social Power.* New York: Harper and Row, 1965.

The Code of the City of Yonkers. Sections 107–11, "Zoning." Rochester, N.Y.: General Code Publishers Corporation, 1993.

Collas, Sara F. "Transgressing Racial Boundaries: The Maintenance of the Racial Order." Paper presented at American Sociological Association Meetings, Los Angeles, Calif., August 8, 1994.

Collins, Sharon. *Black Corporate Executives: The Making and Breaking of a Black Middle Class.* Philadelphia, Pa.: Temple University Press, 1997.

Conley, Dalton. *Being Black, Living in the Red.* Berkeley, Calif.: University of California Press, 1999.

Connolly, Harold X. "Black Movements into the Suburbs: Suburbs Doubling Their Black Population During the 1960s." *Urban Affairs Quarterly* 9 (Sept. 1973).

Cose, Ellis. *The Rage of a Privileged Class.* New York: HarperCollins, 1993.

Cox, Oliver C. *Caste, Class, and Race.* New York: Monthly Review, 1948.

Davidoff, Paul, and Mary E. Brooks. "Zoning Out the Poor." In *Suburbia:*

References

The American Dream and Dilemma, Philip C. Dolce, ed., 135–66. New York: Anchor, 1976.

Davis, Allison, Burleigh B. Gardner, and Mary R. Gardner. *Deep South.* Chicago: University of Chicago Press, 1941.

Davis, F. James. *Who Is Black? One Nation's Definition.* State College, Pa: Pennsylvania State University Press, 1991.

Davis, Richard A. "Ethnic Mythology: If Scholars Define a Myth as Real, It Can Have Real Consequences." *Race and Society* vol. 1, no. 1 (1998), 93–103.

Dawson, Michael C. *Behind the Mule: Race and Class in African-American Politics.* Princeton, N.J.: Princeton University Press, 1994.

Dollard, John. *Caste and Class in a Southern Town.* New York: Harper and Row, [1937] 1949.

Dominguez, Virginia R. *White by Definition,* New Brunswick, N.J.: Rutgers University Press, 1986.

Douglas, Paul. *The Suburban Trend.* New York: Arno Press, 1968.

Downs, Anthony. *Opening Up the Suburbs.* New Haven, Conn.: Yale University Press, 1978.

Drake, St. Clair, and Horace Cayton. *Black Metropolis.* New York: Harper and Row, 1962.

Du Bois, W. E. B. *The Philadelphia Negro.* Millwood, New York: Kraus-Tomson Organization, [1899] 1973.

Edwards, G. Franklin, ed. *E. Franklin Frazier on Race Relations.* Chicago: University of Chicago Press, 1968.

Esannason, Harold A., and Vinnie Bagwell. *A Study of African-American Life in Yonkers from the Turn of the Century.* Elmsford, N.Y.: Harold A. Esannason, 1993. Prepared under a UDAG Grant from the NAACP and the Community Development Agency of Yonkers.

Farley, Reynolds. *Blacks and Whites: Narrowing the Gap.* Cambridge, Mass.: Harvard University Press, 1984.

———. "The Changing Distribution of Negroes Within Metropolitan Areas: The Emergence of Black Suburbs." *American Journal of Sociology* 75 (Jan. 1970).

———, and Walter Allen. *The Color Line and the Quality of Life in America.* New York: Oxford University Press, 1987.

Farley, Reynolds, Howard Schuman, Suzanne Bianchi, Diane Colosanto, and Shirley Hatchett. "'Chocolate City, Vanilla Suburbs': Will the Trend Towards Racially Separate Communities Continue?" *Social Science Research* 7 (1978).

Feagin, Joe R., *White Racism.* New York: Routledge Press, 1995.

―――, and Melvin Sikes. *Living with Racism: The Black Middle-Class Experience.* New York: Beacon Press, 1994.

Fein, Helen. *Imperial Crime and Punishment: The Massacre of Jallianwall Bagh and British Judgement, 1919–1920.* Honolulu: University of Hawaii Press, 1977.

Fields, Barbara J. "Ideology and Race in American History." In *Region, Race, and Reconstruction: Essays in Honor of C. Vann Woodward,* J. Morgan Kousser and James M. McPherson, eds., 183–208. New York: Oxford University Press, 1982.

Fitz-Gibbon. "Father Divine Followers Fight Landmark Status for Home." *Herald Statesman,* 10A, Jan. 7, 1993.

Foner, Nancy. "The Jamaicans: Race and Ethnicity Among Migrants in New York City." In *New Immigrants in New York,* Nancy Foner, ed. New York: Columbia University Press, 1987.

Ford, Richard Thompson. "The Boundaries of Race: Political Geography in Legal Analysis." *Critical Race Theory,* Kimberle Crenshaw, Neil Gotanda, Gary Peller, and Kendall Thomas, eds., 449–64. New York: New Press, 1995.

Frazier, E. Franklin. *The Negro Church in America.* New York: Schocken Books, [1964] 1974.

―――. *Black Bourgeoisie.* New York: Macmillan. [1957] 1962.

―――. *The Negro in the United States.* New York: Macmillan, 1949.

―――. *The Negro Family in the United States.* Chicago: University of Chicago Press, 1939.

Galenson, Walter. "The Historical Role of American Trade Unionism." In *Unions in Transition,* Seymour Martin Lipset, ed., 39–73. San Francisco: Institute for Contemporary Studies, 1986.

Gamson, William A. "Hiroshima, the Holocaust and the Politics of Exclusion." *American Sociological Review* 60 (1) (Feb. 1995).

Gans, Herbert J. *The Urban Villagers: Group and Class in the Life of Italian-Americans.* New York: Free Press, [1962] 1982.

―――. *The Levittowners.* New York: Pantheon Books, 1967.

Glazer, Nathan, and Daniel Patrick Moynihan. *Beyond the Melting Pot: The Negroes, Puerto Ricans, Jews, Italians, and Irish of New York City.* 2d ed. Cambridge, Mass.: MIT Press, [1963] 1970.

Gregory, Stephen. *Black Corona: Race and the Politics of Place in an Urban Community.* Princeton, N.J.: Princeton University Press, 1998.

Gold, Raymond L. "Roles in Sociological Field Observation." In *Issues in*

References

Participant Observation, George J. McCall and J. L. Simmons, eds. Reading, Mass.: Addison-Wesley, 1969.

Goldberg, David Theo. "The New Segregation." *Race and Society* 1 (1), 15–32, 1998.

Goldston, Robert. *Suburbia: Civic Denial.* New York: Macmillan, 1970.

Gossett, Thomas F. *Race: The History of an Idea.* New York: Schocken Books, (1965) 1971.

Gould, Stephen J. *The Mismeasure of Man.* New York: W. W. Norton, 1981.

Gramsci, Antonio. *Selections from the Prison Notebooks of Antonio Gramsci,* Quintin Hoare and Geoffrey Nowell Smith, eds. New York: International Publishers, 1971.

Green, Charles, and Basil Wilson. *The Struggle for Black Empowerment in New York City.* New York: McGraw-Hill, 1992.

Guest, Avery. "The Changing Racial Composition of Suburbs, 1950–1970." *Urban Affairs Quarterly* 14 (Dec. 1978).

Hacker, Andrew. *Two Nations: Black and White, Separate, Hostile, Unequal.* New York: Ballantine Books, 1992.

Hall, Stuart. "Gramsci's Relevance for the Study of Race and Ethnicity." Reprinted in *Stuart Hall: Critical Dialogues in Cultural Studies,* David Morley and Kuan-Hsing Chen, eds. New York: Routledge, 1996a.

———. "What Is This 'Black' in Black Popular Culture?" Reprinted in *Stuart Hall: Critical Dialogues in Cultural Studies,* David Morley and Kuan-Hsing Chen, eds. New York: Routledge, 1996b.

Halliburton, Warren J. *A Pictoral Story of Yonkers and Its People.* Yonkers Board of Education, 1987.

Herrnstein, Richard J., and Charles Murray. *The Bell Curve: Intelligence and Class Structure in American Life.* New York: Free Press, 1994.

Hershberg, Theodore, Alan N. Burstein, Eugene P. Ericksen, Stephanie Greenberg, and William Yancey. "A Tale of Three Cities: Blacks, Immigrants, and Opportunity in Philadelphia, 1850–1880, 1930, and 1970." *Annals of the American Academy of Political and Social Science* 441 (Jan. 1979).

Higginbotham, Evelyn Brooks. "African-American Women's History and the Metalanguage of Race." In *Feminism and History,* Joan Scott, ed. New York: Oxford University Press, 1996.

"Home Development for Negroes Changed to White Community As Builders Cannot Get Montages Placed with Investors." *New York Age* 1 (July 3, 1926).

Jackson, Kenneth. *Crabgrass Frontier.* New York: Oxford University Press, 1985.

Jaynes, Gerald David, and Robin M. Williams. *A Common Destiny: Blacks and American Society.* Washington, D.C.: National Academy Press, 1989.

Johnson, Charles S. *Backgrounds to Patterns of Negro Segregation.* N.Y.: Thomas Y. Crowell Company, 1943.

Johnson, Paul. *A History of the Jews.* New York: Harper and Row, 1987.

Johnson, Yolanda, Mary E. Lawson, Lillian Reilly, Loraine Spencer, Ethel Thibault, and Emelyn Webster. *Yonkers Through the Years.* Yonkers, N.Y.: Yonkers Board of Education, 1962.

Kaplan, Samuel. "Them Blacks in Suburbia." *New York Affairs* 3 (Winter 1976).

Kasinitz, Philip. *Caribbean New York: Black Immigrants and the Politics of Race.* Ithaca, N.Y.: Cornell University Press, 1992.

Keith, Verna M., and Cedric Herring. "Skin Tone and Stratification in the Black Community." *American Journal of Sociology* 97 (3), 760–78.

Kelly, Robin D. G. *Race Rebels: Culture, Politics, and the Black Working Class.* New York: Free Press, 1994.

Kronus, Sidney. *The Black Middle Class.* Columbus, Ohio: Charles E. Merrill, 1971.

Kruger-Kahloula, Angelika. "On the Wrong Side of the Fence: Racial Segregation in American Cemeteries." In *History and Memory in African-American Culture,* Genevieve Fabre and Robert O'Meally, eds. New York: Oxford University Press, 1994.

Kunkel, Peter, and Sara Sue Kennard. *Spout Spring: A Black Community.* New York: Holt, Rinehart and Winston, 1971.

Lake, Robert W. *The New Suburbanites: Race and Housing in the Suburbs.* Center for Urban Policy Research, 1981.

Landry, Bart. *The New Black Middle Class.* Berkeley: University of California Press, 1987.

Lewis, David Levering. *When Harlem Was in Vogue.* New York: Oxford University Press, 1981.

Lewis, Hylan. *Blackways of Kent.* Chapel Hill: University of North Carolina Press, 1955.

Lincoln, C. Eric. *The Black Church Since Frazier.* New York: Schocken, 1974.

Lofland, John, and Lyn H. Lofland. *Analyzing Social Settings.* Belmont, Calif.: Wadsworth, [1971] 1995.

Logan, John R., and Gordana Rabrenovic. "Neighborhood Associations:

References

Their Issues, Their Allies, and Their Opponents." *Urban Affairs Quarterly* 26 (1), 68–94.

MacDonald, John S., and Leatrice D. MacDonald. "Chain Migration, Ethnic Neighborhoods, and Social Networks." *Milbank Memorial Fund Quarterly* 42 (1964), 82–97.

Marshall, Adriana. "New Immigrants in New York's Economy." In *New Immigrants in New York,* Nancy Foner, ed. New York: Columbia University Press, 1987.

Massey, Douglas. "American Apartheid: Segregation and the Making of the Underclass." *American Journal of Sociology* 96 (2), 329–57.

———, and Nancy Denton. *American Apartheid: Segregation and the Making of the Underclass.* Cambridge, Mass.: Harvard University Press, 1993.

———. "Suburbanization and Segregation in U.S. Metropolitan Areas." *American Journal of Sociology* 94 (3), 592–626 (Nov. 1988).

Moynihan, Daniel Patrick. *The Negro Family: A Case for National Action.* United States Department of Labor, Washington, D.C.: Government Printing Office, 1965.

Myrdal, Gunnar. *An American Dilemma.* New York: Harper and Brothers, 1944.

Nelson, William Javier. "Racial Definition: Background for Divergence," *Phylon,* 47 (4), 318–26.

O'Donnell, Noreen. "Caribbean Immigrants Are Reshaping the County," *Herald Statesman,* Feb. 10, 1994, 4A.

Oliver, Melvin, and Thomas M. Shapiro. *Black Wealth, White Wealth: A New Perspective on Racial Inequality.* New York: Routledge, 1995.

Omi, Michael, and Howard Winant. *Racial Formation in the United States: From the 1960s to the 1990s.* 2d ed. New York: Routledge, 1994.

Osofsky, Gilbert. *Harlem: The Making of a Ghetto.* 2d ed. New York: Harper and Row, [1963] 1971.

Palen, J. John. *The Suburbs.* New York: McGraw-Hill, 1995.

Patillo-McCoy, Mary. *Black Picket Fences: Privilege and Peril Among the Black Middle Class.* Chicago: University of Chicago Press, 1999.

Pendleton, William. "Blacks in Suburbs." In *The Urbanization of the Suburbs,* Louis Masotti and Jeffrey Hadden, eds. Beverly Hills, Calif.: Sage, 1973.

Perkins, Aurelia. "Runyon Heights: Portrait of a Neighborhood," *Journal of Philosophy and Social Sciences* 14 (1990), 46–61.

Pinkney, Alphonso. *The Myth of Black Progress.* Cambridge, England: Cambridge University Press, [1984] 1993.

Raskin, A. H. "Labor in Search of a Mission." In *Unions in Transition,* Seymour Martin Lipset, ed., 3–38. San Francisco: Institute for Contemporary Studies, 1986.

Reid, Ira De Augustine. *The Negro Immigrant: Characteristics and Social Adjustment, 1899–1937.* New York: Harper and Row, [1939] 1970.

Rieder, Jonathan. *Canarsie: The Jews and Italians of Brooklyn Against Liberalism.* Cambridge, Mass.: Harvard University Press, 1985.

Ringer, Benjamin B. *We the People and Others: Duality and America's Treatment of Its Racial Minorities.* New York: Tavistock, 1983.

Roberts, Sam. *Who We Are: A Portrait of America Based on the Latest U.S. Census.* New York: Random House, 1995.

Roediger, David R. *The Wages of Whiteness: Race and the Making of the American Working Class.* New York: Verso Press, 1991.

Rose, Harold. *Black Suburbanization.* Cambridge, Mass.: Ballinger, 1976.

Sandor, Gabrielle. "The Other America." *American Demographic,* June 1994, 36–42.

Schnore, Leo, Carolyn Andre, and Harry Sharp. "Black Suburbanization, 1930–1970." In *The Changing Face of the Suburbs,* Barry Schwartz, ed. Chicago: University of Chicago Press, 1976.

Schuman, Howard, Charlotte Steeh, and Lawrence Bobo. *Racial Attitudes in America: Trends and Interpretations.* Cambridge, Mass.: Harvard University Press, 1985.

Schwartz, Joel. "The Evolution of the Suburbs." In *Suburbia: The American Dream and Dilemma,* Philip C. Dolce, ed. New York: Archer Press, 1976.

Sheingold, Dave. "Failure to Spread Subsidized Housing Led to Lawsuit." *Herald Statesman,* June 1, 1992, 5A.

Sigelman, Lee, and Susan Welch. *Black American's Views of Racial Inequality.* Cambridge, England: Cambridge University Press, 1994.

Sowell, Thomas. *Ethnic America: A History.* New York: Basic Books, 1981.

Stack, Carol B. *All Our Kin: Strategies for Survival in a Black Community.* New York: Harper and Row, 1974.

Stearns, Linda Brewster, and John Logan. "The Racial Structuring of the Housing Market and Segregation in Suburban Areas." *Social Forces* 65 (1).

———. "Suburban Racial Segregation as a Non-Ecological Process." *Social Forces* 60 (1981), 61–73.

Steigman, Arnold L. "Mayor-Council Government: Yonkers, New York, 1908–1939—A Study of 'Failure and Abandonment.'" Doctoral Dissertation. Graduate School of Public Administration, New York University, 1967.

Steinberg, Stephen. *The Ethnic Myth: Race, Ethnicity, and Class in America.* 2d ed. New York: Beacon, 1989.

Suttles, Gerald D. *The Social Construction of Communities.* Chicago: University of Chicago Press, 1972.

Taeuber, Karl E. "Racial Segregation: The Persisting Dilemma." *Annals of the American Academy of Political and Social Science* 422 (Nov. 1975).

———, and Alma F. Taeuber. *Negroes in Cities.* Chicago: Aldone, 1965.

Takaki, Ronald. *Strangers from a Different Shore: A History of Asian Americans.* New York: Penguin Books, 1989.

United States District Court Southern District of New York. *United States of America and Yonkers Branch- National Association for the Advancement of Colored People, et al., v Yonkers Board of Education; City of Yonkers; and Yonkers Community Development Agency.* Opinion 80 CIV 6761 (LBS).

Veblen, Thorstein. *The Theory of the Leisure Class.* New York: Penguin Books, [1899] 1979.

"Was There a Fiery Cross?" *Herald Statesman,* May 22, 1939, 1.

Waters, Mary C. *Ethnic Options: Choosing Identities in America.* Berkeley: University of California Press, 1990.

———. "The Role of Lineage in Identity Formation." *Qualitative Sociology* 14 (1), 57–76.

Watkins-Owens, Irma. *Blood Relations: Caribbean Immigrants and the Harlem Community, 1900–1930.* Bloomington: Indiana University Press, 1996.

Weigold, Marilyn E., ed. *Westchester County: The Past Hundred Years, 1883–1983.* Valhalla, N.Y.: Westchester Historical Society, 1984.

Wiese, James Andrew. "Struggle for the Suburban Dream: African-American Suburbanization Since 1916." Ph.D. Dissertation, Columbia University Graduate School of Arts and Sciences, 1993.

Williams, Bruce. *Black Workers in an Industrial Suburb.* New Brunswick, N.J.: Rutgers University Press, 1987.

Williams, Richard. *Hierarchical Structures and Social Value: The Creation of Black and Irish Identity in the U.S..* New York: Cambridge University Press, 1990.

Wilson, Leslie. *Dark Spaces: An Account of Afro-American Suburbanization, 1890–1950.* Ph.D. dissertation in history, City University of New York, 1992.

Wilson, William Julius. *When Work Disappears: The World of the New Urban Poor.* New York: Random House, 1996.

———. *The Truly Disadvantaged: The Inner City, the Underclass, and Public Policy.* Chicago: University of Chicago Press, 1987.

———. *The Declining Significance of Race: Blacks and Changing American Institutions.* 2d ed. Chicago: University of Chicago, 1980.

Winant, Howard. *Racial Conditions: Politics, Theory Comparisons.* Minneapolis: University of Minnesota Press, 1994.

Wirth, Louis. "Urbanism as a Way of Life." Reprinted in *Metropolis: Center of Our Times,* Philip Kasinitz, ed. New York: New York University Press, 1995.

Wolseley, Roland E. *The Black U.S.A.* 2d ed. Ames: Iowa State University, 1990.

Yinger, John. *Closed Doors, Opportunities Lost: The Continuing Cost of Housing Discrimination.* New York: Russell Sage, 1995.

Zukin, Sharon. *Landscapes of Power: From Detroit to Disney World.* Berkeley: University of California Press, 1991.

Zunz, Olivier. *The Changing Face of Inequality: Urbanization, Industrial Development, and Immigrants in Detroit, 1880–1920.* Chicago: University Chicago Press, 1982.

Index